The Structure and Development of Middle Indo-Aryan Dialects

The Structure and Development of Middle Indo-Aryan Dialects

VIT BUBENIK

MOTILAL BANARSIDASS PUBLISHERS
PRIVATE LIMITED • DELHI

First Edition: Delhi, 1996

ISBN: 81-208-1317-0

Also available at:

MOTILAL BANARSIDASS

41 U.A. Bungalow Road, Jawahar Nagar, Delhi 110 007
120 Royapettah High Road, Mylapore, Madras 600 004
16 St. Mark's Road, Bangalore 560 001
Ashok Rajpath, Patna 800 004
Chowk, Varanasi 221 001

PRINTED IN INDIA

BY JAINENDRA PRAKASH JAIN AT SHRI JAINENDRA PRESS,
A-45 NARAINA, PHASE I, NEW DELHI 110 028
AND PUBLISHED BY NARENDRA PRAKASH JAIN FOR
MOTILAL BANARSIDASS PUBLISHERS PRIVATE LIMITED,
BUNGALOW ROAD, DELHI 110 007

To Marcela, Monica and Andrea
for their patience

अतिविस्तृतदुरागमविप्रकीर्णशब्दानुशासनसमूहः
Hemacandra's *Siddha-Hema*, Praśasti 4

CONTENTS

PREFACE

This monograph is based on my research in the area of Indo-Aryan linguistics during the last fifteen years. Its first version (limited to Phonology and Morphology) was written between June and December 1979 at the Centre of Advanced Study in Sanskrit, University of Poona (India) where I held an award of the Shastri Indo-Canadian Institute in the field of Sanskrit linguistics. I must gratefully acknowledge the advice and assistance of Dr. S. D. Laddu (University of Poona) who guided me through Middle Indo-Aryan texts (in Ardha-Māgadhī and Māhārāṣṭrī) and surveyed the phonology and morphology of Prākrits with me. I am grateful to Dr. M.G. Dhadhpale (Deccan College) with whom I read Pāli texts for many penetrating observations regarding their interpretation. Dr. A.M. Ghatage (Deccan College) offered his advice in matters of the morphology of Ardha- Māgadhī. And finally my thanks are due to Dr. H.S. Ananthanarayan (Osmania University) for his help with texts in Māhārāṣṭrī.

After my return to Canada I had been using this short manual for my lectures on Indo-European and Indo-Aryan linguistics at Memorial University. Between 1983-89 my attention was devoted to several major issues in Indo-Aryan syntax (word order, cliticization, modality, ergativity, passive and causative constructions) in the framework of Functional Grammar. During those years my research was supported by several grants from the Vice-President and the Dean of Memorial University, which enabled me to hire research assistants and to go to conferences to present some of the results of my research. I had the opportunity to discuss many of the problems analyzed in this monograph with my European, Canadian and American colleagues. It is my pleasure to mention the names of those scholars whose sincere comments on my presentation of Middle Indo-Aryan data sharpened my perception of philological and linguistic issues involved in my work: Dr. A. Aklujkar (University of British Columbia), Dr. L. Campbell (SUNY Albany), Dr. K. Chari

(University of Ottawa), Dr. M. Deshpande (University of Michigan), Dr. S. Dik (University of Amsterdam), Dr. H.H. Hock (University of Illinois), Dr. G. Holland (Berkeley), Dr. P.E. Hook (University of Michigan), Dr. B. Joseph (State University at Ohio), Dr. R. Schmidt-Brandt (University of Heidelberg), Dr. R. Singh (University of Montreal), Dr. P. Thieme (University of Tübingen), Dr. C. Watkins (Harvard), Dr. L. Zgusta (University of Illinois).

During its final stages consisting of enlarging and completing the final version of the monograph my work has been supported by the generous grant from the Alexander von Humboldt-Stiftung tenable at the Institute für Allgemeine und Indogermanische Sprachwissenschaft, University of Munich in 1986. My gratitude is due to Prof. Dr. Klaus Strunk, who sponsored my work for the Stiftung, for his kind permission to use the facilities and the library of the Institute, and to Prof. Dr. D. Schlingloff for a similar permission to use the holdings of the Institute für Indologie und Iranistik.

And finally, a fellowship grant from the Shastri Indo-Canadian Institute tenable at the Bhandarkar Oriental Research Institute, Pune, in 1991 enabled me to take my MIA studies back to India. Thanks to Dr. R.N. Dandekar, Honorary Secretary, and Dr. S.D. Laddu, Director, I could avail myself of the library of the Institute and enlarge my research into the morphology and syntax of late MIA (Apabhraṃśa). During that period Dr. A.M. Ghatage, Director of the Dictionary of Prākrits, provided invaluable assistance in my perusal of Apabhraṃśa texts and Prākrit grammarians.

It is hardly necessary to say that none of the above-mentioned scholars is in any way responsible for any shortcomings in my work; they remain solely my responsibility.

Pune, December 1991

VIT BUBENIK
c/o Bhandarkar Oriental
Research Institute

ILLUSTRATIONS

LANGUAGES AND DIALECTS

AGr	Ancient Greek
AMg	Ardha-Māgadhī
Ap	Apabhraṃśa
Av	Avesta
Dh	Dhauli
EAp	Eastern Apabhraṃśa
EH	Eastern Hindi
Er	Eṛṛdaguḍi
Gi	Gīrnār
H	Hindi
IA	Indo-Aryan
II	Indo-Iranian
Jg	Jaugaḍa
JMah	Jain Māhārāṣṭrī
JŚ	Jain Śaurasenī
Ka	Kālsī
Kash	Kashmīrī
Lat	Latin
Ma	Mānsehrā
Mah	Māhārāṣṭrī
Mar	Marāṭhī
Mg	Māgadhī
MIA	Middle Indo-Aryan
MnH	Modern Hindi
NIA	New Indo-Aryan
OCSl	Old Church Slavonic
OH	Old Hindi
OIA	Old Indo-Aryan
OLat	Old Latin
OP	Old Persian
Pai	Paiśācī
PIA	Proto-Indo-Aryan

PIE	Proto-Indo-European
Pkt(s)	Prākrit(s)
Ś	Śaurasenī
SAp	Southern Apabhraṃśa
Sh	Shāhbāzgaṛhī
Si	Sindhī
Skt	Sanskrit
So	Sopārā
WAp	Western Apabhraṃśa
WH	Western Hindi

EDITIONS OF MIDDLE INDO-ARYAN TEXTS

Av	*Āvaśyaka-Erzählungen* (ed.) E. Leumann. Leipzig, 1897.
Āyār	*Āyāraṅgasutta* (ed.) H. Jacobi. London, 1882.
BhK	*Bhavisatta Kaha von Dhaṇavāla* (ed.) H. Jacobi. München, 1918.
D	*Dīgha-Nikāya* (ed.) T.W. Rhys Davids and J.E. Carpenter. London, 1890-1911.
Daś	*Daśakumāracarita of Daṇḍin* (ed.) M.R. Kāle. Delhi, 1925/1979.
Dham	*Dhammapada* (ed.) V. Fausbøll. Copenhagen, 1855.
Dkk	*Les chants mystiques de Kānha et de Saraha* (ed.)
Dks	M. Shahidullah. Paris, 1928.
Dn	Hemacandra's *Deśīnāmamālā* (ed.) R. Pischel. Bombay, 1880.
Erz	*Ausgewählte Erzählungen in Māhārāshṭrī* (ed.) H. Jacobi. Leipzig, 1886.
G	*Gaüḍavaho* (ed.) Sh. P. Paṇḍit. Bombay, 1887.
H	*Das Saptaçatakam des Hāla* (ed.) A. Weber. Leipzig, 1881.
Hc	Hemacandra's *Siddha-Hema (Prakrit Grammar)* (ed.) P.L. Vaidya. Poona, 1928.
Hv	*Harivaṁśa-purāṇa* (ed.) L. Aldsdorf. Hamburg, 1936.
JaCo	*The Jātaka together with its Commentary* (ed.) V. Fausbøll. London, 1877-96.
Jc	Puṣpadanta's *Jasahata-Cariu* (ed.) P.L. Vaidya. Poona, 1931.
Ki	Kramadīśvara's *Saṁkṣipta-Vyākaraṇa.*
Kk	*Kālakācārya-caritam* (ed.) H. Jacobi. *ZDMG* 34 (1880), pp. 247-318.
Kp	*Kumārapāla-pratibodha* (ed.) L. Alsdorf. Hamburg, 1929.
Lalitav	*Lalitavigraharājanāṭaka* (ed.) F. Kielhorn. Göttingen, 1893.
Milp	*The Milindapañha being Dialogues between King Milinda*

	and the Buddhist Sage Nāgasena (ed.) V. Trenckner. London, 1928.
MP	Puṣpadanta's *Mahāpurāṇa* (ed.) P.L. Vaidya, Bombay, 1937-41.
Mṛcch	*Mṛcchakaṭikā* (ed.) R.K. Karmarkar. Poona, 1937.
Mt	*Materialien zur Kenntnis des Apabhraṃśa* (ed.) R. Pischel. Berlin, 1902.
Mudr	*Mudrārākshasa* (ed.) M.R. Kāle. Delhi, 1976.
Nāyādh	*Nāyādhammakahā* (ed.) P. Steinthal. Leipzig, 1881.
Pc	Svayaṃbhūdeva's *Paüma-cariu* (ed.) H.C. Bhayani. Bombay, 1953-60.
Pd	Rāmasiṃha's *Pāhuḍa-dohā* (ed.) H.L. Jain. Amraoti, 1933.
PPr	Joindu's *Paramātma-prakāśa* (ed.) A.N. Upadhye. Kolhapur, 1937.
Pu	Puruṣottama's *Prākṛtānuśāsana* (ed.) L. Nitti-Dolci. Paris, 1938.
R	*Rāvaṇavaha oder Setubandha* (ed.) S. Goldschmidt. Strassburg, 1880-84.
RE	*Die Großen Felsen-Edikte Aśokas* (ed.) U. Schneider. Wiesbaden, 1978.
S	*Saṁyutta-Nikāya* (ed.) L. Feer. London, 1884-98.
Sc	*Sanatkumāracarita* (ed.) H. Jacobi. München, 1921.
Śak	*Abhijñāna-Śākuntala of Kālidāsa* (ed.) R.D. Karmarkar. Poona, 1952.
Sūya	*Sūyagaḍaṅgasutta.* Bombay saṃvat 1936.
Ṭhāṇ	*Ṭhāṇaṅgasutta.* Benares saṃvat 1937.
Thera/ī	*The Thera- and Therī-Gāthā* (ed.) R. Pischel and H. Oldenberg. London, 1883.
Uttar	*Uttarajjhayaṇasutta.* Calcutta saṃvat 1936.
Uvās	*Uvāsagadasāo* (ed.) A.F.R. Hoernle. Calcutta, 1890.
Vet	*Jambhaladatta's Version of the Vetālapañcaviṁśati* (ed.) M.B. Emeneau. New York, 1934/1967.
Vikr	*Vikramorvaśīya of Kālidāsa* (ed.) R.K. Karmarkar. Poona, 1932.
Vin	*Vinaya-Piṭaka* (ed.) H. Oldenberg. London, 1879-83.
Vivāhap	*Vivāhappannatti.* Benares saṃvat 1938.
Ys	Joindu's *Yogasāra* (ed.) A.N. Upadhye. Kolhapur, 1937.

INTRODUCTION

The aim of the present monograph is a systematic treatment of the most likely historical processes that are responsible for the variation and change found in phonology, morphology and syntax of Middle Indo-Aryan dialects during the successive stages of their development. I will attempt to explain their development as a function of the (i) time, (ii) space and (iii) social dimension.

(i) The upper limit of this study will be the middle of the 1st millennium B.C. and its lower limit the end of the 1st millennium A.D. For the sake of exposition the traditional trichotomy of these ca. fifteen centuries will be adhered to:

Old (early) stage (represented by Aśokan inscriptions, Pāli and Ardha-Māgadhī)
Middle stage (Māhārāṣṭrī, dramatic Prākrits, the dialects used by the Jainas)
Late stage (represented by Apabhraṃśa and Avahaṭṭha).

(ii) The geographical area of Northern Aryan India will be considered but the Prākrits found outside India (the Ceylon inscriptions and the Kharoṣṭhī documents from Central Asia) will be excluded from my expose.

(iii) Certain dialects will be correlated with social class, occupational group and literary genre. An attempt will be made to throw new light from this angle on problems of variation and ongoing linguistic change in Middle Indo-Aryan.

The principal techniques employed in this type of work are familiar from diachronic studies of other dead languages and dialects. They may be subsumed under the headings of internal and external evidence:

Internal evidence	(i)	the internal structure of the language/dialect itself
	(ii)	spelling conventions and variants found in inscriptions and manuscripts
External evidence	(iii)	representations in other ancient languages
	(iv)	subsequent developments.

In addition to (i) - (iv) the statements of contemporary grammarians are of considerable importance for the reconstruction of the state of affairs in remote centuries (in the case of MIA only Bharata and Vararuci were contemporary).

In the sections dealing with phonology and morphology (Chapters Two and Three) my attention will be devoted to the best documented varieties of MIA, namely: Aśokan Prākrits, Pāli, Ardha-Māgadhī, Māhārāṣṭrī and Apabhramśa. The limits of space prevented the legitimate inclusion of the three types of non-Classical Sanskrit (Jaina, Buddhist and Epic Sanskrit) into the chapters dealing with phonology and morphology. However, in the section dealing with syntax (Chapter Four) it proved necessary to draw on data from late Classical Sanskrit for the sake of statistical accounts and comparisons with dramatic Prākrits.

In my contrastive paradigms (Chapter Three) Old Indo-Aryan forms will be used as a starting point in the discussion of phonological and morphological changes separating OIA and MIA. Pāli, AMg, Mah and Ap forms will be used as points of reference in the discussion of phonological and morphological changes separating the early and the middle, and the middle and the late stages of MIA. Only a limited attempt will be made to relate the late stage of Apabhraṃśa/Avahaṭṭha to the stage of proto-vernaculars when the real break with the synthetic typology begins (declension becomes limited to two cases, direct and oblique, and the nominal forms are fully incorporated into the verbal system).

Chapter Two will present derivational histories of various lexical items in a cross-dialectal spectrum (Item and Process model). A number of phonological rules will be posited, clearly formulated and their operation in various linguistic environments examined (fricative weakening, dental palatalization, affrication, lenition and spirantization, retroflexion). Their interplay will be of fundamental importance for the presentation of individual forms and paradigms

(Chapter Three). The issue of the spatial and temporal diffusion of a linguistic rule will be tackled where permitted by the amount of primary evidence (Chapter Five). In the section dealing with vowels (2.1) phonetic vs. phonological (vs. orthographic) facts which are confused in older treatments will be kept strictly apart. This will allow us to present the cardinal event in the history of MIA—raising of short mid vowels in a new light. The shortening and lengthening processes of MIA will be stated in terms of syllabic heaviness (vs. traditional accounts in terms of segmental clusters).

In Chapter Three my method will be that of a contrastive study. The paradigms from representatives MIA dialects (Pāli, AMg, Mah, Ap) will be juxtaposed to show that MIA dialects are as systematic as Sanskrit even if they possess fewer forms (their losses being compensated for by analytic formations). Older studies present MIA morphology with emphasis on the phonological aspect (i.e., the drivation of individual dialectal forms from their ancestral OIA proto-forms). The paradigmatic presentation of MIA should enhance our comprehension of the cohesion and the trends of the development of individual dialects. In addition, it will permit us to describe more convincingly the operation of proportional analogy whose locus is the paradigm.

MIA syntax deserves a monograph of its own and only a few topics deemed to be of fundamental importance were examined in Chapter Four (word order, citicization of pronominal objects, epistemic and deontic modality, evolution of aspect, passive and the emergence of ergative construction, and causativization). Methodologically, this chapter adheres to the tenets of Functional Grammar (Dik 1980, 1989).

In the last section (Chapter Five) an attempt will be made to bring the MIA dialects into a close relationship with their speakers (the linguistic attitudes of Sanskrit and Prākrit grammarians will be surveyed, and the correlation of dialect with social class, occupational group and literary genre in *Mṛcchakaṭikā* will be examined in some detail).

A linguistic study of a dead language or dead dialects can be contemplated only after a certain amount of philological work (consisting of providing reliable editions of inscriptions and manuscripts, composing grammars, compiling lexica) has been accomplished. My indebtedness to a great number of philological and more recent linguistic studies will be patent in each section. Their bibliography (up to 1960) has been provided by Banerjee (1970). The whole field of older MIA phonology and morphology has been most recently surveyed by O.von Hinüber (1986) *Das ältere Mittelindisch im Überblick* (equipped with an up-to-date bibliography).

For the benefit of those general and historical linguists who are not specialists in Indology I would like to survey briefly the older standard works to which I will be often referring on the following pages.

There are two comparative grammars of MIA. The older one was published in the frame of the *Grundriss der indo-arischen Philologie und Altertumskunde* by R. Pischel at the beginning of this century (1900). The more recent one was composed in India (1960) by Sukumar Sen. Pischel's monumental work *Grammatik der Prakrit-Sprachen* (430 pp.) has a character of a loose compilation of phonological and morphological data (with no section on syntax) which methodologically does not proceed beyond their collection and classification. In *Lautlehre* the orthographic and phonetic (not to mention phonological) facts are often confused; in morphology pandialectal MIA paradigms are presented and their individual forms are discussed atomistically in terms of sound changes from their OIA ancestors. In terms of coverage Pischel did not include Pāli and inscriptional Prākrits into his work. A wealth of new texts, especially in Apabhraṃśa, were published in the meantime. Pischel's work, however, remains valuable for its rich documentation and references to MIA texts available to him.

The gap in the *Grundriss* was filled in by W.Geiger who composed the manual of Pāli (*Literatur und Sprache*) in 1916. As far as its coverage is concerned the manual includes a detailed presentation of phonology and morphology (with no section on word formation and syntax) on the basis of all the available Pāli manuscripts. Geiger's manual is outdated in the same fashion as that by Pischel.

In the early thirties (1933) there appeared a book by J. Bloch which became very influential in India. His masterpiece *Indo-Aryan from the Vedas to Modern Times* (English edition enlarged and revised by A. Master in 1965) surpasses methodologically the previous works on the varieties of Old and Middle Indo-Aryan. In phonetics (Part One) Bloch's approach lies basically in the drawing of isoglosses and heteroglosses which link and separate various Indo-Aryan (also Indo-Iranian and Dardic) languages and dialects in different stages of their development. In his own words

> 'to display side by side and explain, so far as can be explained by such confrontation, the actual facts in the different periods.' (p. 30)

The study of the Noun and Verb (Part Two) is organized diachronically into three sections (Sanskrit - Middle Indian - Neo-Indian). In the paragraphs dealing with Middle Indian main attention is paid to the 'phonetic origin' of the endings and their 'alteration'. The short section dealing with the sentence (Part Three, pp. 303-19) is devoted to the following topics:

(i) Verb 'to be' and the nominal sentence
(ii) Word order
(iii) Linking of sentences (subordination).

Bloch viewed the MIA period only as a transitional stage between OIA and NIA and did not try to elaborate on MIA data synchronically. MIA dialects are not presented systematically but rather atomistically in terms of the phonetic origin of their individual forms (paradigmatic relations obtaining in MIA after various sound changes have taken place are rarely considered). Perusing Bloch contemporary linguists will resent some of his non-descriptive statements à propos Apabhraṃśa, such as Apabhraṃśa being 'only a disfigured Sanskrit' (p. 29) undergoing 'phonetic deterioration' (p. 141).

The only comprehensive study of MIA written in India is that by S. Sen (professor of Indian linguistics at the University of Calcutta). His book, *A Comparative Grammar of Middle Indo-Aryan* (1960), presents a detailed classification of MIA dialects (Chapter III); devotes a rather short section to phonology (Chapter III, pp. 34-73), where the OIA sources of MIA vowels, consonants and consonant clusters are listed, Chapters IV-IX are devoted to morphology of Noun, Pronoun, Verb, and Nominal Stem Formation and Composition. Historical syntax of MIA by the same author appeared earlier in IL (1952/53), pp. 1-140. Sen's treatment of MIA morphology—

as that of Bloch—emphasizes heavily the phonetic aspect. The individual dialects are presented without paradigms and their individual forms are analyzed piecemeal in terms of sound changes from their OIA proto-forms.

Among older studies of MIA produced in India those by M.A. Mehendale and G.V. Tagare are outstanding. Mehendale's *Historical Grammar of Inscriptional Prākrits* (1948) is a detailed study of Prākrit inscriptions in Brāhmī and Kharoṣṭhī (from the earliest times to the 4th A.D.). He correctly emphasizes their value (vis-à-vis that of literary compositions) as

> 'the best available representatives of the living forms of speech which were current in different regions of India in those days.' (p. xv)

Tagare (1948) in his *Historical Grammar of Apabhraṃśa* applied a 'chrono-regional' (=diachronic-diatopical) method of study to the available Apabhraṃśa literature and abstracted from it a number of nominal and verbal paradigms for the regional varieties of Apabhraṃśa.

The situation in the study of MIA syntax is worse than that in phonology and morphology and a comprehensive monograph—using a more up-to-date theoretical framework—remains a desideratum. The work by S. Sen (1952/53) tries to be comprehensive and is valuable for its documentation. H. Hendriksen's *Syntax of the Infinite Verb-Forms of Pāli* (1944) is a significant contribution to the study of Pāli morphosyntax. O. von Hinüber's *Studien zur Kasussyntax des Pāli* (1968) contains well-organized material for the study of the syntax of case. R.A. Singh's *Syntax of Apabhraṃśa* (1980) contains a wealth of syntactic data from the final stages of MIA but does not offer any syntactic framework for their evaluation. New horizons in MIA syntactic studies have been opened by P.K. Andersen in his articles (1980), (1982/83) and (1986), cast in the framework of Functional Grammar (devoted to problems of word order, functional sentence perspective and the origin of the ergative construction in MIA).

M. Deshpande's study *Sociolinguistic Attitudes in India* (1979) has been influential in my thinking about sociolinguistic problems which are inherent in any historical study of regional and literary dialects based on inscriptional and literary evidence.

It goes without saying that the above survey is not meant to be exhaustive. Many other significant works bearing on MIA philology and linguistics (by Alsdorf, Berger, Burrow, Gaefke, Ghatage, Gonda, Grierson, Jacobi, M. Jha, Katre, Lüders. Mayrhofer, Norman, Turner, Vaidya, Vertogradova, Woolner and others) will be referred to and can be found in my bibliography.

CHAPTER 1

CLASSIFICATION OF MIDDLE INDO-ARYAN DIALECTS

1.1 Prehistory of Middle Indo-Aryan Dialects

The historical period of the Indo-Aryan family of the Indo-European phylum begins about 1200-1000 B.C. with the compilation of Rgveda. One of its representatives, the Sanskrit language, in the very earliest period lay in the North-West of India (present Punjab). There were other varieties (or 'dialects') of Old Indo-Aryan but we possess no direct evidence of them. Nevertheless, we must assume the existence of non-Sanskritic dialects of Old Indo-Aryan in order to be able to explain a number of phonological and morphological features of Middle Indo-Aryan. Burrow (1955:45-47) has assembled fragmentary—but convincing—evidence for the dialectal differentiation of the Old Indo-Aryan ancestor of Middle Indo-Aryan dialects.

In phonology Midde Indo-Aryan shows sometimes clusters *j(j)h*, *ggh* in agreement with Iranian γž* but at variance with Sanskrit *kṣ* (Prākrit *jharaï* 'flows', Pāli *paggharati*, cf. Avestan γžar-, vs. Sanskrit *kṣar-*). Proto-Indic *r̥̄* had two reflexes in Old Indo-Aryan: *īr* found commonly in Sanskrit (*jīrṇá-* 'old' < **jr̥̄ná-*) vs. *ūr* which has to be postulated for the Old Indo-Aryan ancestor of Prākrits (witness Prākrit *juṇṇa-* < *jūrṇá-* 'old' < **jr̥̄ná-*). There was a double outcome of the Proto-Indic cluster *-žd-*; the cluster underwent regressive assimilation (*žd* > *dd*) which could be followed by degemination accompanied by compensatory lengthening in Sanskrit: Proto-Indic *nižḍá-* 'nest' > *niḍḍá-* > *nīḍá-*. Pāli *niḍḍa* represents an older form of the word.

Another archaism found in Pāli is *idha* 'here' vs. Sanskrit *ihá* (explainable from *idha* by fricativazation d > δ and a complete loss of δ > ϕ).

In morphology the most striking archaism of Prākrits is the

enclitic form of the 3rd person pronoun *se* (corresponding to Avestan *he, se,* Old Persian *šaíy*) which is not found in Sanskrit (cf. 3.3.2). Among other peculiarities, Burrow (1955:46) mentions the Pāli descendant of an Old Indo-Aryan *aniṭ* (i-less') future *kāhāmi* (<**karṣyāmi*) vs. Sanskrit *kariṣyāmi.* There are participial formations in *-na* in MIA (cf. 3.4.10), corresponding to Sanskrit formations in *-ta* (Prākrit *mukka-* 'releásed' < **mukna* vs. Sanskrit *mukta*). The Ardha-Māgadhī medio-passive imperfective participle in *-mīṇa* continues probably an ancient Indo-Aryan variant of Sanskrit *-māna.* The participle *dinna-* 'given' (vs. Sanskrit *datta*) implies an ancient formation *didāmi* reduplicating with *i* (as in Greek *didōmi*) vs. Sanskrit *dadāmi* (cf. 3.4.10).

We have no direct evidence of the language or dialect divisions in North India in the 6th and 5th c. B.C., when the great religious and social reforms of Buddhism and Jainism were preached in vulgar tongues. In the North-West of India Pāṇini described the standard language of the college of the Brahmins without mentioning any other regional varieties; the social dialects of the lower classes of Śalātura, where Pāṇini was born, were not considered either. The first authentic documents of dialectal differentiation which enable us to make a back-projection to the state of affairs in the 6th/5th c. B.C. are the dialectal inscriptions in which Aśoka addressed his subjects in the middle of the 3rd c. B.C. However, there can be little doubt that their ancestors in the 6th/5th c. B.C. were phonologically and morphologically far enough from the norms of Pāṇinian Sanskrit. This assumption is born out by the following considerations. One of the diagnostic features of Middle Indo-Aryan dialects is the treatment of OIA liquids *r* and *l*. Broadly speaking, the Western dialects kept the opposition between /r/ and /l/ whereas the Eastern ones merged them in favor of the latter one. The alternation between *l* and *r* is very old in the history of Indo-Aryan, dating right back to the period of common Indo-Iranian. It is known (cf. Burrow, 1955:82-4) that the language of Madhyadeśa showed an inclination towards the lateral liquid.[1]

Another of the distinguishing features of Eastern dialects, namely the suffix *-e* in the Nom Sg of *a*-stems (arising through-*aḥ* > *-e*) is found in the Ṛgveda (I.34.5 *sūre duhitā* but *sūro* in VII:69.4). We might speculate that this process could be even more common in a non-Sanskritic dialect of Old Indo-Aryan spoken farther to the east. In other words, there is no reason to doubt that long before the time of the Buddha and Mahāvīra there could have been a dialect in Magadha where the Nom Sg of *a*-stems was in *-e*, and *l* replaced *r* in certain lexical items.

Furthermore, in a small number of words in Sanskrit the *s* which is expected on the basis of comparative evidence is replaced by *ś*; there are also doublets such as *kusūla-kuśūla* 'granary' (Burrow, 1955:97-8). As mentioned by Norman (1980:71), this might indicate a tendency, found only in a restricted area, to replace *s* by *ś* during an early stage of the development of Indo-Aryan. This assumption would not again be inconsistent with the facts of the 3rd c. B.C.

From the very beginning of their existence as literary and 'inscriptional' languages, the Middle Indo-Aryan dialects had to compete with Sanskrit. As is well-known from the history of Sanskrit literature, they lost ground to a more prestigious artificial literary form of Old Indo-Aryan in post-Christian centuries. Only in remote areas outside India proper was the situation different. For instance, in Chinese Turkestan the Middle Indo-Aryan dialect served as an administrative language of the kingdom of Shan-Shan up to ca. 300 A.D. (the bulk of the texts of an administrative character came from Niya; linguistically, their dialect has strong affinities with the northwestern varieties of Aśokan Prākrits). The usual explanation for this state of affairs is sought in the deliberate decision made by the non-native dynasties of northern and western India not to use diverging spoken varieties of contemporary Indo-Aryan but rather the codified form of Old Indo-Aryan in their monumental inscriptions. From the point of view of non-native speakers of Indo-Aryan, the latter variety had an obvious advantage against the diverging vernaculars: the linguistic evolution of Sanskrit was finished and the language was already established as a prestigious vehicle of long literary tradition. The Prākrits, on the other hand, could have been perceived only as administrative languages used by the domestic Mauryan dynasty in eastern India.[2]

1.2 Between Old and Middle Indo-Aryan-Pāli

The Middle Indo-Aryan period is represented by inscriptions, and in literature by Pāli, Prākrits and Apabhraṃśa-Avahaṭṭha. It comprises all the dialects (or Prākrit 'languages') used in an oral form from the middle of the first millennium B.C. down to the time of about 1100 A.D., when further phonological and morphological changes had produced proto-vernaculars which are of an analytic linguistic type. Middle Indo-Aryan dialects can be studied synchronically by themselves or diachronically in their relationship to the OIA dialects (Vedic and Classical Sanskrit). In this study I will try to relate them to the OIA dialects and explain further changes which took place during the MIA period.

It is customary to divide the MIA period chronologically into three stages:

(i) Old (represented by Pāli and inscriptions from the 4th C. B.C. to the 2nd C. A.D.);
(ii) Middle, which includes Māhārāṣṭrī (the language of the lyric poetry and Jain postcanonical literature), the Prākrits of drama (such as Śaurasenī and Māgadhī), the dialect of the Jain Canon (so-called Ardha-Māgadhī) and Paiśācī (known only from the statements of Prākrit grammarians);
(iii) New (represented by literary works composed in Apabhraṃśa and Avahaṭṭha).

Pāli was the only one among Middle Indo-Aryan languages that became a vehicle of a great culture. There is no place in this monograph to enumerate all the religious, philosophical, scientific and artistic works that were written in Pāli. Linguistically, Pāli represents the earliest stage of the development of Middle Indo-Aryan languages which is still very close to Old Indo-Aryan. Pāli's intermediate position between Old and Middle Indo-Aryan provides us very often with hard evidence for the intermediate linguistic stages between Vedic Sanskrit and later Prākrits.

Pāli's origins are controversial. There are essentially two basic views regarding this problem, depending on whether a greater weight is given to its eastern ('Magadhisms') or its western features. According to the former hypothesis, Pāli is based on the eastern dialect (Ardha-Māgadhī?) and later on the early literary works composed in it were 'westernized'. The antithetical view considers Pāli to be the literary language based on the western dialect. This is the position taken by Lüders (1954) according to whom the Pāli of the Ceylonese Canon is a western Middle Indian dialect. The comparison of Pāli with the contemporary language of the chancellery of Aśoka seems to point in the western direction (the Gīrnār version of Aśokan edicts from Kāthiāwār being closest to Pāli). The eastern elements (so-called Magadhisms) may be accounted for by the assumption that the 'Urkanon' was compiled in an eastern dialect similar to the Māgadhī (according to Lüders the oldest Buddhist texts were composed in Old Ardha-Māgadhī). The two unmistakable eastern features of Pāli are the following: *-e* instead of *-o* (< *aḥ*) as in *bhikkhave* 'monks' (Skt. *bhikṣavaḥ*), and *l* instead of *r* in a considerable number of words (there are also instances of hypercorrections, cf. Elizarenkova-Toporov, 1976:18).

There are several chronological layers in Pāli literature:

(i) the language of the metrical parts of the Canon (Gāthās) contains the most archaic forms, some of which are found in Vedic Sanskrit: Nom Pl in *-āse* (cf. Vedic 'double' plural *-āsaḥ*); *-bhi* in the Instr Pl of *a*-stems (cf. Vedic *tebhiḥ* vs. Classical *taiḥ*); the absolutive in *-(t)vāna* (cf. Vedic *tvāna* vs. Classical *-tvā*); etc.

(ii) the language of Canonical prose which does not include any significant number of archaisms and which may be considered standard Classical Pāli;

(iii) the language of post-canonical prose (e.g., of the *Milinda-Pañha*);

(iv) the language of later works (displaying a wide spectrum of forms ranging from Sanskritisms to neologisms which do not conform to the rules of Classical Pāli).

1.3 Geographical Dialect Continuum in Northern India in the 3rd c. B.C.

With the inscriptions of Mauryan king Aśoka (ca. 272-231) we are for the first time on a firmer ground in terms of diachrony and diatopicality, since these are datable with a relative precision to the middle of the 3rd c. B.C. Mehendale (1948:1) called them a 'remarkable survey of Indo-Aryan languages' as they were spoken in the Mauryan empire during the 3rd c. B.C. The heartland of Mauryan empire, the region of Magadha, rose to prominence during the 4th and 3rd c. B.C. During the Mauryan period Māgadhī, the language of its capital Pāṭaliputra, became the administrative language of

North India. Aśoka's decrees were inscribed all over India in local Prākrits on the basis of presumably a Māgadhī version (there are also Greek and Aramaic translations of Aśoka's decrees). This fact was probably the cause of the belief that Māgadhī was the 'root language' of all these languages[3].

Aśokan edicts are supplemented by short (and fragmentary) inscriptions dated to the three pre-Christian centuries: Mahāsthān Stone Plaque Inscription (from North Bengal), Jogīmārā Cave Inscription (from Central India), Sohgaurā Copper-Plate Inscription (from North-West Bihar), Besnagar Pillar Inscription (from Madhya Pradesh), Hāthigumphā Cave Inscriptions (from Orissa), and some others.

The extant Aśokan edicts come from several distinct geographical areas of India: Northern Punjab, Gangetic basin, the delta of the Mahānadī in Orissa, Kāthiāwār in Gujarat, Deccan, and the basin of Tungabhadra. The Indo-Aryan dialects as spoken in the 3rd c. B.C. can be subdivided on the basis of these inscriptions into four geographical areas:

(i) the North-Western dialect group is represented by the two versions of the Rock Edicts incised in Kharoṣṭhī script at Shāhbāzgaṛhī and Mānsehrā;

(ii) the (South-)Western dialect is represented by the Gīrnār Rock Edicts in Junagarh (Kāthiāwār);

(iii) the Central and Eastern dialect sub-groups: the Central subgroup is represented by the version from Kālsī (near Dehradun), the Topra Pillar Edict (Delhi) and the Jogīmārā Cave Inscription; the Eastern sub-group is represented by the inscriptions from the delta of the Mahānadī (the versions incised at Dhauli and Jaugaḍa in Orissa), all the Minor Rock Edicts and Pillar Edicts, the Mahāsthān Stone Plaque Inscription, the Sohgaurā Copper-Plate Inscription and the Hāthigumphā Cave Inscriptions;

(iv) the Southern dialect group is represented by the inscriptions from the Deccan, the whole group of the inscriptions in the Tungabhadra basin (Maski, Siddapur, Kopbal, Eṟṟdaguḍi), and Sopārā (north of Bombay) on the western coast.

The geographic distribution of Aśokan Rock Edicts is shown on Map 1.

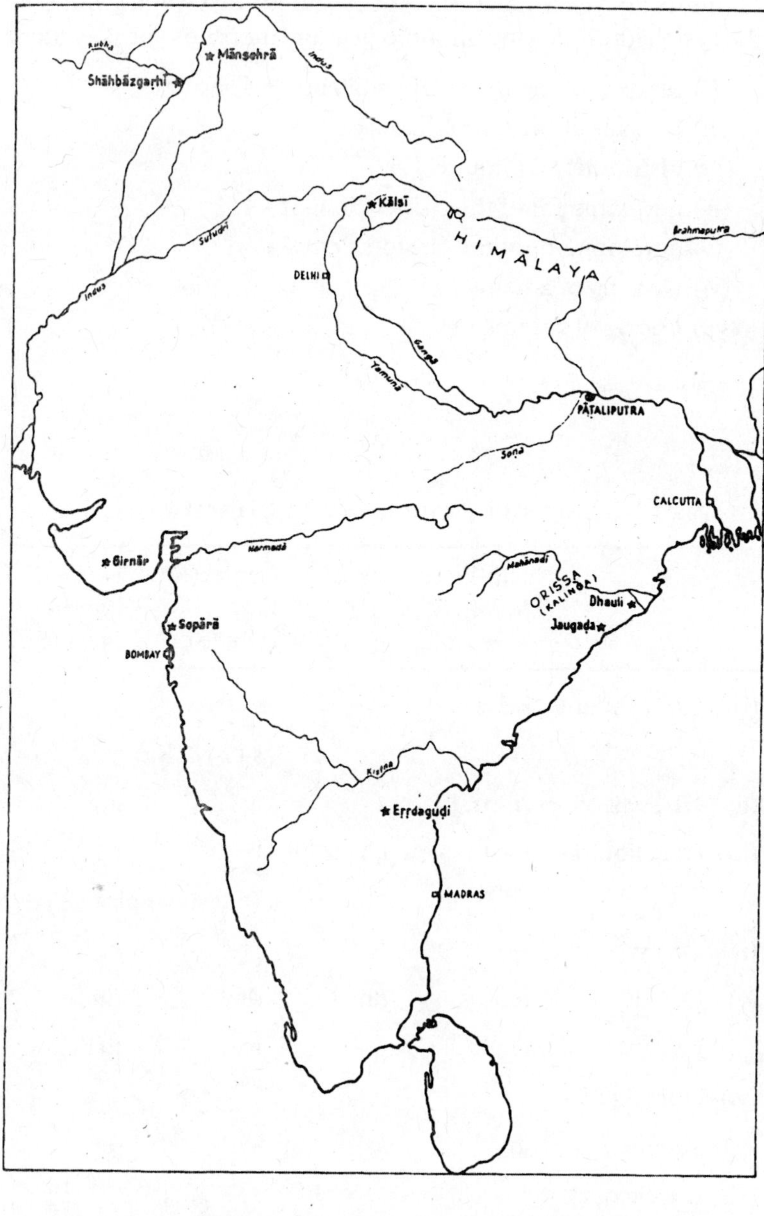

Map 1. Aśokan Rock Edicts according to Schneider (1978)
(Reproduced by kind permission of Otto Harrassowitz).

In correspondence with these major geographical areas the Middle Indo-Aryan dialects may be classified into several groups[4] on the basis of the following phonological and morphological features:

(i) reflexes of the three OIA sibilants (s, ś, ṣ)
(ii) reflexes of the OIA syllabic r
(iii) distribution of liquids 1, r
(iv) development of the cluster sibilant + v
(v) development of the clusters dental stop + v
(vi) Nom Sg of *a*-stems
(vii) Loc Sg of *a*-stems

Chart 1-1. Diagnostic Features of MIA Dialects (3rd c. B.C.)

	North-West (Sh, Ma)	West (Gi)	Center(Ka) East (Dh, Jg)	South (Er) South-West (So)
(i) OIA sobilants	s, ś, ṣ	s	s	s
			s (ś, ṣ) (Ka)	
(ii) OIA syllabic ṛ	ri, ru, i	a	a, i	a, i
(iii) OLA liquids	l, r	l, r	l	l
			(r at some places)	
(iv) OIA sv	sp	sv	sv	sv
(v) OIA dv	duv	db	duv	duv
tv	tv	tp	tv	t (Er)
(vi) Nom Sg of *a*-stems	-o	-o	-e	-e
(vii) Loc Sg of *a*-stems	-e, -aspi	-e, -amhi	-a(s)si	-a(s)si

(i) The three sibilants of OIA survive only in the North-West (Sh and Ma) and to a certain degree in the Center (Ka). Elsewhere they merged into a simple sibilant spelled *s. duva[ḍa]śa* 'twelve' vs. *duvādasa* (Dh) [Edict III.B], *suśruṣatu* 'they should listen' (Ma, Sh) vs. *susuṣātu* (Ka) vs. *susūsatu* (Jg) [Edict X.A], *savrapaṣaḍani* 'all the religious societies' (Ma) vs. *ṣāvāpāṣaṃ[ḍān]i* (Ka) [Edict XII.A] but *savrapaṣaḍana* (Ma) vs. *ś[a]vapāśaḍāna* (Ka) [Edict XII.B].

(ii) Syllabic *ṛ* of OIA had a number of reflexes in MIA, but it is only in the North-West where the consonantal component *r* remained (*ṛ*> *ri* or *ru*). Elsewhere the reflexes are *a* or *i* (*i* is not found in Gi). Examine the reflexes of OIA *dṛḍha* 'firm' and *mṛga* 'animal':

dridha (Ma, Sh) [Edict VII.E] mrigaviya hunt (Ma) [Edict VIII.B]

	mrugaya (Sh)
daḍha (Gi)	magavyā (Gi)
diḍha (Ka, Er)	migaviyā (Ka, Er)

a and *i* are found also in the North-West in some forms. Thus OIA *kṛta* 'made' appears as *kaṭa* in the West (Gi), Center (Ka) and the South (Er); in the North-West there exists a bewildering variety of forms:

Edict II.A	Edict V.D	Edict V.I	Edict Vi.C
Ma [ka]ṭa	kaṭe	kaṭa	kiṭaṃ
Sh [kr]i[ṭa]	ki[ṭ]raṃ	kiṭa	kiṭaṃ

(iii) The distinction between OIA liquids *l* and *r* is maintained only in the North-West (Sh, M) and West (Gi). Elsewhere they merged in favour of *l*

rājā 'king' vs. *lipi* ' writing' in the West corresponds to *lājā* and *lipi* in the East. In the East a half of the places studied by Mehendale (1948:183 ff.) preserve the contrast /r/ : /l/.[5]

(iv) Only in the North-West is the cluser *sv* dissimilated into *sp*: *spagraṃ* (< OIA *svarga*) 'heaven' (Ma, Sh) vs. *svagaṃ* elsewhere [Edict VI.L].

(v) Only in the West (Gi) the clusters *dv* and *tv* assimilate into *db* and *tp*:[6]

dbādasa twelve (Gi) vs. *duvadaśa* (M)
tadātpano 'presence' (Gi) vs. *tadatvāye* (Ka)

(vi) The *a*-stems display the ending *-o* (Nom Sg of Masc) in the West vs. the ending *-e* in the East. This morphological distinction (*o*- vs. *e*-dialects) is coextensive with the phonological distinction of *r*- vs. *l*-dialects. Thus *jano* 'men' (Masc) in the West corresponds to *jane* in the East.
-e is found in the East even for the Western Nom Sg Neuter *-aṃ*:
dāne 'gift' (Ka) vs. *dānaṃ* (Gi) [Edict XII.B] (but in XII.L even Kālsī displays *dānaṃ*), *phale* 'fruit' (Ka, Er) vs. *phalaṃ* (Sh, Gi) [Edict XII.N] (but also Mānsehrā displays *phale*).

(vii) The Loc Sg of *a*-stems in the East has only the suffix *-a(s)si* (of a pronominal origin < *-asmin*), whereas in the West the OIA suffix *-e* survived. But even here the suffixes of a pronominal origin made their inroad:
-aspi (*-asmin*) in the North-West and *-amhi* (< *amsi* < *asmin*) in the West: *praṣaḍaspi* 'in the religious society' (Sh) vs. *pāsaṃḍamhi* (Gi) vs. *pāsaṃḍasi* (Er) [Edict XIII.J].

This distribution of phonological and morphological features in inscriptional Prākrits has some interesting parallels to that found in certain literary dialects. Chart 1.2 shows the relationship between Buddhist Pāli and Jaina Ardha-Māgadhī, on the one hand, and

Chart 1.2. Literary vs. Inscriptional Prākrits.

	Pāli	Ardha-Māgadhī	Western Aśokan	Eastern Aśokan
(i) OIA sibilants	ś, s	ś, s	s	s ś (only in the Jogīmāra Cave)
(ii) OIA liquids	l, r (*l* for *r* rarely)	l, r (*l* for *r* rarely)	l, r	l, r (5 places) l for r (4 pl.)[5]
(iii) Nom Sg of *a*-stems	o, e (very rarely)	o, e (fairly consistently)	o	o (Udayagiri,[7] Sāranāth)

Western and Eastern inscriptional Prākrits, on the other hand. The three most salient features are shown, namely: reflexes of OIA sibilants, OIA liquids, and the forms of Nom Sg of *a*-stems.

It may be observed that the inscriptional pattern of Northern India in the 3rd and 2nd c. B.C. is, broadly speaking, in agreement with the pattern of dialect geography which may be postulated on the basis of the literary Prākrits. Of particular importance are the facts that only one site (the Jogīmārā cave) among the Eastern inscriptional sites shows the typical Māgadhī *ś* (instead of *s*) and that less than half of the places display merger of OIA liquids in favor of *l*. In other words, the strict Māgadhī dialect (with all three features *ś*, *l*, and *-e*) was confined to a rather small area; the greater part of the Eastern regions shows only two of the three features; and the periphery of the region possesses none of the Māgadhī characteristics. Pāṭaliputra, the capital of Mauryan empire, is usually considered as the focus where 'strict' Māgadhī must have been spoken. Elsewhere in Magadha there was less strict Māgadhī spoken. This dialect—called traditionally Ardha-Māgadhī—did not merge OIA sibilants *ś* and *s*, and liquids *l* and *r* (*l* is used for *r* rarely)[8], but used fairly frequently *-e* in the Nom Sg of *a*-stems. Comparing Pāli with strict Māgadhī, it appears that Pāli did not merge OIA sibilants *ś* and *s*, and liquids *l* and *r* (*l* is used for *r* rarely), and used very rarely *e* in the Nom Sg of *a*-stem. Pāli is therefore closer to the Western type (such as Prākrit of Gīrnār) and farther away from Māgadhī than Ardha-Māgadhī is.[9]

While the Eastern group of Aśokan inscriptions resembles in its phonological and morphological features the Māgadhī of the classical drama, there are no inscriptional equivalents of the two principal literary Prākrits, although they have local names: Śaurasenī and Māhārāṣṭrī.

1.4 Literary Prākrits

Excluding Pāli, the following are the two groups of the most important literary Prākrits as preserved in Sanskrit drama, Prākrit poetry and Jain writings:

(i) Māhārāṣṭrī, Śaurasenī and Māgadhī (used in Sanskrit drama, Māhārāṣṭrī also in poetry);

(ii) Ardha-Māgadhī (in Jain Canon), Jain-Māhārāṣṭrī and Jain-Śaurasenī (in post-canonic writings).

Māhārāṣṭrī, according to the grammarians, was the Prākrit par excellence, the 'standard' Prākrit. While the grammarians describe its features, in the case of other Prākrits they mention only how they deviate from the 'standard' Prākrit. According to Daṇḍin (6th c. A.D.), Māhārāṣṭrī was the most 'excellent' Prākrit.[10] It was based on the living tongue of the north-western part of the Deccan (along the river Godāvarī) and the beginnings of its literary cultivation go back to the 4th c. A.D. Its prestige might be due to the fact that it was spoken in the dominions of the powerful dynasty of Sātavāhanas (the Andhra dynasty) which established itself in this part of India with the capital city Pratiṣṭhāna (the modern Paiṭhan on the north bank of the Godāvarī in the Aurangābād district). In the 1st c. B.C. the Sātavāhanas were paramount sovereigns of Trans-Vindhyan India and their power was restored in the 2nd c. A.D., when they ruled over Mahārāṣṭra, Kāthiāwār, Central India, Berar and Mālwā. The Prākrit inscriptions of Sātavāhana kings were found at Nāsik, Nānāghaṭ, Sāñci, Kārle, Kaṇheri, Amarāvati and Cina. In any case, only Māhārāṣṭrī among the other Prākrit dialects used in Sanskrit drama became literary *koine* (e.g., the speakers of various dialects in Sanskrit drama recite their poetic passages in Māhārāṣṭrī). Some magnificient poetic works were composed in this dialect: *Setubandha* (or *Rāvaṇavaha*) relates the story of Rāma, but it is supposed to commemorate the building of a bridge of boats by the king of Kashmir, Pravarasena, in Srinagar; the *Gauḍavaho* celebrates the conquest of Bengal by Yaśovarman of Kanauj (the end of the 7th c. A.D.); *Sattasaī* (*Saptaśatakaṃ* of Hāla, identified with the king Sātavāhana (2nd c. A.D.), is an anthology of lyric verses composed by many poets.

As far as its relationship to OIA is concerned, it is the most advanced dialect of the middle stage of MIA. Some of its salient features are the following:

(i) The three sibilants of OIA *s* (dental), *ś* (palatal) and *ṣ* (retroflex) merged here into one dental sibilant *s;*

(ii) All intervocalic voiceless stops were voiced and spirantized (cf. 2.2.6). Subsequently, the resulting voiced fricatives were reduced to zero ($k > g > \gamma > \phi$), e.g., OIA *prākṛta*, Mah *pāua*:

	prākṛta
Cr > *C*, *ṛ* > *u*	pākuta
voicing of intervocalic stops	pāguda
spirantization	pāγuδa
voiced intervocalic fricatives > ϕ	pāua

Similarly, all murmured voiced stops were spirantized and ultimately lost their consonantal component but kept their murmur as a segment (*kh*>*gh*>*γh*>*h*), e.g., OIA *mukham* 'face', Mah *muhã*; OIA *katham* 'how', Mah *kahã*; OIA *dadhi* 'curds', Mah *dahi*.

	mukha	katha	dadhi
voicing of intervocalic stops	mugha	kadha	
spiratization	muγha	kaδha	daδhi
voiced intervocalic fricatives > ϕ	muha	kaha	dahi

Intervocalic voiced retroflex stops (originating from voiceless retroflex stops which in their turn may originate by retroflexion of plain voiceless stops) do not undergo spirantization. Contrast the development of OIA *prākṛta* 'Prākrit' and *prābhṛta* 'present, offering':

	prākṛta	prābhṛta
Cr > *C*, *ṛ* > *u* (+ retroflexion)	pākuta	pābhuta
voicing	pāguda	pābhuḍa
spirantization	pāγuδa	pāβhuḍa
voiced interocalic fricatives > ϕ	pāua	pāhuḍa

(iii) Final -*aḥ* of OIA becomes -*o in* Mah.

Śaurasenī is deemed to be the Prākrit of the Madhyadeśa (Śūrasena was the name of the country around Mathurā). However, as mentioned under 1.3, we have absolutely no inscriptional evidence for this Prākrit. In Sanskrit drama it is spoken by women and the Vidūṣaka 'clown, jester' (in the late drama *Karpūramañjarī* even by the king). Apart from these dramatic passages, there are no independent literary works in Śaurasenī. The following are its main phonological and morphological features:

(i) The three sibiliants of OIA merged here into one dental sibilant *s*;

(ii) Its intervocalic stops were reduced to zero as in Mah with the exception of the voiced dental stop (plain or murmured) whether the original or arising from the voiceless one: *t(h)* > *d(h)*. In other words, the environment for spirantization includes here only the peripheral stops *b* and *g*. Thus we find Ś *gada* 'gone' (< OIA *gata*) versus Mah *gaa* (*gata* > *gada* > *gaδa* > *gaa*), Ś *jāṇādi* 'he knows' (< OIA *jānāti*) versus Mah *jānai*; Ś *jīvadha* 'you live' (< OIA *jīvatha*) versus Mah *jīvaha*;

(iii) Final *-aḥ* of OIA becomes here *-o* as in Mah.

Māgadhī, on the other hand, possesses rich inscriptional evidence. Dramatic Māgadhī may be viewed as a stylized literary variety based on the dialects of eastern India. In Sanskrit drama Māgadhī is spoken by people of low social status. Sanskrit drama supplies us with precious evidence for a number of its regional and occupational varieties (e.g. Śākārī, Cāṇḍālī, Ḍhakkī; cf. under 5.3). Its salient phonological features:

(i) The three sibilants of OIA merged here into one palatal sibilant *ś* (< *ś*, *ṣ*, *s*), e.g., OIA *śuṣka* 'dry' > Mg *śuśka;*

(ii) The two liquids of OIA *r* and *l* merged into *l*, e.g., OIA *rājā* 'king', Mg *lājā*;

(iii) Intervocalic stops in Mg are reduced to zero as in Ś (i.e., with the exception of the voiced dental stop, whether the original or that arising from the voiceless one), e.g., OIA *bhaviṣyati* 'he will be' Mg *bhaviśśadi* (cf. Ś *bhavissadi*). However, the environment for spirantization in Mg includes also the voiced palatal affricate (plain or murmured): OIA *j(h)* > Mg *y(h)*. Thus we find Mg *ayya* 'today' (from OIA *adya* > *ajja*) versus Mah *ajja*.

Chart 1.3 summarizes these phonological features in addition to the distribution of the suffixes of the Nom Sg (*o* ~ *e*):

Chart 1-3. Diagnostic Features of Dramatic Prākrits

OIA	Śaurasenī	Māgadhī	Māhārāṣṭrī
Sibilants			
ś, ṣ, s	s	ś	s
Liquids *l, r*	l, r	l	l, r

Intervocalic stops			
b	> β > ϕ	> β > ϕ	> β > ϕ
d	d	d	> δ > ϕ
j	j	> y	ǰ
g	> γ > ϕ	> γ > ϕ	> γ > ϕ
Nom Sg *-aḥ*	-ō	-ē	-ō

It is generally assumed that dramatic Prākrits do not represent the actual speech of the people they are supposed to typify. Nevertheless, they are based upon it and they remain for us pieces of valuable evidence regarding phonology, morphology and syntax of Middle Aryan dialects. This value diminishes with time. The later dramas, written by dramatists who learnt their Prākrit as a 'classical' language, present us with Prākrits following strictly the rules of Prākrit grammarians. For instance, the tyrannic use of the passive causative in Sanskrit and Prākrit sections of Mudrārākṣasa (ca. 800 A.D.) belongs to the realm of artificial linguistic usage (cf. under 4.5).

As mentioned above, the Prākrits were cultivated by the religious sects of Jainas who made them a vehicle for their literary works. The oldest Jain sūtras were composed in Ardha-Māgadhī (some of its features are: Nom Sg of masculine *a*-stems in *-e*, Loc Sg of *a*-stems in *-ṃsi*; *-itthā* as the singular suffix of the preterite in all persons, and *-īsu* as the plural suffix in all persons; cf. under 3.4.5) These form the Canon of the Śvetāmbara sect (comprised of 45 *āgamas*). This collection of writings was arranged by Devaḍḍhi Gaṇin in the 5th c. A.D. The oldest poetic work (*kāvya*) in Jain literature is the *Paümacariya* (a version of the Rāmāyaṇa) dated to the 3rd c. A.D., which already contains a number of linguistic features of the following linguistic stage (Apabhraṃśa).

The non-canonical books of the Śvetāmbaras (consisting mainly of the collections of stories) were written in a form of Māhārāṣṭrī, called Jain Māhārāṣṭrī. The upper and lower limits of their literary activity are given between ca. 500 and 800 A.D. by Jacobi (1886:XVIII). The starting point of their literary activity seems to be the conclusion of their Canon in the middle of the 5th c. A.D. (454) and we may assume that they had been using Māhārāṣṭrī for several centuries until Sanskrit replaced Māhārāṣṭrī as the literary *koine* of educated people. To judge by our manuscripts, the differences between 'general' and Jain Māhārāṣṭrī seem to be unimportant. As the most salient one Jacobi (1886:XXII) mentions the use of the palatal glide to avoid the hiatus in the environment after vowels before *a* (cf. 2.2.6):

OIA	Māhārāṣṭrī	Jain Māhārāṣṭrī
gata 'gone'	gaa	gaya
hṛdaya 'heart'	hiaa	hiyaya

The canon of the Digambara sect was written in a dialect which in some respects resembles Śaurasenī and has therefore been termed Jain Śaurasenī. Thus what is typical of the evolution of the Middle Indo-Aryan during its middle period is a simultaneous or overlapping use of a number of literary koines by various religious sects and social groups. These koines during their existence had always been enriching themselves from the literary sources of prestigious Sanskrit[11].

1.5 Apabhraṃśa

The last stage of MIA is known as Apabhraṃśa. The term comes from *Mahābhāṣya* of Patañjali (ca. 2nd c. B.C.) where it meant 'aberrant, off standard' in speech. There is more evidence which allows us to conclude that Apabhraṃśa was a linguistic stage of Middle Indo-Aryan as early as 300 A.D. From the 6th c. A.D. this term or Avahaṃsa (or Avahaṭṭha) designated a literary dialect in the works of grammarians and rhetoricians. During this period Prākrits became stylized and artificial (as Sanskrit in the last pre-Christian centuries). Up to 1100 A.D. Apabhraṃśa denoted the literary form of provincial speeches and from the 12th century A.D. onwards Apabhraṃśa was a classical language like Sanskrit and Prākrit.

The earliest document of Apabhraṃśa are the Apabhraṃśa songs in the Fourth Act of Kālidāsa's *Vikramorvaśīya.* Apabhraṃśa was used for literary purposes mostly by the Jaina writers. Three types of literary works in Apabhraṃśa are extant:

(i) biographical studies of the Jaina saints (*Purāṇas* and *Caritakathās* 'biographical tales');
(ii) theological and didactic works (*Dharmakathās* 'pious tales' and *Dohās* 'educative couplets and quadruplets');

(iii) compendia of stories (*Kathānakakāvyās* 'poetic tales').

The earliest specimen of (i) is Svayaṃbhūdeva's (ca 7th c.) *Paüma-cariu.* The most important 10th c. Apabhraṃśa literary work is Dhaṇavāla's *Bhavisattakahā.* The most important author of (ii) was Muni Rāmasiṃha (*Pāhuḍadohā*). Most of the works of the Jaina writers of Rajasthan and Gujarat were composed in the Western Apabhraṃśa. However, a number of non-Jaina writers wrote in a language which is usually described as the Eastern Apabhraṃśa (*Dohās* of Kānha, Saraha and Tillo). Western Apabhraṃśa corresponds to the 'Śaurasenī region' (Grierson, LSI, Vol. I.1): modern Gujarat, Rajasthan and western Gangetic Doab. Eastern Apabhraṃśa comprises the provinces where the modern descendants of Māgadhī are spoken: Bengal, Bihar and Orissa. There was also a southern Deccani variety of Apabhraṃśa (cf. Tagare, 1948:18 ff.) spoken in the Māhārāṣṭrī region (Grierson, LSI, Vol. I.1): modern Mahārāṣṭra, Berar and adjoining districts.

The following three phonological phenomena may serve as the salient diagnostic features of the Western and Eastern varieties of Apabhraṃśa (cf. Tagare, 1948:24-6):

(i) the OIA cluster *kṣ* became unexceptionally *kh* in EAp (fricative weakening). In the West, from the beginning of the 7th C. A.D., *k* was fronted in the anticipation of the retroflex sibilant and assumed the place of the more front palatal affricate *k* → *c*/-*ṣ* (cf. 2.2.3.i). Contrast EAp *khetta* 'field' (< *kṣetra*), *akkhara* 'syllable' (< *akṣara*) with WAp *acchi* 'eye' (< *akṣi*), *vaccha* 'tree' (< *vṛkṣa*);

(ii) OIA *v* became unexceptionally *b* in EAp but it remained unchanged (with some sporadic *b*'s) in WAp and SAp;

(iii) OIA sibilants merged in favor of *ś* in the East, but in favor of *s* in the West and South.

There is no mention of Apabhraṃśa in the oldest Prākrit grammar by Vararuci. The first among the Prākrit grammarians to mention it were Hemacandra and Puruṣottama. Puruṣottama (12th c.) classified Apabhraṃśa as a major MIA language with three varieties or dialects:

Nāgaraka 'belonging to Nāgara' (probably the common city dialect(s), i.e., the *lingua franca* used by merchants that ran among cities), *Upanāgaraka* 'belonging to the periphery of Nāgara' and *Vrācaḍaka* 'belonging to (the country of) Vracaḍa'.

Puruṣottama also mentions *Laukika*[12] as different from Apabhraṃśa. Dharmadāsa in his *Vidagdhamukhamaṇḍana* (before 1160) distinguished between the earlier and the later phase of the popular literary language; the former he called Apabhraṃśa and the later Laukika (i.e., belonging to the *loka* 'common people'). According to Kramadīśvara (12th c.), Apabhraṃśa means primarily a later phase of Prākrit.

In any case, it seems that the focal area of Apabhraṃśa was Rajasthan and Gujarat. From here Apabhraṃśa spread through the whole of North India during the last two centuries of the first millennium and became North India's literary koine. It should be mentioned that Apabhraṃśa literary works display various degrees of Prākrit influence. According to Bloch (1965:21), the mixed character of Apabhraṃśa is attributable to the multilingualism/dialectism of its poets (like the Rajput bards). Thus Apabhraṃśa texts contain various archaisms and dialectisms.

The following stage in the history of Indo-Aryan languages is known under the Sanskrit term *Abhibhraṣṭa* (i.e., *apabhraṣṭa* 'fallen away') which is used synonymously with MIA *Avahaṭṭha* 'fallen down'). Some of the early writers (Dharmadāsa) and many later writers called it Laukika ('belonging to the common people'). Avahaṭṭha became a literary koine of Northern India by the 8th c. and continued to be used so until it was replaced in this function by the emerging NIA languages (from the 10/11th c. onwards).

At present it is impossible to establish exactly how the above-mentioned MIA dialects relate through their Apabhraṃśa-Avahaṭṭha descendants to individual modern North Indian languages and dialects. However, without trying to be exact about diatopicality and diachrony, it is possible to see broad connections and developmental tendencies. Let us compare the conjugation of the present in Apabhraṃśa with that in Old Gujarātī:[13]

	Apabhraṃśa	Old Gujarātī
Sg 1	karaũ	karauṃ
2	ahi	aṃ
3	ai	ai

Pl 1	ahũ	auṃ
2	ahu	au
3	ahĩ	aiṃ

The forms of the suffixes of the 1st and 3rd Sg are identical, and the plural forms of Old Gujarati resulted from their ancestral forms by the loss of intervocalic *h*.

The changes separating the old and the middle, and the middle and the late stages of MIA will be investigated in detail under 3.1.4. At this point I want to mention that the most drastic changes occurred between the middle and the late stage. This can be shown on the declension of *a*-stems (*putraḥ* 'son'):

		Old Prākrits	Middle Prākrits	Late Prākrits
	Sanskrit	Pāli	AMg	Ap
Sg N	putraḥ	putto	putto	puttu
A	am	ã	ã	,,
I	eṇa	eṇa	eṇã	e, ĩ
G	asya	assa	assa	aha, -ahu
Abl	āt	asmā	ā(o)	,,
L	e	asmĩ	āsi	ahĩ, -ĩ, e
Pl N	āḥ	ā	ā	a
A	ān	e	,,	,,
I	ebhiḥ	ehi	ehĩ	ahĩ, -ehĩ
G	ānām	ānã	ānã	ahã
Abl	ebhyas	ehi	ehinto	,,
L	eṣu	esu	esũ	ahĩ, -ehĩ

Old and Middle Prākrits created a new type of the opposition of the direct (Nom, Acc) to the oblique cases (Instr, Gen, Abl, Loc) in both numbers: a monosyllabic ending in the direct case vs. a dissyllabic ending in the oblique case (trisyllabic in the Abl in AMg). In Apabhraṃśa, in addition, a new opposition of the singular to the plural in oblique cases based on the presence of a nasalized vowel started emerging: V vs. Ṽ, plain vs. nasalized ultima of the ending signalized the opposition between the singular vs. plural oblique case (i.e., here we are reaching the NIA state of affairs). In morphological terminology, the cumulative exponence of grammatical significates of OIA and earlier stages of MIA gave way gradually to new types of semi-agglutinative exponence in MIA. Ultimately, the nasalization of the ultima became obligatory in the plural oblique cases in Ap, whereas it was only optional during the previous stage (as shown by AMg).

With the risk of oversimplification and idealization we may relate the MIA dialect continuum to the NIA dialect continuum through their Apabhraṃśa-Avahaṭṭha stages in the following crude schema:

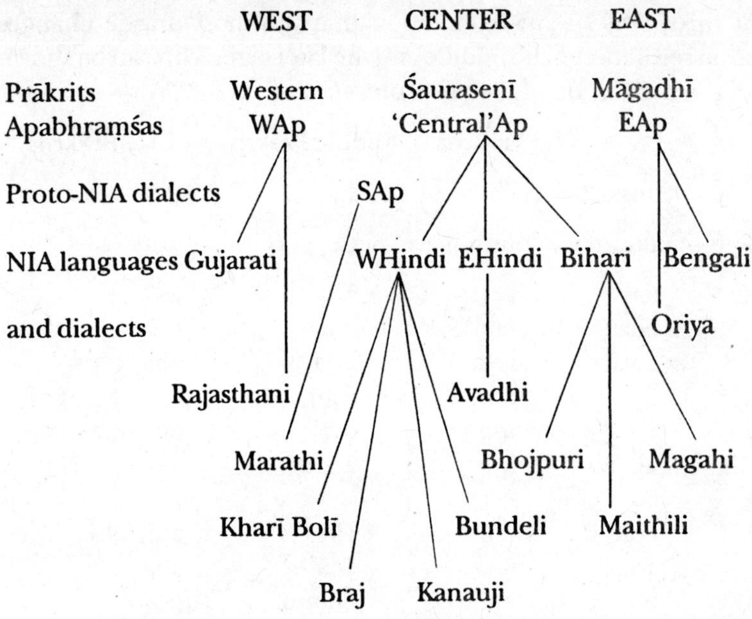

A more detailed diagram of the development of the Indo-Aryan languages (based on Grierson's LSI) is found in Chatterji (1926:6). More recently, Cardona (1974) arranged the Indo-Aryan languages into geographical divisions, with little attempt to construct a formal *Stammbaum*.

1.6 Evidence of Medieval Indian Grammarians

Finally, a few words about the studies of Prākrits by Medieval Indian grammarians whose evidence sometimes corroborates and sometimes contradicts that of Prākrit and Apabhraṃśa manuscripts.

Traces of the only genuine (?) Prākrit grammar (with material from pre-Christian centuries) are perhaps the fragments preserved in Chapter XVII (XVIII) of the Bharatīya-Nāṭyaśāstra (cf. 5.2).

The oldest Prākrit grammar preserved to us is *Prākṛtaprakāśa* by Vararuci Kātyāyana. The eight books (ca. 420 sūtras in Sanskrit) deal only with Māhārāṣṭrī. It is possible that Vararuci's rules were abstracted from a collection of popular songs similar to Hāla's collection *Sattasaī* (cf. Scharfe 1977:192) and that he lived in the 3rd/4th c. A.D.

Nitti-Dolci (1938:14 ff) demonstrated that Book X (on Paiśācī) and Book XI (on Māgadhī) were not written by Vararuci himself but by the rhetorician Bhāmaha (7th c.?). Some time after Bhāmaha Book V was divided into two and another book on Śaurasenī was added, making a total of 12 books. The original title of Vararuci's work was probably *Prākṛtasūtra*, while the usual title *Prākṛtaprakāśa* designated only the commentary by Bhāmaha.

All the other grammarians of the Eastern and Western Schools lived and worked in later centuries when the Prākrits they were describing stopped being used as living languages. Instead, they had to rely on the grammatical tradition and their own study of manuscripts of Prākrit works.

The Eastern School of Prākrit grammarians followed Vararuci's rules for Māhārāṣṭrī in their descriptions of dramatic Prākrits, Paiśācī and Apabhraṃśa. The earliest among them was Puruṣottama, the author of *Prākṛtānuśāsana* (preserved in a single manuscript), who lived in the 12th c.

Among the Western grammarians the earliest was Hemacandra Sūri of Gujarat (1088/89-1172/73). The first seven chapters of his grammar deal with Sanskrit and the eighth chapter is devoted to Prākrit (1119 rules). Hemacandra's 'transfer' rules for Prākrits follow the rules of Sanskrit grammar and close with the statement that in all remaining respects Prākrit is like Sanskrit (*śeṣaṃ saṃskṛtavat siddham*). Hemacandra's formulations depend on those by Vararuci and his treatment of Māgadhī, Paiśācī and Śaurasenī shows the influence of a lost treatise (cf. Scharfe 1977:193). Hemacandra described the language of the canonical Jain scriptures, the Ardha-Māgadhī, which he called *ārṣa* '(language) of the saints' (almost all the special forms have been verified from the texts). On the other hand, his sūtras of the Māgadhī section correspond to those of Bhāmaha (with some minor differences). Of particular importance is Hemacandra's description of Western Apabhraṃśa (illustrated with many *dohā*'s 'stanzas' taken from the contemporary poetry) since this variety was a direct ancestor of Old Gujarati spoken by Hemacandra (cf. 1.5).

Kramadīśvara, the author of *Saṃkṣiptasāra*, is generally placed between Hemacandra and Vopadeva (of the 13th c.). Like that of Hemacandra his grammar deals with Sanskrit in the first seven chapters and only the eighth chapter is devoted to Prākrit. The author followed Vararuci in his exposition.

Prākṛtaśabdānuśāsana of Trivikramadeva (about 13th c.) consists of ca. 1036 sūtras and follows Hemacandra in the presentation of the material. The third book of his work is valuable because of many Apabhraṃśa stanzas quoted in it.

Among the late grammars composed by Eastern grammarians *Prākṛtasarvasvam* of Mārkaṇḍeya Kavīndra (patronized by Mukundadeva, the king of Orissa) and *Prākṛtakalpataru* of Rāmasarman may be mentioned. Both lived in the 17th c. when any direct observation of the living usage of Prākrits can be ruled out.

NOTES

(1) In Iranian IE *r* and *l* appear indiscriminately as *r*; in the language of the Rgveda this is predominantly the case; and in Classical Sanskrit both *l* and *r* are found. The dialect at the basis of the Ṛgvedic language lay to the north-west, while the classical language was formed in Madhyadeśa and in its further development it was subject to the continuous influence of the dialectal forms of Magadha. Thus in Classical Sanskrit the distribution of *r* and *l* found in many basic words of the vocabulary continues the distribution established by the Vedic literature, but in other cases *l*-forms based on the dialect of Madhyadeśa prevail. For details see Burrow (1955:82-3).

(2) For instance, king Rudradāman's inscription in Gīrnār, dated to the 2nd c. A.D., was composed in Sanskrit ca. 400 years after Aśokan inscriptions had been incised in various dialects of Middle Indo-Aryan and ca. 300 years after the victories of king Khāravela of Kaliṅga (Orissa) had been eulogized in the MIA vernacular (Hāthigumphā inscription).

(3) Cf. Buddhaghoṣa's statement that Māgadhī is the root-language of all people: *Māgadhikāya sabba-sattānaṃ mūlabhāsāya* (Vism 441, 34).

(4) No attempt will be made to relate systematically to these groups the dialect of the Ceylon Inscriptions (1st c. B.C. - 3rd c. A.D.) and the dialect-groups of

the Central Asian Kharoṣṭhī documents (3rd c. A.D.). For their characteristics cf. Sen (1960:12-18).

(5) In the East the distinction between *r* and *l* is maintained at some places: Sītābeṅgā (Choṭa Nagpur Division), Bodh-Gayā (Bihar), Barābar Hill (north of Gayā in Bihar), Udayagiri (in the Puri District of Orissa), and Sāranāth (north of Benares). The OIA liquids merged in favor of *l* at the following places: Piprāhwā (in the Biradpur Estate of the Basti District south-east of the ruins of Kapilavastu), Sohgaura (on the right bank of Rāptī in the United Provinces), Jogīmārā (Choṭa Nagpur Division), Mahāsthān (Bogrā District of Bengal). For examples see Mehendale (1948:189-90).

(6) In a further development the clusters *tp* and *db* in initial position were simplified by dropping the initial dental stop. Thus in WAp (around 500 A.D. ?) there are forms such as *paĩ* 'you' (< OIA *tvayam*) and between 600-1000 A.D.) *be* 'two' (< OIA *dvau*). See Tagare (1948:92-7) for data and situation in other Ap dialects.

(7) The Nom Sg of masculine *a-* stems in *-o* appears in the inscriptions of Udayagiri and Sāranāth; elsewhere *-e* is used. In the case of the Nom Sg of the neuter stems *-e* is found at Sohgaura, Piprāhwā and Mahāsthān; *-aṃ* at Bodh-Gayā, Udayagiri, Sāranāth and Mahāsthān. For examples see Mehendale (1948:196).

(8) Pischel (1900, § 17) quotes Abhayadeva as saying: *Ardha-Māgadhī bhāṣā yasyāṃ rasor laśau Māgadhyām ityādikaṃ Māgadha-bhāṣā-lakṣaṇaṃ paripūrṇaṃ nāsti* 'The Ardha-Māgadhī language in which the characteristics of the Māgadhī language exemplified in such statements as "in Māgadhī *śa* replaces *sa* and *la* replaces *ra*" are not fulfilled'. Abhayadeva thus assumes that the language is called 'Half-Māgadhī' because it has only half its characteristics.

The alternative explanation, quoted by Ghatage (1941:2), that the name could mean 'current in half the country of Magadha' seems less likely.

(9) On the basis of this evidence, Norman (1980:68) concluded that both Ardha-Māgadhī and Pāli had their home somewhere in Magadha; the latter in a region somewhere near the border with Kaliṅga (Orissa). On the other hand, Waldschmidt in his edition of Lüders (1954) classified Pāli as an essentially western MIA language because it displays several features in common with the inscription from Gīrnār.

(10) Kāvyādarśa (1.35): *Mahārāṣṭrāśrayāṃ bhāṣāṃ prakṛṣṭaṃ prākṛtaṃ viduḥ.*

(11) As summarized aptly by Sen (1973:7): 'In the literary scene in India through the centuries, a spoken form of the current language was never preferred for literature—the language used for literary purposes always harked back to an older literary language which already had an established place'.

(12) Sen (1973:13) uses Puruṣottama's (and others') term Laukika and Advayavarjra's (and others') term Abhibhraṣṭa (or Avahaṭṭha) in the meaning of Proto-New Indo-Aryan, defined by him as 'the popular literary and standardized form of the transitional stage between Middle and New

Indo-Aryan'.

(13) The Apabhraṃśa forms are quoted according to Hemacandra (IV, 382 ff.); Old Gujarati forms according to *Kriyāratnasamuccaya*, composed 1410 A.D. A propos the *anusvāra* in the 2nd Sg, Jacobi (1918:56*) mentions that it is written only once. It should be kept in mind, however, that the WAp texts may show the above forms only exceptionally. Thus Bhavisatta Kaha (Jacobi, 1918:40*) displays *karaũ* only once vs. 69 instances of *karami*; in the 3rd Pl *karahĩ* occurs 10 times vs. karanti 65 times. Forms such as *karami* and *karanti* can, of course, be evaluated as archaisms.

CHAPTER 2

PHONOLOGY

2.1 Phonological System of MIA Dialects: Vowels

Using the traditional pseudoarticulatory diagram the vocalic phonemes of OIA may be represented as shown below:

OIA Vocalic System

ī, i	u, ū	āi, ai	au, āu
ē	ō		
a, ā			

Note: /a/ was realized as schwa[ə] (cf. Pāṇini 8.4.68)[1]

The OIA triangular system possessed vowels of three heights on both axes. The feature of length was phonemic on high and low vowels (and diphthongs); however, no contrast existed with mid vowels which were only long in both open and closed syllables (CV: and CV:C, where V: = ē and ō).

OIA diphthongs were monophthongized in MIA: *ai* > *ē*, *au* > *ō*. If the diphthong occurred in a closed syllable the resulting long mid vowel was shortened (2.1.2) and later on raised (2.1.3). For instance, OIA *vairamaṇī* 'abstinence' > Pāli *vēramaṇī*, but *vaidya* 'doctor' > Pāli, Mah *vĕjja*. Diphthongs which remained in MIA are found in Sanskritisms (data in Pischel 1900:55-58) and interjections (*ai*).

Early MIA completed this diagram by creating short mid vowels. These resulted from OIA long mid vowels *ē* and *ō* (original ones or those monophthongized in overweight (2.1.2a) and pretonic/posttonic heavy syllables (2.1.2b)).

Early MIA Vocalic System

ī, i u, ū

ē, e o, ō

a, ā

Short mid vowels could be phonemicized only if they appeared in open syllables, where the contrast /ē/ : /ĕ/ was possible (i.e., not in closed syllables where only short vowels existed). Short vowels in open syllables could arise in several ways:

(i) if the double consonant in heavy syllables was degeminated without compensatory lengthening:

$$C\,e\,C_x.\ C_x\,V \longrightarrow C\,e.\ C_x\,V$$

(ii) when the syllable boundary was moved after the rule of metathesis applied in clusters of *h* + nasals or liquids (cf. 2.2.iv). Thus when the structure of Ś, Mg *gĕṇ.hadi* 'takes' (OIA *gṛhṇāti)* changed to *gĕ.ṇhadi* (i.e., under the assumption that *ṇh* represents a unitary phoneme), we find a short mid vowel in an open syllable;

(iii) another opportunity arose in instances where the dyadic cluster was resolved by epenthesis. Thus OIA *jyōtsnā* 'moonlight' underwent shortening of the vowel and simplification of the triadic cluster in MIA *j(y)ŏs.nā.* This form developed in two directions: AMg *dŏ-siṇā* shows the epenthesis of *i* while preserving short *ŏ* which now appears in an open syllable; Mah *jŏ.ṇhā* shows the fricative weakening of *s*, metathesis of *ṇh* and resyllabication of the form (under the assumption of *ṇh* being a unitary phoneme): *jŏh.nā* > *jŏn.hā* > *jo.ṇhā* > (cf. Pāli *juṇhā*);

(iv) finally, a short mid vowel could arise in an open syllable if the shortening of an originally long mid vowel was not accompanied by the compensatory gemination of the following consonant. As shown in 2.1.2b, in.middle and late MIA dialects the shortening process spread to heavy syllables (i.e., those containing long vowels in open syllables), especially, if the

OIA accent was located on the preceding or the following syllable. Vowel shortening in this environment might have been accompanied by compensatory gemination of the following consonant. If gemination did not take place, the mid vowel would appear in an open syllable: OIA *-evám* 'thus' > Mah *ĕv.vã* ~ *ĕ.vã.*

In the late MIA system of long and short vowels, vowels short *i* and long *ē* became closer to one another than to long *ī* and short *e*, respectively; and the same is true about the *o* and *u* vowels:

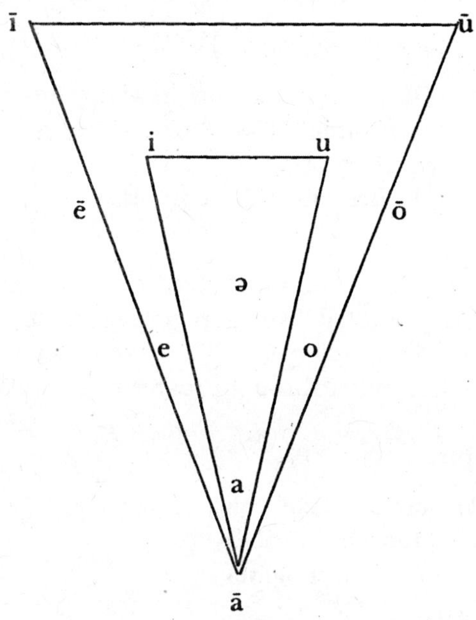

As will be shown in 2.1.3, the MIA spellings Ē (*ē-kāra*) and Ō (*ō-kāra*) for [i] and [u] may be interpreted as indicating that the value of short *i* and *u* was lax [ɪ] and [ʊ], i.e. that Ap reached already a NIA state of affairs with four degrees of aperture (closed, half closed, half open, open):

Apabhraṃśa Vocalic System

ī				ū
	ɪ		ʊ	
	ē		ō	
		ə		
	ɛ		ɔ	
		ā		

For [ɨ] and [ʉ] cf. 2.3.

2.1.1 *Compensatory Lengthening of Short Vowels*

Two types of OIA consonantal clusters were assimilated (cf. 2.2.2) and the resulting geminate (preserved in Pāli) was degeminated (during later stages of MIA) with a concomitant compensatory lengthening of the preceding short vowels: $V \rightarrow V{:} / — C_x C_x$, when $C_x \rightarrow \phi$.

(a) *r* followed by a consonant (especially sibilant). Here the geminate resulted through regressive assimilation (2.1.1a);
(b) *s* followed by glides (*y, v*), *r* , and a sibilant. Here the geminate resulted through progressive assimilation (2.1.1b).

Some examples:

	OIA		Pāli	
(a)	kartum 'to make'		kattabba ~ kātabba (gerundive)	Ś, Mg kādū
				Mah, AMg, JMah kāū
	sarva 'all'		sabba	Ap sāva
	nirṇayati			AMg, JMah nīṇei

In AMg even the loss of *l* may be accompanied by compensatory lengthening, e.g. *vāgala* 'bark (of a tree)' (< OIA *valkala*).

	OIA	Pāli	
(b)	paśyati 'sees'	passati	AMg, JMah pāsai
	śiṣya 'disciple'	sissa	AMg, JMah sīsa
	manuṣya 'man'	manussa	AMg, JMah maṇūsa

aśva 'horse'	assa	Mah, AMg, JMah āsa
śvaśrū 'mother-in-law'	sassū	Mah sāsū
utsava 'holiday'	ussava	Mah, AMg, JM, Ś ūsava

In grammatical morphology the degemination of *ss* (< *sy*) had certain consequences for the remodelling of nominal and verbal paradigms. Compensatory lengthening accounts for the length in the Gen Sg: *-asya* > *-assa* > *-āsa* > *-āha* (3.2.1) and in the future: *-iṣy* > *-iss* > *-īs* and *-īh* (3.4.6) (vs. Bloch, cf. Footnote 3 to 3.2.1).

2.1.2 *Shortening of Long Vowels*

There are essentially two environments for the shortening of OIA long vowels in MIA: overweight syllables and pretonic/posttonic heavy syllables.

(a) Long vowels in overweight syllables were shortened:

V: → V / — CC. Examples for low and high vowels:

OIA gātra 'limb' MIA	gatta (Mah, AMg, JMah)
grīṣma 'summer'	gimha (Mah, AMg, Ś, Mg, Ap)
ūrdhva 'upright'	uddha (Mah, JMah, Ś, Mg, Ap)

Similarly, the long mid vowels *ē, ō* of OIA (occurring in both open and closed syllables) remained long only in open syllables whereas in closed syllables they were shortened:

prēkṣyate 'perceives'	pĕcchai (Mah, AMg, JMah)
anyōnya 'each other'	aṇṇŏṇṇa (Mah, AMg, JMah, Ś)

Thus the syllabic pattern of OIA *dē.vaḥ* 'god' remained unchanged, dē.vō, whereas that of OIA *ōṣ.ṭhaḥ* 'lip' changed into MIA *ŏṭ.ṭh-ō*.

Traditionally, the change in the syllabic pattern of MIA vis-à-vis that of OIA was explained by taking recourse to the so-called 'Law of Mora' (see Geiger (1916/1943:63-4)). According to this law, our terminology could be reworded as follows:

light syllable (CV) contains 1 mora
heavy syllable (CV:, CVC) contains 2 moras
overweight syllable (CV:C) contains 3 moras

As we saw above, MIA dialects did not possess overweight syllables, or, diachronically, the overweight syllables were replaced by the heavy ones (i.e., the three-mora syllables by the two-mora syllables). Since the heavy syllables can be of two types: (i) those containing a short vowel before a consonant cluster (CVC.C); (ii) those containing a long vowel before a single consonant (CV:C), there were two ways to achieve this aim:

(i) shortening in overweight syllables and keeping C.C : OIA *jīrṇaḥ* > Pāli *jiṇṇo* 'old';
(ii) keeping the long vowel but resolving the cluster by various processes, e.g., by fricative weakening: OIA *apēkṣā* > Pāli *apēkhā* 'expectation' (2.2.3).

(b) In middle and late MIA dialects (Mah, AMg, JMah, JŚ, Ap, but rarely in other dialects, e.g. dramatic Pkts) the shortening process spread from the overweight syllables to the heavy ones. In these dialects the long vowels (in open syllables) are often shortened if the OIA accent was located on the preceding or the following syllable:

$$V{:} \rightarrow V \qquad \left\{ \begin{array}{l} \acute{V}\;\_\_\_\_ \\ \\ \_\_\_\_\;\acute{V} \end{array} \right\}$$

Examples of vowel shortening in posttonic syllables:

OIA kúlāla 'owl' — AMg kulala
prásīda 'have mercy!' — Mah pasia (but Ś pasīda, Mg pasīda)
úlūka 'owl' — Mah ulua, AMg uluga

Shortening in pretonic syllables:

sthāpáyati 'makes X stand' — Mah, AMg, JMah ṭhavei (but see 3.4.9)
nīta 'led' — Mah ṇia

The shortening process of the long vowels may be accompanied by the compensatory gemination of the following consonant if the word was accented on the ultima. Thus we find:

OIA ēvám 'thus' — Mah, Ś, Mg, Ḍh ĕvvā̃ but also ĕvā̃ (cf. 2.1)
krīḍā́ 'play' — AMg, JMah kiḍḍā but also AMg, JMah kīḍā

yauvaná 'youth'	Mah, AMg, JM, Ś, Ap jŏvvaṇa
tailá 'oil'	Mah, AMg, JM, Ś, Mg tĕlla

Also the palatal glide in the same environment is geminated; *-yy-* is further affricated (cf. 2.2.7). Hence the MIA optatives and passives in *-jj-*:

OIA dēyā́t 'give' (Opt) Mg, JMah dĕjjā (via *dĕyyā́t*)
dīyáte 'give' (Pass) Mah, JMah dijjai (via *diyyáte*)

2.1.3 *Raising of Short Mid Vowels*

Short mid vowels arising through the shortening of OIA long vowels before consonant clusters (2.1.2) were raised during the middle period of MIA. Our evidence comes from the spellings with graphemes I (*i-kāra*) and U (*u-kāra*) for *ĕ* and *ŏ* found in AMg, Ś, Mah, JMah. (Earliest examples are found in Pāli, cf. 3.4.5.) Here are some examples (assembled by Pischel, 1900:73):

AMg miccha 'barbarian' vs. Mg, JM, Ś, Ap mĕccha (< OIA mlēccha)
AMg chitta 'field' khitta vs. Mah chetta (< OIA kṣētra)
JMah uṭṭha 'lip' AMg huṭṭha vs. AMg, Mah, JM ŏṭṭha (< OIA ōṣṭha)

In addition, during the same period, mid short vowels were raised word-finally in disyllabic suffixes after the long penultima *metri causa*.[2] Our evidence comes from Mah, AMg, JMah, JŚ. An example from Mah [H 15]:

pucchiāi muddhāe 'asked (and) perplexed' (Gen Sg) where we find *pucchiāi* instead of *pucchiāe* (OIA pṛṣṭāyā mugdhāyāḥ)

During the middle period of MIA (evidence of Mah, AMg, JMah, JŚ) the raising rule did not apply across the word boundary before enclitics. Thus we find:

Mah tumhĕ=ttha 'you=are' [R 3.3] not * *tumhi=ttha*
(cf. Vedic yuṣmē=stha)
JM purisŏ=tti 'the man=PART' (Pischel, 1900:74)

In the latter example, the shortening rule before CC applied across the word boundary before the enclitic, V: → V / — = CC, but the raising rule was blocked: *purisō=tti* → *purisŏ=tti* (i.e., not **purisu=tti*).

During the late period of MIA (evidence of Ap) the raising rule applied across the whole phonological spectrum without any restrictions.

In our data from the middle period of MIA there are also examples which seem to indicate the opposite process of lowering of high short vowels. Here is some evidence:

OIA itthā 'thus'	Mah, AMg, JMah, Mg ĕttha
	Ap ĕtthu
āgamiṣyant 'go' (Part Fut)	AMg āgamĕssa
puṣkara 'lotus'	Ś pŏkkhara
pustaka 'book'	Ś pŏtthaa

From the way these facts are presented in Pischel (1900:96 ff.) and Tagare (1948:59) one might conclude that we are dealing with a phonological process of the lowering of short high vowels in the environment before consonant clusters (*ĭ* > *ĕ*/-*CC* and *ŭ* > *ŏ*/—*CC*).[3]

In my opinion there was no lowering process of high short vowels of a phonological nature in MIA. I think that we are only dealing with attempts at the phonetic spelling of high lax vowels [ɪ] and [ʊ] by graphemes Ē (*ē-kāra*) and Ō (*ō-kāra*).

On similar grounds we may dismiss Pischel's (1900:101) further evidence for the lowering of high vowels, namely that of those arising through the shortening of high long vowels before consonant clusters: ū > ŭ > o / — CC.[4]

The best we can do with these mutually exclusive processes is to assume that the products of the raising rule were not identical with short OIA vowels (*i* and *u*) but that they were lax [ɪ] and [ʊ], i.e., realized lower and more towards the center than *i* and *u*. Hence the suitability of the graphemes Ē and Ō for the products of the raising rule.

To return to our original problem of the raising of short mid vowels, we may remind ourselves of a typological parallel from the history of Latin. As is well-known, the cardinal change which separated Classical from Vulgar Latin was merger of high short (lax) vowels (*i, u*) and mid long (tense) vowels (*ē, ō*)—hence the identical reflexes for Classical Latin *i* and *ē* (*u* and *ō*) in Modern French (e.g. *poir* < **pirus* and *voile* < * *vēlum*). In late Classical Latin the similarity of *ĭ* and *ē* is shown by the occurrence (already in republican inscriptions) of E for short *ĭ* and I for long *ē* (e.g. TREBIBOS, MENUS, MINSIS, for *trĭbibus, mĭnus, mēnsis*). The open articulation of short *i* is shown by its frequent rendering in Greek as *e* (e.g. *Lepedos* = *Lepidus*), and conversely by the rendering of Greek *e* by Latin I (e.g. *PHILUMINA* = *Philouménē*). The similarity of short *ŭ* and long *ō* is likewise illustrated (cf. Allen, 1973:132 for data) and the open articulation of *ŭ* is shown by the use of *u* to render Greek *o*, e.g. *purpura* = *porphúrā*).

It is tempting to hypothesize that here Ap inagurates the development of the NIA phonological type based on four degrees of aperture instead of three as in the previous OIA type. It goes without saying that its exact phonetic reconstruction is beyond the powers of historical linguistics. Thus it is conceivable that phonetically the four degrees of aperture on the front axis could be [i, ɩ, e, æ] (as in Modern Panjabi) or [i, e, ɛ, a] (as in Modern Gujarati or Hindi).

2.2 Phonological System of MIA Dialects: Consonants

MIA dialects were remarkably stable in their system of plosives vis-à-vis that of OIA. The basic pattern of five articulatory positions (*k, c, ṭ, t, p*) combined with features of voice (*k-g*), aspiration (*k, kh*) and murmur (*g-gh*) remained unchanged during the MIA period (it survived, with various additions or losses, until NIA times). Major changes, in terms of loss and acquisition of phonemes, will be noticed in the subsystems of liquids, sibilants and nasals:

(i) syllabic liquids (complete loss)
(ii) sibilants (reduction in number)
(iii) nasals (phonemicization of [ṇ])
(iv) murmured nasals and the lateral liquid (acquisition).

(i) The loss of OIA syllabic /ṛ/ took place in all MIA dialects (with the exception of Niya and the Ap of the grammarians). For its treatment in inscriptional Prakrits see 1.3. There are three vocalic reflexes of /ṛ/: *a, i,* and *u* depending on the dialect and environment (in the West only *a* is found). In Pāli we find *i* before *i, u* before *u* and after labials, and *a* elsewhere:

OIA	Pāli
kṛta 'done'	kata
ṛṣi 'sage'	isi
ṛju 'straight'	uju
pṛcchati 'he asks'	pucchati

Long /ṝ/ becomes *ī* and *ū* in identical environments. Examples can be found in the inflection of *ṛ*-stems: AMg *piūṇã* ~ *piīṇã* 'fathers' (Gen) < OIA *pitṝṇām*; *māīṇã* 'mothers' (Gen) < OIA *mātṝṇām* (cf.3.2.5). Syllabic / l / becomes *ili* according to the grammarians (Vr.I,33): OIA *klpta* 'created' > *kilitta*.

(ii) As already mentioned in 1.3, the three sibilants of OIA *s* (dental), *ś* (palatal) and *ṣ* (retroflex) merged into one dental *s* (in most MIA dialects) or into palatal *ś* (in eastern Pkts). (Only in Niya and other North-Western inscriptional Pkts are all the three preserved.)

Put in the terminology of autonomous phonology, the feature of place stopped being contrastive with sibilants in MIA times. Only one subdialect of Māgadhī, namely Ḍhakkī (as preserved in Mṛcch), shows both dental *s* and palatal *ś*. In this subdialect dental *s* continues both *s* and retroflex *ṣ* of OIA, and ś continues ś. Formally:

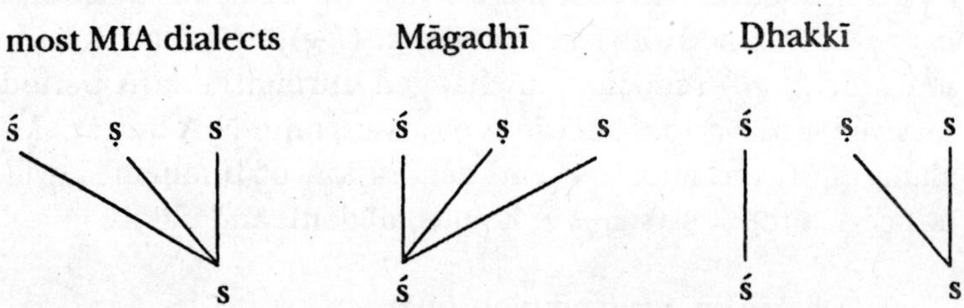

Here are some examples:

OIA	Pāli	Māgadhī	Dhakkī
su- 'well'	su-	su-	su-
daśa 'ten'	dasa	daśa	daśa
puruṣa 'man'	purisa	puliśa	puliso

(iii) Barring Sanskrit as a metalanguage, palatal [ñ] was only an allophone of /n/ in the environment of palatal affricates (*c, j*). In several MIA dialects this allophone was phonemicized as a result of various phonological processes. In Pāli the OIA cluster *jñ* became *ññ* (by regressive assimilation) and the geminate *ññ* was simplified in initial position:

OIA	rājñā 'king' (Instr)	Pāli raññā [5]
	jñāpayati 'make X know Y'	ñāpēti

In Cūḷikāpaiśācī (according to Hemacandra) *ñ* appears intervocalically in grammatical forms such as *rāciñā* (OIA *rājñā*) and *rāciño* (OIA *rājñaḥ*). For the intrusive vowel cf. JMah *rāiṇā* (< *rājinā* < *rājñā*); Paiśācī, according to the grammarians, devoiced all voiced stops; hence the development from OIA *rājñā* > *rājiñā* > *rāciñā* (cf. Pischel, 1900:167).

Ap *vuñai* (Hc.4,392) and Mg *vaññadi* 'walk' may be derived from undocumented **vrajñāti* (vs. OIA *vrajati*) by regressive assimilation in the cluster *jñ* and the subsequent degemination of *ññ* in intervocalic position (cf. Pischel,1900:167).

(iv) In OIA the feature of murmur was functional in the subsystem of plosives (where it functioned contrastively); elsewhere, it appears only with retroflex *ḷ* in isolated lexical items (cf. RV *voḷhā* 'draught horse' ~ *voḍhar*). In MIA murmured nasals and the lateral liquid resulted through metathesis from OIA clusters *hm, hn, hṇ* and *hl*:

OIA	brāhmaṇa 'brahman'	Ś, Mg bamhaṇa
	madhyāhna 'midday'	Mah, AMg, JM, JŚ, Ś majjhaṇha
	gṛhṇāti 'takes'	Ś, Mg geṇhadi
	prahlāda 'delight'	AMg palhāa [6]

In terms of autonomous phonology, it may be said that the feature of murmur became phonemic in the subsystem of nasals and liquids (l), anticipating the situation in NIA.

In Pāli murmured glides arose in the same fashion:

OIA	mahyam 'me' (Dat)	Pāli mayhā
	jihvā 'tongue'	jivhā

During the later stages of MIA murmured *yh* was not stable and the palatal glide was affricated (*y* > *j*); cf. AMg, Mah *majjha*, Ap *majjhu*. Also *vh* developed further in that the labio-dental fricative underwent closure (*v*> *b* to judge by its orthography); cf. AMg, JMah *jibbhā*.

2.2.1 *MIA Consonant Clusters*

A high number of dyadic and triadic consonant clusters was typical of OIA. Dyadic clusters of Sanskrit occurring in medial position are displayed in Chart 2.1 (marked with 0). For the sake of a contrastive study, this chart also lists dyadic clusters of Pāli (marked with x).

The high number of consonant clusters was drastically limited in MIA by several phonological processes:

(i) epenthesis ($\phi \rightarrow V/C — C$);

(ii) various assimilations in place and manner of articulation (2.2.2).

Geminates arising through (ii) could be simplified (with a concomitant lengthening of the preceding short vowel, cf. 2.2.1).

Chart 2.1 shows some conspicuous differences in the phonotactic possibilities of Sanskrit and Pāli (e.g. Sanskrit allows for 41 clusters of the type

$$\left\{\begin{array}{c}\text{glide}\\ \text{liquid}\\ \text{sibilant}\\ \text{h}\end{array}\right\} + \text{stop},$$

while Pāli tolerates only one (*sm*); the opposite type

$$\text{stop} + \left\{\begin{array}{c}\text{glide}\\ \text{liquid}\\ \text{sibilant}\\ \text{h}\end{array}\right\}$$

has 57 tokens in Sanskrit but only 10 in Pāli). Among the most salient phonotactic innovations of MIA was the simplification of the onset and the coda of the word. Starting with the initial position, Sanskrit,

Chart 2-1. Sanskrit and Pāli Dyadic Clusters (in medial position)

	-k	kh	g	gh	ṅ	c	ch	j	jh	ñ	ṭ	ṭh	ḍ	ḍh	ṇ	t	th	d	dh	n	p	ph	b	bh	m	y	r	l	v	ś	ṣ	s	h
k-	⊗	⊗				0									0	0	0			0					0	0	0	0	⊗		0		
kh																										0	0						
g			⊗	x															0	0						0	0		0				
gh																				0					0	0	0						
ṅ	⊗	⊗	⊗	⊗	0										0										0	0							
c						⊗	⊗			0															0	0							
ch																									0	0							
j								⊗	⊗	0															0	0			0				
jh																																	
ñ						⊗	⊗	⊗	x	x																							x
ṭ											⊗	x														0							
ṭh																										0	0						
ḍ			0	0									⊗	x												0	0	0					
ḍh																										0	0						
ṇ											⊗	⊗	⊗	⊗	⊗										0	0			0				
t	0	0														⊗	⊗			0	0	0			0	⊗	0		⊗		0		
th																										0	0						
d			0	0														⊗	⊗	0			0	0	0	0	0		⊗				
dh																				0					0	0	0		⊗				
n																⊗	⊗	⊗	⊗	⊗	0				0	0	0					0	x
p																0			0	0	x				0	0	0	0	0			0	
ph																																	
b			0					0										0	0	0			⊗	⊗		⊗	⊗		0				
bh																				0						0	0		0				
m																				⊗	⊗	x	0	⊗	⊗	0	0	0	0				x
y																										⊗			0				x
r	0		0	0		0	0	0							0	0	0	0	0		0		0	0		0			0	0	0		
l	0																				0	0			0	⊗		⊗	0				⊗
v																				0						0	0		0				x
ś						0	0													0						0	0	0	0	0			
ṣ	0	0									0	0			0						0	0			0	0			0				
s	0	0														0	0			0	0	0			⊗	0	0		⊗			⊗	
h															0					0					0	0	0	0	⊗				

as is well-known, allows for dyadic clusters of several types in this position:

$$\text{stop} + \left\{\begin{array}{c}\text{nasal}\\\text{liquid}\\\text{glide}\\\text{sibilant}\end{array}\right\}$$

(*kn*,[7] *kr, ky, kṣ*) but not stop + stop (*pt-, *bd-, *kt-, *gd-); nasal + glide (*ny, nv*); liquid + glide (*ly, lv* in metalanguage); glide + glide (*vy*);

$$\text{sibilant} + \left\{\begin{array}{c}\text{stop}\\\text{nasal}\\\text{liquid}\\\text{glide}\end{array}\right\} \quad (\textit{st, sn, sr, sy})$$

In MIA only the two following cluster types are allowed in this position: (i) consonant + glide and (ii) stop + *r* (*ṇh, mh* and *lh* may be interpreted as unitary phonemes, cf. 2.2.iv). Examples of (i) occur in the oldest stages of MIA. Thus in Pāli we find unassimilated *tv* and *dv* in *tvā̃* 'you' (~ *tuvā̃*) and *dva*- 'two' (but *bārasa* 'twelve'); *sv* is documented in *sve* 'tomorrow' (*e*! not *o* < OIA *śvas*); *ty* occurs in *tya*-'that' OIA *tya*-, and there are quite a few examples of *by* (<OIA *vy*): *byañjana* 'sign' (~ *vyañjana*), *byatta* 'experienced' (~ *vyatta* <OIA *vyakta*), etc. Examples of (ii) are limited in Pāli to the cluster *br* seen in numerous derivatives and compounds of *brahma*-, e.g. *brāhmaṇa* 'brahman' (vs. *bamhaṇa* in other MIA dialects). The cluster C + *r* occurs initially, according to the grammarians, in various lexical items (*doha* ~ *droha* 'injury'), names (*Praāvadi* ~ *Prajāpati*), and borrowings (*dramma* < AGr *drakhmā*).

Medially, the same wealth of dyadic clusters as in initial position is found in Sanskrit (in addition, homorganic clusters of stops such as -*kt*-, -*pt*-, -*tk*-, -*tp*-, etc. are permissible). In MIA only the following types of dyadic clusters existed:

(i) geminates
(ii) nasal + stop (as in Sanskrit)
(iii) stop + *r*
(iv) sibilant + stop (only in Māgadhī)

Examples for (iii) are found in the older stages of MIA. Thus in

Pāli we find unassimilated *tr* and *dr* in *tatra* 'there' (~ *tattha*), *citra* 'variegated' (~ *citta*), *bhadra* 'happy' (~ *bhadda*). *Ky* and *gy* are found in borrowings from Sanskrit (*vākya* 'word', *ārogya* 'health'). Prākrit grammarians also mention various names showing unassimilated clusters in medial position (*Inda ~ Indra, Rudda ~ Rudra*).

As Chart 2-1 shows, in Pāli in non-geminate clusters whose second member is a stop the first member is typically a nasal (as in Sanskrit); the only other possibility is the combination with the labial nasal stop: *s* + *m*. According to the grammarians, in Māgadhī sibilants could form clusters with stops in all the five articulatory positions (*sk, sc, sṭ, st, sp*), and the glottal fricative could occur before the velar stop (*hk*). Evidence of Māgadhī dramatic passages is ambivalent; thus against *sk(h)* of the grammarians we find *kkh* (also *kk*) in our manuscripts; against *sṭ* (corresponding to OIA *ṣṭ(h)*) *ṭṭh* or *śṭ* in the manuscripts; *sp(h)* vs. *pph* or *ṣp* (data and other details in Pischel, 1900:207-14). The most sensible explanation of this state of affairs would seem to assume an existence of two dialects of Māgadhī: that one which is described by the grammarians did not change the OIA clusters of the sibilant + stop, whereas the other one, in agreement with the other MIA dialects, metathesized the sequence *s* + *C* → *C* + *s* and weakened the sibilant *s* > *h* (2.2.3). The Mg cluster *st* corresponds to OIA *st(h)*, but there is some evidence that OIA *st* > Mg *śt* by dissimilation in the place of articulation, e.g., Mg *haśta* 'hand', OIA *hasta* (cf. Pischel, 1900:213-4). Mg *śṭ* in *suśṭu* 'aptly' (OIA *suṣṭhu*) could be explained along the same lines as a result of dissimilation in retroflexion for OIA *ṣṭ* (or dissimilation in the place of articulation from 'Proto-Māgadhī'* *śṭ*).

The Mg cluster *śc* continues OIA *śc*, e.g. *aścalia* 'marvelous' (< OIA *āścarya*), while the other dialects show here the effects of metathesis and fricative weakening (Mah, Ś *accharia*).[8]

The Mg cluster *hk* (corresponding to OIA *kṣ*) appears, according to Hemacandra, in several lexical items such as *yahke* (OIA *yakṣaḥ*) and *lahkaśe* (OIA *rākṣasaḥ*). On the other hand, Somadeva has *śk* in all instances (*bhiśkā*, OIA *bhikṣām*, *laśkidā*, OIA *lakṣitam*; etc.); cf. Pischel (1900:222) for details.

According to Hemacandra (4,289), Māgadhī possessed also the clusters of the type sibilant + nasal (*sṇ* and *sm*): *Visṇu* (OIA *Viṣṇu*), *usma* 'vapour' (OIA *ūṣman*), but *gimha* 'summer' (OIA *grīṣma*). Dramatic Mg, as far as our manuscripts go, displays only forms showing effects of fricative weakening; thus in Mṛcch we find *gimha*, *paṇha* 'question' (OIA *praśna*), *uṇha* 'hot' (OIA *uṣṇa*), etc.

Synchronically, Māgadhī spellings with *s* such as *śuska* 'dry' (OIA *śuṣka*), *suśṭu* 'aptly' (OIA *suṣṭhu*) present certain problems for the phonemization of this dialect, since only palatal / *ś* / existed in free position. Here we have to assume dissimilatory processes in the place of articulation (*ś*→ *s*/ — *k* and *ś*→ *s*/— *t*). On the other hand, *ṣ* in Mg *ciṣṭhadi* 'stand' (< OIA *tiṣṭhati*), if considered an allophone of /*ś*/, could have resulted through assimilation in retroflexion: *ś*→ *ṣ*/ — *ṭ*.

One of the most salient phonological features of MIA is the wealth of geminates in comparison with OIA. Our Chart 2.1 obscures the facts of the productivity of various phonological process which produced these geminates[9]. We should also establish the fact that IA languages do not possess reduplicatory processes of a morphophonological nature as those found, e.g., in Semitic languages. Reduplicatory processes of OIA were of a phonetic nature and they were responsible for certain peculiarities of pronunciation whereby *ch* and nasals (*ṅ* nd *n*) were lengthened in external sandhi (e.g. /tava#chāyā/ could be pronounced [tavac:hāyā], / pratyaŋ āste/ as [pratyaŋ:āste], etc.). However, geminates could arise as a 'by-product' of various assimilatory processes in both internal and external sandhi. Geminated dental stops arise in both types of sandhi: *tt* < *d*, *t* + *t*; *tth* < *t* + *sth*; *ddh* < *dh* + *t*; *nn* < *t*, *d* + *n*. Geminated palatals and retroflex stops appear in external sandhi:

cc(h) < *t#c(h)*; *jj(h)* < *t* + *j(h)*; *ṭṭ(h)* < *t* + *ṭ(h)*; *ḍḍ(h)* < *t* + *ḍ(h)*.

The cluster *cch* arises also from *t* + *s* (cf. 2.3). Geminated velar and palatal stops may arise only in those rare instances when the final consonant of the first word is either *-k* or *-p* followed by another word beginning with *k-* or *p-*, respectively: e.g., *prāk-kāla* 'former age' (*prāñc* 'former'), *appati* 'ocean' (< *ap* + *pati*). There are also certain lexical items showing geminates internally, but some of them are obviously nursery words (*akkā* 'mother', *attā* 'mother') or onomatopoeia (*akkhala* exclamation of joy) or words of an obscure origin (*aṭṭaṭṭa* 'very high', *aḍḍati* 'join', mentioned by the lexicographers).[10]

In MIA, on the other hand, the geminates arise internally through a number of highly productive phonological processes which will be studied in the next section (2.2.2). Due to the loss of final consonants, geminates across the word boundary arise in MIA only rarely in composition (but many compounds were inherited from OIA) and before enclitics; thus in MAg we find *chac = ca* 'and six' (OIA *ṣaṭ = ca*), *chap = pi* 'also six' (OIA *ṣaḍ = api*).

The final position was heavily constrained in OIA. No dyadic clusters (with the exception of *r* + voiceless unaspirated stops) were allowed in it; and among single consonants only oral and nasal stops (*k, ṭ, t, p,* but not * *c#*; *m, n, ṇ,* but not * *ñ#*, and the voiceless velar fricative (*visarga*)) were allowed before the pause.

In MIA absolutely no consonants were tolerated in final position; thus in MIA we find only open syllables before the pause (reminiscent of the 'law' of open final syllable in OCSl). This constraint had, of course, far reaching consequences for the fate of OIA consonant stems (athematic declension), cf.3.1.

Finally, a few comments regarding triadic clusters. Phonotactic rules for triadic clusters in OIA, in terms of major classes of consonants: S(top), N(asal), Si(bilant), L(iquid) and G(lide), allow for the twelve following cluster types:

$$\begin{Bmatrix} \text{S} \\ \text{Si} \end{Bmatrix} \text{S} \begin{Bmatrix} \text{L} \\ \text{G} \end{Bmatrix} \quad \begin{Bmatrix} \text{S} \\ \text{Si} \end{Bmatrix} \begin{Bmatrix} \text{N} \\ \text{L} \\ \text{G} \end{Bmatrix} \text{G}, \quad \text{S Si} \begin{Bmatrix} \text{N} \\ \text{G} \end{Bmatrix}, \ \text{N S} \begin{Bmatrix} \text{S} \\ \text{N} \\ \text{Si} \\ \text{L} \\ \text{G} \end{Bmatrix}$$

In terms of constraints on positions we may formulate two major rules:

(i) if C_1 = S or Si then C_3 = N, L, G
(ii) if C_1 = N then C_3 = S, N, Si, L, G

There are no triadic clusters in MIA. OIA triadic clusters were reduced to dyadic clusters by epentheses, assimilation, palatalization and fricative weakening as the dyadic clusters were. Thus OIA *arghya* 'valuable' ends up as *aggha* in Mah; *uddyota* 'shining' > Mah *ujjoa;* etc. Clusters with C_1 = nasal end up as single consonants in that the nasal becomes a feature of nasality on the preceding vowel: *Paṅkti* 'set of five' > Mah *pāti* (via *pātti*); *Vindhya* > Mah *Vījha*; etc.

Clusters containing a sibilant show effects of fricative weakening. For instance, *astra* 'weapon' > Mah *attha* (via *-htr-* > *-htt-*); in the case of *ṣṭv*, instead of expected *ṭṭh* (via *-hṭv-* > *-hṭṭ-*), we find *sv* or *ss*: OIA *dṛṣṭvā* 'having seen' > Pāli *disvā* (here C_2 > ϕ), AMg *dissā* (*v* > *s*/ *s* —).

Clusters with a sibilant as C_2 (*kṣṇ, tsn*) could be simplified in essentially two ways depending on whether C_1 was dropped or short *i* was inserted between C_2 and C_3. Hence several descendants of OIA *tīkṣṇa* 'sharp' in Pāli (*tiṇha, tikhiṇa, tikkha*), and of OIA *jyotsnā* 'moonlight' in other dialects (Mah *joṇhā*, AMg *dosiṇā*). In terms of our rules:

	kṣṇ	tsn	kṣṇ	tsn	kṣṇ
epenthesis	-	-	kṣiṇ	tsin	-
simplification	ṣṇ	sn	-	sin	-
fricative weakening	hṇ	hn	khiṇ	-	khṇ
metathesis	ṇh	nh	-	-	-
assimilation	-	-	-	-	kkh

2.2.2 *Pāli Geminate Clusters*

With the exception of *n, r, v, h* all Pāli consonants may occur geminated. Their OIA sources are surveyed in Chart 2.2. Several phonological processes are responsible for their appearance:

(i) regressive and progressive assimilation in place and manner of articulation in OIA clusters containing stops, nasals, liquids and glides (with the exception of iii);

(ii) fricative weakening in OIA clusters containing the sibilant as a first or second member (to be studied in 2.2.3);

(iii) dental palatalization in OIA clusters containing the dental or retroflex stop as a first member and the palatal glide as a second member (to be studied in 2.2.4). Also *ts* (the original one or that arising through metathesis or epenthesis, cf. 2.2.3) undergoes dental palatalization.

Chart 2-2. The OIA Sources of Pāli Geminate Clusters

	stop + {nasal, liquid, glide}					{liquid, stop} + stop			stop + sibilant	sibilant + stop	
kk	kn	kr	kl	ky	kv	rk	lk	tk			
kkh				khy				tkh	kṣ	sk, skh	ṣk, ṣkh
gg	gn	gr		gy	gv	rg		dg			
ggh	ghn	ghr		ghy		rgh		dgh			
cc				ty, cy		rc					
cch				thy, chy		rch			kṣ, ts, ps		
jj				dy, jy		rj					
jjh				dhy							
ññ	jñ			ṇy, ny							
ṭṭ											
ṭṭh		ṭhr									ṣṭ, ṣṭh
ḍḍ											
ḍḍh		ḍhr				rdh					
ṇṇ						rn					
tt	tm	tr		ty	tv	rt	pt	kt			
tth										st, sth	
dd		dr		dy	dv	rd	bd				
ddh		dhr		dhy	dhv	rdh	bdh	gdh			
nn											
pp	pn	pr		py	pv	rp	lp	tp			
pph								tph		sp, sph	ṣp, ṣph
bb		vr, br		vy, by	dv	rv	lv, lb	db			
bbh		bhr		bhy	dhv	rbh		dbh			
mm				my		rm					
ss		sr		sy	sv	rs					
ll				ly	lv						
yy				ry							

Under (i) we may distinguish between assimilatory processes taking place in (a) homorganic and (b) heterorganic clusters (from the point of view of the manner of articulation).

(a) Homorganic clusters underwent regressive assimilation (i.e., they were reduced to the geminate form of the second member):

tk(h) > kk(h)	dg(h) > gg(h)
pt, kt > tt	bd(h), gdh > dd(h)
tp(h) > pp(h)	db(h) > bb(h)

Examples of voiceless unaspirated stops:[11]

prāpta 'obtained'	patta
ukta 'said'	vutta
utpāda 'appearance'	uppāda

(b) Heterorganic clusters were reduced to the geminate form of the 'stronger' consonant from the point of view of its occlusion: (oral) stop - nasal (stop) - liquid - glide (in descending order). Consequently, the clusters of the type (oral or nasal) stop + nasal, liquid or glide; liquid + glide; and also sibilant + liquid or glide underwent progressive assimilation:

$$k + \left\{\begin{matrix} n \\ r,\ l \\ y,\ v \end{matrix}\right\} \rightarrow kk \quad n + y \rightarrow \tilde{n}\tilde{n} \quad l + y, v \rightarrow ll \quad s + \left\{\begin{matrix} r \\ \\ y, v \end{matrix}\right\} \rightarrow ss$$

Under (b) we have to do with classical examples of progressive assimilation in the manner of articulation, whereby nasals and liquids are assimilated completely to the preceding stop:

OIA	śaknoti 'he can'	Pāli	sakkoti
	cakra 'wheel'		cakka
	śukla 'white'		sukka

There are several problematic cluster types here. In the case of the cluster *tm* the more expected reflex is *tt*, cf. Pāli *atta(n)* 'soul' <OIA *ātman*. Mah and Ap, however, show almost always *appa* which can be explained by coalescence: (dental) stop + labial (nasal) = labial stop.[12]

OIA *dv* shows two reflexes in MIA: *dd* (with progressive assimilation) and *bb* (with regressive assimilation), e.g., OIA *dviṣṭa* 'hated one' > Pāli *diṭṭha* 'enemy', OIA *dvādaśa* 'twelve' > Pāli *bārasa*. For its treatment in inscriptional Pkts see 1.3. Similarly OIA *dhv* > *ddh* (with progressive assimilation) and *bbh* (with regressive assimilation), e.g., OIA *ūrdhvan* 'high' > Pāli *ubbhā* 'up'.

A propos the OIA clusters of the type consonant + palatal glide we may assume that they resulted in geminates in MIA through two different phonological processes: in the case of peripheral stops (*k*, *p*) and the sibilant we may assume straightforward assimilation in the manner of articulation: *y*→ *k*/*k*- (also *v*→ *k*/*k*-):

OIA	śakya 'possible'	Pāli	sakka
	pakva 'cooked'		pakka
	-asya (Gen Sg)		-assa

In the case of dental stops (oral and nasal) and liquids we have to assume dental palatalization preceded by affrication (in the case of stops, cf. 2.2.4). The development of *sacca* 'true', *kaññā* 'girl' and *kalla* 'well' is shown below:

	satya	kanyā	kalya
affrication	$sat^{s}ya$	-	-
palatalization	$sat^{ś}a$	kañā	kal'a
gemination	$satt^{ś}a$	kaññā	kal'l'a
depalatalization	-	-	kalla

The process of gemination may be here understood as a preservation of the syllabic structure of the word which was changed by palatalization:

sat.ya > *sa.t^{ś}a* > *sat.t^{ś}a*

The development of the cluster *ry* was exceptional in that it shows regressive assimilation: *r*→ *y*/-*y*. Resulting *yy* remained in Pāli and Māgadhī but it was affricated in other dialects: *yy* > *jj*. Here are some examples: OIA *ārya* 'lord' > Pāli and Mg *ayya* vs. *ajja* in Mah (and other dialects); OIA *sūrya* 'sun' > Mg *suyya* (but Pāli *suriya* shows epenthetic *i*).

On the other hand, the clusters of the type liquid + (oral or nasal) stop, and also liquid + sibilant underwent regressive assimilation (as homorganic clusters):

{r,. l} + k → kk   r + ṇ → ṇṇ   r + ṣ → ss

In this case we are dealing with regressive assimilation in the manner of articulation, whereby liquids are assimilated completely to the following stop:

OIA	tarka 'conjecture'	Pāli takka
	valkala 'bark garment'	vakkala
	karṇa 'ear'	kaṇṇa
	varṣa 'rain'	vassa

2.2.3 *Fricative Weakening in MIA Dialects*

This process of the weakening of the sibilant into the glottal fricative (*s* > *h*) is responsible for some of the most drastic changes which remodelled the morphophonemic pattern of OIA. Its environment was primarily the postconsonantal position (*s* → *h*/ *C*—): OIA *bhikṣu* 'monk' > Pāli *bhikkhu.* However, even clusters of the type sibilant + stop show effects of this process after the sequence sibilant + stop has been metathesized: OIA *śuṣka* 'dry' Pāli *sukkha* (via *sukṣa*).

It should be noted that this process existed already in OIA where it operated across word boundary (in external sandhi). For instance, *ucchuṣyati* 'dries up' may be derived from *ut* + *śuṣyati* as follows:

	ut + śusyati
affrication	$ut^{ś}$śuṣyati
fricative weakening	$ut^{ś}$huṣyati
gemination	$utt^{ś}$huṣyati
	(ucchuṣyati)

It is of interest to observe that in similar cases, i.e. those involving morpheme boundary, MIA dialects do not show effects of fricative weakening but rather those of regressive assimilation in the manner of articulation (*t* → *s*/ -*s*): *ut* + *śuṣyati*> *utsusyati*> *ussussati* (Pāli). -*ss*- may be degeminated and the preceding vowel compensatorily lengthened: Mah *ūsava* 'holiday', AMg *ussava* (< OIA *utsava*).

In OIA the glottal fricative could also arise through the dissimilation of *s* before another *s*: *s* → *h*/ —*s* (cf. 2.2.7). Classical examples are found in the inflection of *s*-stems before the ending of the Loc Pl, e.g. *manaḥsu* 'minds' (< *manas*+*su*).

In this section I want to examine in some detail linguistic diffusion of this process. Its interplay with paradigmatic restrictions will be studied in 3.2.1 and 3.4.6. In the Indic branch of II[13] languages the rule of fricative weakening started operating at a certain point in the transitional period between Old and Middle IA stages. We may study its linguistic diffusion systematically in the following three environments:

(i) before and after voiceless stops
(ii) before nasals
(iii) intervocalically

(i) Fricative weakening in the environment before and after voiceless stops.

Preconsonantal *s* is metathesized[14] and the rule *s* → *h* operates. Postconsonantal *s* is weakened immediately, e.g., Ś *sukkha* 'dry' and *akkhi* 'eye' can be derived from OIA *śuṣka* and *akṣi* as shown below:

	śuṣka	akṣi
metathesis	sukṣa	-
fricative weakening	sukha	akhi
gemination	sukkha	akkhi

Similarly ṣk(h) and kṣ become kkh

ṣṭ(h)	ṭṭh
st(h)	tth
sp(h)	pph

In the case of *s* in front of *t* and *p* we may assume that fricative weakening applies before metathesis, e.g., MIA *atthi* 'he is' and *puppha* 'flower' can be derived from OIA in the following manner:

	asti	puṣpa
fricative weakening	ahti	puhpa
metathesis	athi	pupha
gemination	atthi	puppha

One might wonder whether the same result *atthi* would be reached if we allowed fricative weakening to take place after metathesis: *asti* > *atsi* > *athi* > *atthi*. There is some evidence that the latter solution might be preferable in the case of the sequence *s* + *nasal* since we find forms such as AMg *aṃsi* [ãsi] corresponding to Pāli *amhi* (< OIA *asmi* 'I am'), which indicate that the intermediate step was *ms* by metathesis from *sm*:

		asmi	
metathesis		aṃsi	
fricative weakening	amhi	ãsi	nasalization

It would seem, however, that metathesis would create an environment for affrication and palatalization and that the outcome would be **acchi* and **puccha* (*asti* > *atsi* > *a*t^s*si* > *a*$t^ś$*hi* > *acchi*). In addition, some dialects did not metathesize the output of the fricative weakening. For instance, Old Hindi *puhup* 'flower' can be derived from OIA *puṣpa* directly by the fricative weakening, whereas Ś *puppha* shows the result of metathesis. Contrast their development:

	puṣpa	puṣpa
fricative weakening	puhpa	puhpa
metathesis	-	-
gemination	-	puppha
epenthesis	puhup	-

MnH *phup* 'flower' derives from OH *puh(u)p,* not from Ś *puppha.*

The development of clusters *ts* and *ps* was more complicated in that the rule of fricative weakening was preceded by palatalization (or rather affrication). Both *ts* and *ps* of OIA end up as *cch* in MIA and so does *kṣ* in some dialects. It is easier to understand what happened in the latter case: *k* was apparently fronted in the anticipation of the retroflex *ṣ* (= regressive assimilation in place of articulation) and assumed the place of the more front palatal affricate c.[15] Formally, *k* → *c*/-*ṣ*. A similar explanation is wanting for *ts*, where we have to assume spontaneous affrication *ts* > t^s*s*. The resulting t^s*s* underwent fricative weakening, palatalization and gemination. As far as *ps* is concerned, we may assume that there appeared an intrusive consonant *t* between *p* and *s, p* was assimilated to *t*, and then *ps* and *ts* underwent the same development. Thus the development of Pāli *acchi* 'eye' (< OIA *akṣi*), *vaccha* 'calf' (< OIA *vatsa*) and *accharā* 'nymph' (< OIA *apsaras*) may be reconstructed in the following manner:

	akṣi	vatsa	apsarā
intrusive consonant	-	-	ap^{t}sarā
assimilation	at^{ś}ṣi	-	at^{t}sarā
affrication	-	vat^{s}sa	at^{s}sarā
fricative weakening	at^{ś}hi	vat^{s}ha	at^{s}harā
palatalization	-	vat^{ś}ha	at^{ś}harā
gemination	att^{ś}hi	vatt^{ś}ha	att^{ś}harā

The split of *kṣ> kkh ~ cch* is difficult to describe diatopically and diachronically. Broadly speaking, in EAp *kṣ* underwent fricative weakening > *kkh*; WAp originally treated *kṣ* in the same fashion but there is some evidence that by 600 A.D. *kṣ* could undergo assimilation before fricative weakening > *cch* in initial and medial position: *chāra* 'caustic' (< OIA *kṣara*) ~ *khattiu* 'warrior' (< OIA *kṣatriya*); *acchi* 'eye', *vaccha* 'tree' (< OIA *vṛkṣa*). In SAp the reflex *cch* predominates over *kkh* (cf. Tagare 1948:87-8 for details). NIA languages show both reflexes, e.g., *ūkh* 'sugar cane' (Eastern Hindi) vs. *ūs* (Marathi), *mākhī* 'fly' (H) vs. *dacchin* (Eastern H), etc.[16]

(ii) Fricative weakening in the environment before nasals.

S in the environment before nasals was regularly weakened to *h*. There is some evidence that in the older stages of MIA the development did not proceed further. Thus in Bhāsa's dramas we find forms such as *hṇāīadi* 'bathing takes place' (vs. Ś *ṇhāīadi* < OIA *snāpyate*) where *s > h/- n*.

During the later stages the metathesis followed the fricative weakening quite regularly:

śn	ṇh	praśna 'question'	paṇha
śm	mh	Kāśmīra 'Kashmir'	Kamhīra
ṣṇ	ṇh	uṣṇa 'hot'	uṇha
ṣm	mh	grīṣma 'summer'	gimha
sn	ṇh	snāna 'bathing'	ṇhāṇa
sm	mh	asme 'we'	amhe

The development of some of the above forms:

	grīṣma	Kāśmīra
shortening /-CC	g(r)iṣma	Kaśmīra
fricative weakening	gihma	Kahmīra
metathesis	gimha	Kamhīra

The rule of fricative weakening could be blocked for various reasons. Thus we find only *rassi* 'ray' (from *rasmi*) never **ramhi.* Here the cluster *sm* develops to *ss* by complete assimilation of *m* to *s* (*sm* > *ss* or with metathesis *sm* > *ms* > *ss* ?). Initial *sn* ends up usually as *ṇ* or *siṇ* (by epenthesis):

śmaśāna 'cemetery'	masāna
sneha 'affection'	ṇehā ~ siṇeha

However, the rule of fricative weakening *s* → *h* did not operate inside the nominal paradigms. Most notably, the locative ending -*Vsmi* in MIA dialects is unaffected by this rule. There are essentially three reflexes of *Vsmi*: *Vmmi, Vssi* and *Ṽsi.* Mah has *Vmmi* with the complete assimilation of *s* to the nasal (either *sm* > *mm* or with metathesis *sm* > *ms* > *mm*); Ś shows the opposite assimilation of the nasal to *s* (*ms* > *ss*); AMg loses *m* before *s* but nasalizes the vowel (cf. 3.2.1 and 3.3.2):

OIA	Ś	Mg	AMg	Mah
tasmin	tassiṃ	taśśim	taṃsi	tammi
etasmin	edassiṃ			eammi (~ eassiṃ)
(loke)			logaṃsi	

The sequence of historical events can be reconstructed in these three steps:

	asmi	asmi	asmi
metathesis	amsi	amsi	amsi
regressive assimilation	assi (Ś)	— progressive	ammi (Mah)
nasalization	—	āsi (AMg)	—

(iii) Fricative weakening intervocalically:

The rule of fricative weakening did not operate intervocalically during the middle stage of MIA. Thus in Mah there are only several lexical items which show its effect:

dhaṇuha 'bow' from *dhaṇuṣa* (thematized *dhanus*)
paccūha 'morning sun' from *pratyūṣa*
(but on the other hand, there is *paccusa* 'dawn')
pāhāṇa 'stone' from *pāṣāna* (cf. Hindi *pāhān*)
anudiahaṃ 'day by day' (vs. Ś *aṇudiasaṃ*) from *anudivasam*

In grammatical morphology the earliest examples of fricative weakening are found in the Gen Sg of *a*-stems in the Māgadhī passages of Mṛcch (cf.3.2.1). Here the pronominal form *tāha* and the nominal forms in *-āha* derive from OIA *-asya* via assimilation, degemination (+ compensatory lengthening) and fricative weakening: *-asya* > *-assa* > *-āsa* > *-āha* (but cf. Footnote 3 to 3.2.1). Notice that fricative weakening could apply only after degemination. This fact may be evaluated as a piece of evidence for the late date of fricative weakening.

2.2.4 *Dental Palatalization in MIA Dialects*

Another far-reaching phonological process which remodelled the sound pattern of OIA was palatalization. This process was limited in MIA to dental (both plain and aspirated) stops in the environment before the palatal glide:

OIA		Pāli	
	nitya 'permanent'		nicca
	mithyā 'false'		micchā
	adja 'today'		ajja
	adhyātman 'belonging to self'		ajjhatta
	kanyā 'girl'		kaññā

Also the lateral liquid probably underwent this process: OIA *kalya* 'well' > Pāli *kalla.* If yes then we have to assume depalatalization from *kal'l'a* (alternatively, we may explain *kalla* and *kalya* by simple assimilation: *y* → *l*/ *l*- as in the case of peripheral stops, cf. 2.2.2). In the case of the palatal nasal *ññ* no depalatalization took place since /ñ/ became a phoneme in Pāli and other MIA dialects (cf. 2.2).

On the other hand, the dental sibilant was not palatalized by the following palatal glide (notice that OIA contrasted /ś/ and /s/ even before *y*, e.g. *syālaka* 'wife's brother' and *śyāma* 'black'). Here the glide was assimilated to the preceding sibilant: *y*→*s*/ *s*—, as seen in the Gen Sg of *a*-stems: OIA *-asya* > Pali *-assa*, cf. 2.2.2.

(alternatively, we might explain *-assa* from palatalized *-as's'a* as in the case of palatalized *l'l'*.)

Retroflex oral stops do not undergo palatalization either. The clusters of the type retroflex stop + glide show effects of the progressive assimilation in the manner of articulation: *y*→ *ṭ*/ *ṭ*—, as seen in the following data:

OIA	nāṭya 'dancing'	Ś ṇaṭṭaa (< nāṭyaka)
	ṭhy ?	
	kuḍya 'wall'	Mah kuḍḍa
	āḍhya 'wealthy'	Mah, AMg aḍḍha

Also the cluster retroflex nasal + glide develops in the same way. In Pāli (and in Mg according to Hemacandra) the result is the palatal geminate *ññ* vs. retroflex geminate *ṇṇ* in other dialects: Pāli *puñña* 'virtue' (< OIA *puṇya*) vs. Mah *puṇṇa*; Pāli *kammaṇṇa* 'workable' (but also *karmaṇiya* with epenthetic *i* < *karmaṇya*).

There was no velar palatalization in MIA. As we saw in 2.2.2, the clusters velar stop + palatal glide undergo assimilation in the manner of articulation: *y*→*k*/ *k*-. What looks superficially as velar palatalization, namely, the development of the cluster *kṣ* > *ch*, can actually be explained by assimilation in the place of articulation *k* → *c*/ -*ṣ* (i.e., velar > palatal/— retroflex).

In the older studies of MIA palatalization is treated in the same fashion as the assimilation of nasals and liquids to preceding stops.[17] As shown in 2.2.2b, this may be a satisfactory solution for peripheral stops (*k, p*) and the sibilant. However, in 2.2.3 we saw that also the cluster *ts* develops in the same fashion as *ty* in that both end up as the palatal affricate (*vatsa* > *vaccha* and *satya* > *sacca*). To give a unitary treatment to these two clusters we have to assume that the palatalization of *ty* was preceded by affrication whereby *s* appeared as an intrusive consonant in the sequence *ty* → *t y*. Palatalization changes *s* to *ś* by coalescing *s* and *y*, and gemination restores the syllabic structure lost by this coalescence. Thus Pāli *nicca* 'permanent' and *ajja* 'today' may be derived from OIA *nitya* and *adya* as follows:

	nit.ya	ad.ya
affrication	nit^{s}.ya	ad^{z}.ya
palatalization	ni.t^{ś}a	a.d^{ź}a
gemination	nit.t^{ś}a	ad.d^{ź}a

In the case of the palatalization of the cluster *ts* we are most likely dealing with a spontaneous process, i.e., that which is not conditioned by the palatal glide (neither OIA nor MIA possessed the dental affricate /t^{s}/ as a phoneme); hence the converging development of OIA *ty* > *cc*, *ts* and *tsy* > *cch* seen in Pāli *nicca*, *vaccha* and *maccha* 'fish' (< OIA *matsya*):

	nit.ya	vat.sa	mat.sya
affrication	nit^{s}.ya	vat^{s}.sa	mat^{s}.sya
fricative weakening	-	vat^{s}.ha	mat^{s}.hya
palatalization	ni.$t^{\acute{s}}$a	va.$t^{\acute{s}}$ha	ma.$t^{\acute{s}}$ha
gemination	nit.$t^{\acute{s}}$a	vat.$t^{\acute{s}}$ha	mat.$t^{\acute{s}}$ha
	(nicca)	(vaccha)	(maccha)

Palatal geminates arise in Pāli also from sequences palatal affricate + palatal glide: *cy* > *cc* and *jy* > *jj*:

OIA ucyate 'it is said' — Pāli vuccati
pravrajya 'having gone forth' — pabbajja

Here, of course, we do not have to go through affrication since we are dealing with affricates. Also, the assimilation of the palatal glide to the preceding palatal affricate resulting in a geminate does not make much sense. The same objection, however, should be levied against the traditional treatment of the clusters containing the palatal glide which we adopted in 2.2.2. Clearly, the assumption of hypothetical assimilatory processes such as *y* → *k*/*k*- does not advance our understanding of the origin of geminates in MIA. The real momentum for their appearance was of an acoustic nature in that the duration of palatalized consonants is longer than that of their plain counterparts. Thus even *ss* and *kk* could be explained through the palatal stage *s's'* and *k'k'* (with subsequent depalatalization). A unitary treatment of all the classes of the consonants discussed above can be outlined in the following fashion:

	ty	ny	ly	ḍy	sy	ky
affrication	t^{s}y	-	-	-	-	-
palatalization	$t^{\acute{s}}$y	ñy	l'y	-	s'y	k'y
gemination	t$t^{\acute{s}}$	ññ	l'l'y	ḍḍy	s's'y	k'k'y
depalatalization	-	-	ll	ḍḍ	ss	kk

2.2.5 *Affrication*

During the middle MIA period (i.e. not in Pāli) the palatal glide in initial position changed into the palatal affricate (with the exception of Mg and P); here are some examples:

OIA *yadi* 'if'	Ś, Ḍh, Ap *jai* but Mg *ya(d)i*
yathā 'as'	Mah, AMg, JMah, Ap *jaha* but Mg *yadhā*

Also the geminate *y* which arises medially through compensatory gemination (2.1.2b) is affricated: OIA *dēyā́t* 'give' (Opt), Mg *dĕjjā* < *dĕyyā́t*. What seems to be the opposite process, namely, *j* + *y* in Mg, is a parallel process to the spirantization of voiced stops /V-V and will be treated in 2.2.6. As we saw in 2.2.4, affrication is of fundamental importance for our understanding of palatalization which operates on its output:

	satya	ārya	yadi
assimilation	-	ayya	-
affrication	$sat^{s}ya$	$ad^{z}ya$	$d^{z}yadi$
palatalization	$sat^{ś}a$	$ad^{ź}a$	$d^{ź}adi$
gemination	$satt^{ś}a$	$add^{ź}a$	-
d > δ > ϕ	-	-	$d^{z}ai$

This process was of an epenthetic/prothetic nature, whereby an intrusive sibilant appeared between the dental stop and the palatal glide (ϕ → *s*/ *t-y*), and the affricate before the word initial glide (or the syllable-initial glide after another glide): #*y* → $d^{z}y$ (*-yy-* → $-d^{z}y$-). The derivation of *sacca* 'true', *ajja* 'noble' and *jai* 'if' is given above.

Y in intervocalic position is not affricated but deleted (see 2.2.6).

2.2.6 *Lenition and Spirantization*

Lenition (voicing) affected all the articulatory positions of both plain and aspirated stops in intervocalic position. In the same environment spirantization operated on the output of lenition (but also the original voiced stops were affected) with the exception of the retroflex stop *ḍ*. The output of spirantization was not stable and the voiced fricatives γ, δ, *y*, β / *v* were deleted (→ ϕ) in most MIA dialects. Schematically:

k → g → γ → φ
c → j → y (j > y > φ only in Mg; OIA *j* also in Mah)
ṭ → ḍ
t → d → δ → φ (δ > φ only in Mah)
p → b → β /v → φ

Here are some examples from Mah: *uaa* 'water' (< *uδaγa* < *udaga* < OIA *udaka*); *gaa* 'elephant' (< *gaya* < OIA *gaja*); *riu* 'enemy' (< *riβu* < *ribu* < OIA *ripu*); also the original palatal (*y*) and labiodental (*v*) fricatives were deleted: *chāā* 'shade' (< OIA *chāyā*), *jīa* 'alive' (< OIA *jīva*). In AMg, JM and JŚ there appeared a phonetic glide in hiatus which arose as a consequence of the deletion of the voiced fricative (indicated by *ẏ* in the Jaina editions of the manuscripts). According to Hemacandra (I, 180) *y* arose only in the environment of low vowels / *a* — *a* but he also acknowledged its existence before/after *i*: *piẏai*, i.e. [piyai], 'drinks' (< *piβaδi* < *pibadi* < *pibati*); *sariẏā* [sariyā] 'river' (< *sariδā* < *saridā*, cf. OIA *sarit*). The oldest manuscripts spell *ẏ* after all vowels before *a*; *hiẏaẏa* 'heart' (< OIA *hṛdaya*), *loẏa* 'world' (< OIA *loka*). The deletion rule did not operate with equal force in all articulatory positions. As shown in 1.4, the peripheral fricatives γ and β/*v* are reduced to zero in all dramatic Prākrits, but the dental fricative undergoes deletion only in Mah. In the case of the palatal affricate arising from OIA *dy* only Mg shows the result of spirantization *j* > *y*. The distribution of descendants of OIA *gata* 'gone' and *adya* 'today':

	Ś	Mg	Mah
gata	gada [gaδa]	gada [gaδa]	gaa
adya	ajja	ayya	ajja

Also OIA *j* is spirantized in Mg according to the grammarians (the manuscripts of dramas spell *j* instead of *y*):

OIA	jñāyate 'is known'	Mg yāṇiyyadi
	jhaṭiti 'instantly'	yhatti (spelled *jhatti* in Mṛcch)

The previous statements are only gross approximations and we are in need of detailed studies of individual authors. For instance, the dramas of Bhāsa (earlier than Kālidāsa but later than Aśvaghoṣa) have been studied for these phenomena by Printz (1921:15) whose findings can be reworded in the following manner:

(a) deletion of original intervocalic voiced consonants

g > ϕ regularly
j > ϕ frequently
d > ϕ rarely

(b) deletion of intervocalic voiced consonants arising through lenition

k > g > ϕ regularly
c > j > ϕ regularly
t > d > ϕ rarely
p > b > ϕ rarely

In Ap the situation with respect to deletion is similar to that found in Mah. Hemacandra (4, 396) lists some Ap lexical items which show voiced plain and murmured stops in intervocalic position, e.g., *ṇāagu* 'leader' (< OIA *nāyakaḥ*), *āgado* 'come' (< OIA *āgataḥ*); also in grammatical morphology: *karadi* 'makes' (< OIA *-ti*). Here we may assume that in some dialects the voiced fricatives were more stable, i.e. their spirantization was not followed by their deletion: [*ṇāaγu*], [*āγaδo*], etc.

In the case of murmured stops (the original ones or those arising through the lenition of voiceless aspirated stops) spirantization did not affect the palatal and the retroflex stops. Schematically:

kh → gh → γ h → h
ch → jh
ṭh → ḍh
th → dh → δh → h
ph → bh → β /vh→ h

Some examples from Mah: *muha* 'face' (< *muγha* < *mugha* < OIA *mukha*); *vahū* 'woman' (< *vaδhū* < OIA *vadhū*); *ṇaha* 'sky' (< *naβ ha* < OIA *nabhas*). *bh* in the root *bhū* 'be' was reduced to *h* even in initial position. But the starting point was here the postvocalic position in derivatives, such as *anu-bhū*, or the close juncture when *bhū* functioned as a clitic. Thus we find AMg, JM *havai*, JŚ *havadi*; Mah, JMah, Ap *hoi*, JŚ *hodi*, all from OIA *bhavati*.

The rule of lenition was blocked if the original accent was located on the following syllable. In this case the intervocalic voiceless stop is geminated:

OIA	ukhá 'boiler'	AMg	ukkhā (not * ughā)
	jitá 'conquered'	JMah	jitta
	nakhá 'nail'	Mah	ṇakkha

As far as the words with voiced intervocalic stops before the original accent are concerned, we have to assume that they were reaccented. Thus AMg *nakkha* 'nail' shows the expected voiceless geminate (< OIA *nakhá*) but there is also the form *naha* which shows effects of lenition, spirantization and deletion. Here the starting point must have been reaccented *nákha* (i.e. accented according to MIA rules): *nagha* > *naɣha* > *naha*. Derivatives with the suffix *-ka* were probably accented on the ultima in OIA. Hence the voiceless geminate in some lexical items in MIA: Mah *sīsakka* 'head' (OIA *śīrṣaka*), Mg *haḍakka* 'heart' (**hṛdaka*). But even here we find both variants: Mg *aakka*~*aaga* 'goat' (OIA *ajaka*); Mg *hak(k)e*~*hag(g)e* 'I' (**ahakam*); Ap *ṇāakka*~*ṇāagu* 'leader' (OIA *nāyaka*).

This reduplicatory process before the accent is of the same nature as that labelled 'compensatory gemination' (2.1.2), where gemination was rationalized in terms of the compensation for the loss of vocalic length. However, if we assume the existence of preaccentual shortening in MIA (V: V̍ : → VV:), resembling iambic shortening in Latin, we may dispose of the term 'compensatory' and give a unitary treatment to geminates arising before the original accent in intervocalic position. The possible development of *nakkha* 'nail' and that of *nĕḍḍa* [*níḍḍa*] 'nest' is shown below:

	nakhá	nīḍá
preaccentual shortening		niḍá
preaccentual gemination	nakkhá	niḍḍá
reaccentuation	nákkha	níḍḍa [níḍḍa]

Finally, it should be mentioned that lenition operated across word boundary if the following word was a clitic. The following clitics show the effects of lenition: *tāvat* 'so much' *tu* 'but' and *te* 'you'. Some examples from Mṛcch:

OIA	tiṣṭha tāvat 'wait for a while'	S ciṭṭha = dāva
		Mg ciṣṭha = dāva
	mastakaṃ te 'your head'	Mg mastaā = de
	praśnaṃ te 'your question'	Mg paṇhā = de

Here lenition was not followed by deletion (obviously, the identity of the clitic would be destroyed).

2.2.7 *Retroflexion*

In OIA retroflexion affected only two consonants, namely the dental stop and sibilant (*n* and *s*) in very restricted environments:

(i) *s* was retroflexed after high vowels (*i* and *u*), *r* and *k* (the so-called *ruki*-rule): *s* → *ṣ*/ (i, u, r, k) —

(ii) and *n* was retroflexed after *r* and *ṣ* (which results from *s* through the *ruki*-rule): *n* → *ṇ*/ (ṣ, r)—.

A propos the *ruki*-rule, even preceding *ē* and *ō* retroflex *s* → *ṣ* (i.e. they are to be understood as underlying diphthongs *ai* and *au*). We might prefer to say that synchronically the *ruki*-rule operates before non-low vowels in Sanskrit. As is well-known, the *ruki*-rule is not blocked by the intervening glottal fricative which arises through the fricative weakening of *s* before another *s* (*s* → *h*/-*s*). Classical examples are found in the inflection of *s*-stems before the ending of the Loc Pl. Contrast the derivation of *manaḥsu* 'minds' (Loc) and *sarpiḥṣu* 'clarified butters' (Loc), *cakṣuḥṣu* 'eyes' (Loc):

	manassu	sarpissu	cakṣussu
fricative weakening	manahsu	sarpihsu	cakṣuhsu
retroflexion		sarpihṣu	cakṣuhṣu

The dental nasal could be retroflexed even at a distance; the intervening segments which did not block retroflexion are limited to any vowel, peripheral stops (*k, p*), glides (*y, v*) and the glottal fricative (*h*). See the derivation of forms *brahmaṇyaḥ* 'kind to Brahmins', *dūṣaṇam* 'abuse' and *niṣaṇṇaḥ* 'seated':

	brahmanyaḥ	dūsanam	nisadnaḥ
assimilation	-	-	nisannaḥ
ruki-rule	-	dūṣanam	niṣannaḥ
n → *ṇ*/ (r, ṣ)—	brahmaṇyaḥ	dūṣaṇam	niṣaṇṇaḥ

On the other hand, retroflexion is blocked in forms such as *arcanam* 'worship' (palatal stop intervenes), *arṇavena* 'ocean' (Instr) (retroflex nasal intervenes), *ardhena* 'half' (Instr) (dental stop intervenes).

In MIA the scope of the application of retroflexion rule(s) became much larger in that in addition to *n* all dental stops were affected (*n* → *ṇ*, however, more regularly than the other dental stops). Furthermore, while in OIA retroflexion had a character of progressive assimilation (the rules applied by carry-over), in MIA retroflextion acquired also a character of regressive assimilation (i.e., the rules operated also anticipatorily).

In Pāli we find this state of affairs in its initial stage. Dental stops are retroflexed after *r* which then disappears; alternative spellings, however, indicate that the rule was not categorical: *paṭhama* 'first' (< OIA *prathama*); *paṭi* ~ *pati* 'towards' (< OIA *prati*). Retroflex *ḍ* in *ḍasati* 'bites' (OIA *daṃś*) and *ḍahati* 'burns' (OIA *dah*) are examples of 'spontaneous' retroflexion. Retroflex *ṇ* in *sakuṇa* 'bird' (< OIA *śakuna*) occurs after the high vowel *u*, but for *ṇ* in *ñāṇa* 'knowledge' (< OIA *jñāna*) a similar explanation is wanting; and alternative spellings *sanati* ~ *saṇati* 'sounds' (OIA *svan*) may be taken as indicative of the uncertainty of speakers in retroflexing *n* between low vowels.

Data from later MIA dialects demonstrate further spread of retroflexion rule. In AMg *nijjūḍha* 'ousted' (< OIA *niryūtha* 'ousted') *th* was retroflexed after the high vowel (and after *r*); *ḍh* in AMg *ḍhaṅka*, Mah *ḍhaṅkha* 'crow' (< OIA *dhvāṅkṣa*) may be explained as resulting from the anticipation of *k* or, perhaps, by 'spontaneous' retroflexion in initial position. *ḍh* in Mah *ḍhakkai* 'covers' (< OIA *sthagáyati* with the pretonic reduplication of the consonant) can be explained along similar lines.

The dental nasal was most susceptible to retroflexion in most dialects. In Ś, Mah, Mg, Ap (less in AMg, JM, JŚ) *n* was retroflexed initially and medially even in the environment of *a*. See some examples from Mah: *ṇa* 'not' (< OIA *na*), *ṇaaṇa* 'leading' (< OIA *nayana*), *ṇihāṇa* 'putting down' (< OIA *nidhāna*) *ṇūṇā* 'now' (<OIA *nūnam*), etc.

In AMg *n* is retroflexed before the palatal glide, whereas in Pāli (2.2.2) it is palatalized. (Both processes are of an assimilatory nature, whereby the dental stop is realized farther back in the anticipation of the palatal glide.) As we saw in 2.2.2, also the OIA cluster *jñ* ends up as *ṇṇ* in AMg but *ññ* in Pāli. While in the latter case we are dealing with straightforward assimilation in the manner of articulation (the oral stop becomes a nasal stop before another nasal stop), in the former case we have to assume that the palatal affricate was spirantized (cf. 2.2.6 for evidence that *j*> *y* in Mg). The development of AMg *raṇṇā* 'king' (Instr) vs. Pāli *raññā* (< OIA *rājñā*) and AMg *aṇṇa* 'another' vs. Pāli *añña* (< OIA *anya*) is shown below:

	rājñā	anya	rājñā	anya
j> *y*	raynā	-	-	-
assimilation (in place)	rayṇā	aṇya	-	añya
assimilation (in manner)	raṇṇā	aṇṇa	raññā	añña

In AMg and also in JM the result of retroflexion is noticeable in the passive participle of some of those roots which ended in *ṛ* in OIA. Thus we find *kaḍa* 'made' (< OIA *kṛta*), *haḍa* 'taken' (< OIA *hṛta*), *maḍa* 'dead' (< OIA *mṛta*). Here we possess precious evidence that the process of retroflexion was older than that of the vocalization of syllabic *r*; obviously, the latter process could run its course only after *r* had retroflexed the following dental stop. *t* in this environment was retroflexed (*t*→ *ṭ*/ *r*-) only in AMg (and less regularly also in JM and Mg); see some dialectal forms of 'done':

AMg kaḍa	Mg kaḍa	*kada*	Mah, Ap kaa
			Ap ki(d)a

Their historical development:

	kṛta	kṛta	kṛta
retroflexion	kṛṭa	-	-
vocalization of *ṛ*	kaṭa	kata	kita
lenition	kaḍa	kada	kida
spirantization	-	kaδa	kiδa
deletion	-	kaa	kia

In many cases retroflexion cannot be explained in terms of a retroflexing environment and we have to assume either spontaneous retroflexion or various analogical processes (or an interplay of both). For instance, both *gada* and *gaḍa* 'gone' (< OIA *gata*) are found in Mṛcch; is the latter by analogy with *maḍa* 'dead' (where *t* → *ṭ/ṛ-*)? What to say about AMg, JM *paḍai* 'falls' (< OIA *patati*)? *ḍ* can be 'rationalized' in the passive participle, e.g., JM *paḍiya* where *t* → *ṭ/—i*; thence it could spread to other phonological environments (such as before *a*) in other grammatical forms.

2.3 *Accent*

We possess no direct evidence (in terms of texts provided with accent marks) regarding the accent pattern of MIA. Certain conclusions, however, may be reached on the basis of various vocalic phenomena, such as vocalic changes, syncopation, shortening and lengthening, above all in Pāli (cf. Geiger 1916:47-9). It is generally assumed that Pāli was accented as Classical Sanskrit. Classical Sanskrit, as is well-known, differed from Vedic Sanskrit in the accentuation of polysyllabic words. In Vedic, in trisyllabic and quadrisyllabic words the accent could fall on any syllable of the word; its position was determined by the morphological class of the word irrespectively of the phonological character of the following syllable (heavy or light). For instance, in the 1st conjugation the antepenult and preantepenult are accented in forms such as *bhávāmaḥ* 'we are' and *ábhavāma* 'we were' in spite of their penult being a heavy syllable. On the other hand, the accent may fall on the heavy penult in the 9th conjugation but only in some forms: *gṛbhṇā́mi* 'I take' vs. *ágṛbhṇīma* 'we took'. These complicated accentual matters were governed by rules of a morphophonological nature, such as the accent falls on the radical syllable in the 1st conjugation but on the postradical syllable (=thematic vowel) in the 9th conjugation (in certain persons); the augment is always accented, etc. These complicated morphophonological rules were replaced in Classical Sanskrit by simple phonological rules based on the character of the following syllable. These rules are taught in the following manner:

(a) in disyllabic words the first syllable is accented;
(b) in trisyllabic words the penult is accented if it is heavy (the initial syllable if the penult is light);

(c) in quadrisyllabic words the penult is accented if it is heavy; if the penult is light the antepenult is accented; if both the penult and antepenult are light then the first syllable will be accented.

Thus the above words are to be accented *bhavā́maḥ, abhavā́ma,* etc. Among the most typical consequences of this new MIA accent pattern is the so-called weakening (Schwächung) of posttonic short *a* to *i* and (in the environment after labials) to *u*. See some data:

	'moon'	'possessing sons'	'ninety'
Vedic Skt	candrámāḥ	putrávant	navatí
Classical Skt	cándramāḥ	pútravant	návati
Pāli	cándimā	púttimā	návuti

The penulimate and desinential accent in these words was moved to the initial syllable in the MIA period. Given the fact that short *a* was realized as schwa [ə] in Sanskrit, the so-called weakening in MIA might be interpreted as an attempt at the phonetic spelling of palatal [ɨ] and velar [ʉ] schwa: [candɨmā], [navʉti]. A complete reduction of posttonic a̲ is seen in *oka* [ʊkə] 'water' from OIA *udaká* (<údəkə) via útkə >úkkə. The *a*~*i* alternation in paradigms, such as that found in the future in Pāli (*dakkhasi*~ *dakkhisi* 'you will see', *dakkhati* ~ *dakkhiti* 'he will see') is not of a phonological nature. Here the opposition is that between the full stressed vowel *dakkhāmi* 'I will see' and the reduced unstressed vowel spelled in two fashions [dakkhəsi] and 'narrower' [dakkhɨsi].

There are vocalic changes which make us believe that there was vocalic reduction in the pretonic syllable. Most notably the shape of compounds with *dvi-* 'two' seems to be evidence for this process. Thus Pāli *d(v)ípada* 'biped' (< OIA *dvípad* ~ *dvipád*) vs. *dujíhva* 'double tongued' (OIA *dvíjihva*) may be quoted in this context. Pāli *dujíhva* may be explained from OIA *dvíjihva* by the MIA reaccentuation (stress the heavy penult) and the coalescence of labidental *v* and palatal schwa *ɨ* resulting in a round vowel:

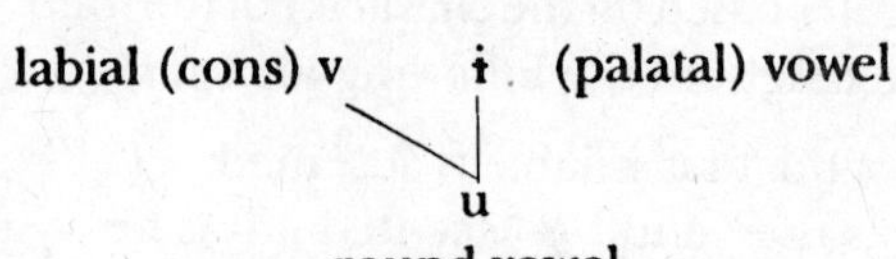

Mah *duuṇa* 'double' may be similarly explained from OIA *dvíguṇa* ~ *dviguṇá*. Since the first *u* should not be stressed (otherwise it could not be derived from vɨΣΣ) we might be in the possession of evidence that the Vedic free accent survived until late centuries in some dialects. Unfortunately, analogical formations diminish the value of this reasoning (thus there are Pāli *dvibhū́mika* 'two floored' and *dúvidha* 'double' < *dvívidha*).

The shortening and lengthening of vowels may also be quoted as evidence. Pāli *gahita* 'taken' (OIA *gṛhītá*) and *álika* 'false' (< OIA *álīka*) show that the long penult could be shortened before and after the original accent. On the other hand, a short vowel in the initial syllable might be lengthened (phonetically?): *ā́linda* 'terrace' (<OIA *álinda*). Instead of lengthening, gemination took place in *úmmā* 'flax' (< OIA *úmā*).

In middle and late MIA dialects (Mah, AMg, JMah, JŚ, Ap) long vowels in open syllables are often shortened if found in posttonic or pretonic syllables (cf. 2.1.2). The shortening process of the long vowels may be accompanied by the compensatory gemination of the following consonant if the word was accented on the ultima: OIA *yauvaná* 'youth' > *yōvaná* > *yŏvvaná* > *jŏ́vvana* (Mah and other dialects).

If compensatory gemination is really conditioned by the following accent we might be in the possession of another piece of evidence for the late survival of the OIA accent into the MIA period.

NOTES

(1) Deshpande (1975) has convincingly argued that there is no evidence to show that the traditional interpretation of *a* being a closed vowel (*saṃvṛta*) is wrong. However, *a* probably opened in Bengal and in some of the Jaina traditions (Hemacandra holds that *a* is an open sound, and says that according to 'others', i.e. the Pāṇinīyas, it is a closed sound).

(2) This condition has been stated somewhat confusingly by Pischel (1900:74) as follows: 'im Auslaut von Casusendungen hinter langen Vocalen, wenn das Metrum eine kurze Silbe erfordert'.

(3) Pischel (1900:96) '*i* kann vor Consonantengruppen zu *ĕ* werden (Vr.1,12; Hc.1,85...)... (§125) 'Wie *i* zu *ĕ* (§119), so kann vor Consonantengruppen *u* zu *ŏ* werden (Vr. 1, 20; Hc.1,116...)'.

(4) Pischel (1900:101) 'Wie *u* ... so kann auch *ū* vor Consonantengruppen zu *ŏ* werden: AMg. *kŏppara* = *kūrpara* (Hc.1,124;...), neben M. *kuppara* ... Wie *o* aus *u* (§66), so wird auch *o* aus *ū* gedehnt, wenn eine ursprüngliche Consonantengruppe vereinfacht wird'.

(5) In Mg, according to Hemacandra (4,293), *jñ* also becomes *ññ*; however, the manuscripts spell *ṇṇ*, e.g., in Mṛcch *jaṇṇa* 'sacrifice' (OIA *yajña*), *viṇṇavia* 'having declared' (OIA *vijñāpya*). Regarding *raññā* 'king' (Instr) vs. *raṇṇā* (Mg) cf. 2.2.7 and 3.2.6.

(6) *lh* (instead of *ḍh*) in several lexical items, such as *krosṭuka* > **kodhua* > *koḷhua* 'jackal', is mentioned by Hemacandra (Deśīnāmamālā 2,65).

(7) The clusters of the type voiceless stop + dental nasal are of a rare occurrence: *pnā* 'the braided hair of Śiva' (lexicographers), *knath* 'hurt' (Dhātupāṭha xix, 38).

(8) Historically, Mg *śc* continues PIE **sk* (*gaśca* 'go' < **g^{w}m-sk*- vs. O and MIA *gaccha*) and PIA *ts(y)* (*maśca* 'fish' vs. MIA *maccha*).

(9) Units such as *kkh, ggh*, etc. will be considered aspirated geminates [kk^h] (or more correctly [$k{:}^h$]) not geminated aspirates *khkh*.

(10) There are also examples of *-bb-* and *-mm-*: *abbindu* (< *ap-bindu*) 'tear' and *ammaya* (< *ap-maya*) 'consisting of water'.

(11) It may be observed that OIA dyadic clusters of two stops have always [+cor] sound as the first or the second member. Peripheral stops do not form clusters (**kp* or **pk*).

(12) Its voiced counterpart, *dm*, undergoes unexpected regressive assimilation in *chadma* 'roof' > *chamma* (according to Hemacandra 2,112), or it may be resolved by epenthesis seen in *padma* 'lotus' > Pāli *paduma* > JMah, Ś *pauma* (also *chauma*). *Pŏmmā* (in Hemacandra) should be derived from *pōmā* through the shortening of *ō* and the compensatory gemination of *m* (not from *padmā* as suggested by Pischel 1900:124).

(13) It is well-known that this rule did not operate in Vedic and Classical Sanskrit. On the other hand, in closely related Iranian dialects (Cuneiform Persian and Avestan) the rule of fricative weakening applied across the whole phonological spectrum, that is initially and medially (intervocalically), and changed the PIE voiceless dental fricative **s* into *h*. Contrast the following lexical items and grammatical forms in Skt and Av:

Skt		Av	
	sarva 'all'		haurva
	bharasi 'you carry'		barahi
	manasā 'mind' (Instr)		manaṅhā

The application of this rule was blocked in the environment (a) before voiceless stops and the dental nasal, and (b) after *t*:

asti 'he is'	asti
matsyaḥ 'fish'	masyo

(14) If, however, *s* occurs before the boundary in a compound it is not metathesized and consequently not weakened; e.g., OIA *niś+cala* > Ś *nic+cala*. In Mg *ś* remains unassimilated: *niś+cala* (cf. 2.2.1.iv).

(15) It could well be that we may explain in this fashion the origin of *ch* in Ap *chaha* 'six' (cf. also Pāli *cha*, Hindi *chah*, etc.). All the previous explanations derive *ch* in 'six' form *ṣ* of OIA (*ṣaṭ* 'six'), e.g. Pischel (1900/1965:156) gives *ṣa*>*ṣha*>*cha*. Starting from PIE **kswes* (cf. Av *xšaš*), which could be a doublet of a more common **sweks* (cf. AGr *heks*, Lat. *sex*, etc.),

we reach *kṣaṣ* (by the II change *e>a*, *ruki*-rule and cluster simplification). At this point, an OIA ancestor of Ap would shift *k* to *c* before *ṣ* (whereas Vedic Sanskrit simplified the initial cluster *kṣ* to *ṣ*) and *ṣ* later on underwent fricative weakening to *h*. Schematically:

	PIE *kswes	~	*sweks
e>a	kswas		
ruki-rule	kṣwaṣ		
Cluster simplification	kṣaṣ	*Frication*	xšvaš (Av)
k → *č*/-*ṣ*	čṣaṣ	ṣaṣ (Skt)	
Fricative weakening	čhah (Ap)		

(16) For their derivational histories cf. my paper 'Fricative weakening in Middle Indo-Aryan dialects', Indian Linguistics 48 (1987).

(17) Mayrhofer (1951:66) follows Pischel when he talks about 'die Assimilierung der Dentale + *y* nach vorheriger Palatalisierung des Dentales: so wurden *ty> (cy) > cc*; *thy> (chy) > cch*' etc.

CHAPTER 3

MORPHOLOGY

3.1 Some General Characteristics of Middle Indo-Aryan Morphological Developments

Before examining in some detail the three morphological subsystems—nominal (3.2), pronominal (3.3) and verbal (3.4)—let us outline several general tendencies and characteristics of MIA morphological developments. As mentioned in 2.2.1, absolutely no consonants were allowed in final position in MIA. In terms of morphology it means that the rich declensional system of consonant stems of OIA was reduced to the vowel-ending type only. Of course, the old system did not break down all of a sudden and we find a number of earlier surviving forms in both early and late MIA texts. We will see that various analogical extensions gradually levelled down the rich morphological system of OIA. As a paradigm case we may mention the thematization of *nt*-stems in Ardha-Māgadhī. Examine the data for the Nom and Acc Sg of the participle *bharant-* 'carrying':

Athematic Declension

	OIA	MIA	
		early	middle
	(Sanskrit)	(Pāli)	(AMg)
Sg Nom	bharan	bharã	bharãto
Acc	bharantam	bharantã	bharantã

Thematic Declension

Sg Nom	devaḥ	devo	devo
Acc	devam	devã	devã

The early MIA dialects (represented by Pāli) still preserve the imparisyllabic pattern of the Nom:Acc of the thematic declension in OIA. During the middle stage of MIA (represented by AMg) the nominative form *bharā̃* became an archaism and a new form with -*ō* borrowed from the thematic declension replaced it. In other words, the parisyllabic pattern of the Nom:Acc of the thematic declension was extended to the athematic declension.

But even the thematic stems were remodelled in MIA dialects. Already in Buddhist Sanskrit we witness the typical form of the Gen Sg of *u*-stems -*oḥ* being replaced by the *a*-stem ending -(*a*)*sya:* Classical Sanskrit *bhikṣoḥ* (Gen Sg) 'monk' vs. Buddhist Sanskrit *bhikṣusya.* Similar situation existed in MIA dialects. We may examine the following data from Pāli in contrast with Sanskrit:

Thematic Declension

		a-stems	*u*-stems
Sanskrit	Sg Nom	devaḥ	bhikṣuḥ
	Acc	devam	bhikṣum
	Gen	devasya	bhikṣoḥ
Pāli	Sg Nom	devo	bhikkhu
	Acc	devā̃	bhikkhū̃
	Gen	devassa	bhikkhussa

In this case the innovation of Buddhist Sanskrit, Pāli (and other MIA dialects) consists of remodelling the OIA parisyllabic pattern Nom/Acc:Gen existing in *u*- (and *i*-) stems according to the imparisyllabic pattern of *a*-stems. Superficially, this process looks like the opposite of what happened between *a*-stems and athematic *nt*-stems. However, even *nt*-stems imitate the imparisyllabic pattern Nom/Acc:Gen of *a*-stems; but it took a longer time for this innovation to take place and we find it accomplished only during the middle stage of the MIA period. Examine the following data:

		Sanskrit	Pāli	Ardha-Māgadhī
Sg	Nom	bharan	bharan	bharāto
	Acc	bharantam	bharantā̃	bharantā̃
	Gen	bharataḥ	bharatō	bharātassa

A complex interplay of analogies was thus involved in the formation of MIA paradigms. We may note at this point that these are not without parallels. For instance, in the early Medieval Greek the old imparisyllabic pattern of consonantal stems existing in late Koine was replaced by a new parisyllabic one, modelled on the pattern of thematic stems. The following data are instructive:

			o-stems	*Consonantal stems*
Koine Greek	Sg	Nom	lógos 'word'	patér 'father'
		Acc	lógon	patéra
		Gen	lógou	patrós
Early Medieval Greek	Sg	Nom	lógos	patéras
		Acc	lógon	patéran
		Gen	lógou	patéra

A shared feature of all the thematic stems (also *a*-stems) was that their Acc Sg ended in *-n*. This *-n* was extended to the Acc Sg of consonantal stems, producing forms such as *patéran* (which replaced the original *patéra*); around this new Acc Sg a new paradigm was modelled after the pattern of thematic stems, which consisted of adding *-s, -n, -ϕ* after the thematic vowel:

$$\frac{\text{lógon}}{\text{lógos}} = \frac{\text{patéran}}{X} \qquad \text{where } X = \text{patéras}$$

The salient feature of the MIA nominal paradigms is the complete loss of the category of dual and the reduction in the number of cases. The Dat merges with the Gen, leaving only a few historical remnants, and in late MIA the Instr merges with the Loc. During the later stages of MIA (represented by Ap) we will witness dichotomization of paradigms into direct (Nom, Acc) and indirect cases. The latter group of cases is based on the morphological syncretism of the Instr and Loc, on the one hand, and that of the Dat, Gen, Abl, on the other hand. At the end of the MIA period there appeared a tendency towards the fusion of these two groups anticipating the general oblique case of NIA languages.

During the earlier stages of MIA the three genders of OIA remained but their alignment with nominal morphology was simplified. Thus the three-way distinction of gender is essentially preserved in Pāli morphology. However, various lapses in agreement demonstrate that the inherited system started being eroded. For instance, in Dhammapada 104 we read *attā jitā* 'the Self is conquered' (instead of *attā jito*); in Dham 194 *tapo sukho* 'the penitence is bliss' (instead of *tapo sukhaṃ*); in Therī 518 we find *sakhiyo tīṇi janiyo* 'we three friends' with the neuter form of 'three' (instead of Fem *tisso*). Athematic neuters in *-as* are sometimes inflected as thematic masculines; and also thematic neuters are sometimes inflected as masculines (and vice versa). The neuter plural form *-āni* became 'redundant' and could also be used with Masc and Fem nouns.[1] A starting point could be the polysemy of the suffix *-ā* in the Masc Pl and Neut Pl (the latter grammatical meaning was 'polymorphous' in that it could be expressed by two suffixes *-ā* and *-āni*):

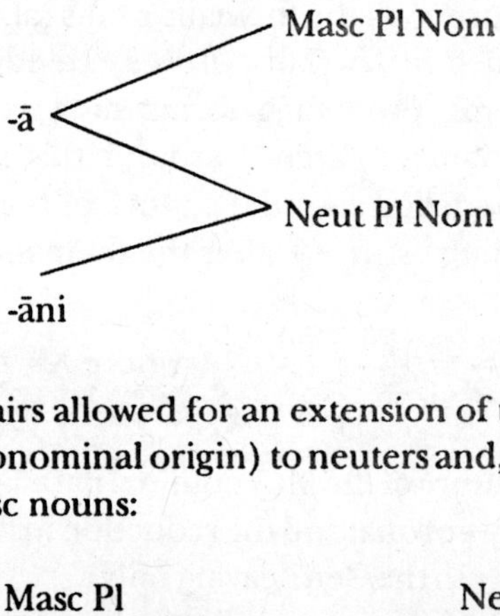

This state of affairs allowed for an extension of the Masc Pl Acc *-e* (which is of a pronominal origin) to neuters and, vice versa, Neut Pl Acc *-āni* to Masc nouns:

	Masc Pl	Neuter Pl
Nom	dhammā 'rights'	rūpāni ~ rūpā 'forms'
Acc	dhamm *e* ~ dhamm *āni*	rūp *āni* ~ rūp *e*

Athematic neuters in *-as* and *-an* became a target for various levellings in all MIA dialects. In Mah and JMah the neuters in *-as* were reassigned the Masc gender because of the phonological identity of their suffixes (both end in *-o* < OIA *-aḥ*): *maṇo* 'mind' (Masc) vs. OIA *mano* (*manaḥ* Neuter). In AMg the neuters in *-as* are commonly used as masculine nouns and both form their Nom Sg in *-e*: *maṇe* 'mind', *tave* 'penitence' (< OIA *tapaḥ*), *tame* 'darkness' (< OIA *tamaḥ*). In Ś and Mg (and occasionally also in AMg) the athematic neuters in *-as* are treated as thematic (*a*-stem) neuters: AMg *vayā* 'age' (OIA vayas), *seyā* 'glory' (OIA śreyas), etc.

In 1.3 we saw an erosion of the Masc-Neuter distinction in Eastern Aśokan dialects, where *-e* functioned as the single suffix in the Nom Sg of *a*-stems replacing both Masc and Neuter suffixes. Similarly, in AMg thematic neuters were reassigned the Masc gender. As in Pāli, the reason behind this change was the polysemy of the suffix *-ā* which is found already in Vedic Sanskrit. The OIA alternation of the type *trīṇi sthānāni* ~ *trīṇi sthānā* 'three places' is continued in MIA; see the data from AMg:

> *tao ṭhāṇāṇi* (Ṭhāṇ 143) or *tao ṭhāṇāĩ* (Ṭhāṇ 158)
> *tao ṭhāṇā* (Ṭhāṇ 163, 165)

The next step would be a metaplasmus of the neuter singular suffix *-ā* by the masculine suffix *-e* (but also the neuter suffix of *s*-stems): *ṭhāṇe*. Old thematic neuters in AMg could have both suffixes *-o* and *-e* as could their masculine counterparts (cf. 3.2.1). In dramatic Mg the suffix *-e* is found, e.g. *pavahaṇe* 'wagon' (OIA *pravahaṇaṁ*), whereas in Ś only *-o* is used: *pavahaṇo* [Mṛcch].

Athematic neuters in *-an* became first thematic neuters since phonologically *-an* ended up as *-ā*. Thus we find Mah *kammā* (<OIA *karman*), Mah, Ś *ṇāmā* 'name' (<OIA *nāman*). These forms shared the fate of original thematic neuters according to the grammarians (Vr, Hc) and were provided with the suffix *-o*: *kammo, jammo* 'birth' (< OIA *janman*).

In Ap the crumbling system of gender was further recategorized by metaplasmus. The primary force behind these innovations was phonological change. During the late MIA period final long vowels were shortened and *ā*-stems (Fem) could no longer be distinguished from *a*-stems (Masc/Neuter). As will be shown in 3.2.1.2, this entailed massive borrowing of the *a*-stem suffixes (Masc/Neuter nouns) into original *ā*-stems (Fem nouns). Furthermore, in Ap the distinction between Masc and Fem *i*- and *u*-stems was completely lost and there developed a common set of endings made up of (originally) Masc and Fem forms (some of these endings could also be used with Fem *a*-stems). This state of affairs arose as a consequence of the convergence of *a*-stems (Masc/Neuter) with *u*-stems (Masc/Fem), caused by the phonological process of raising of mid short back vowel *ŏ* > *u* (cf. 3.2.2 for details). As in other MIA dialects, the 'redundant' suffix of the Neuter Pl *-aĩ* (< OIA *-āni*) could be used with Masc nouns in the Acc Pl. The same suffix is found even with pronouns: *amhaĩ* 'we' (~*amhe*), and *tumhaĩ* 'you' (~*tumhe*), cf. 3.3.1.

3.2 Nouns

OIA possessed a great number of nominal inflectional types: stems in *-a, -i, -u, -an,* -C(onsonant) and *-nt.* In MIA all consonantal stems were thematized (e.g. in Pāli *vijju* < *vidyut* is inflected as a *u*-stem; *bharanto* < *bharanṭ-* as an *a*-stem). As far as the vocalic stems are concerned, the original variety of OIA is kept intact. OIA paradigms may still serve as classical examples of the so-called fusional exponence (= fusion of significates); consider, for instance, the Gen, Abl and Loc of the *a*- vs. high vowel stems:

Sg	Acc	devam	agnim	bhikṣum
	Gen	devasya	agneḥ	bhikṣoḥ
	Abl	devāt	agneḥ	bhikṣoḥ
Pl	Nom	devāḥ	agnayaḥ	bhikṣavaḥ

MIA dialects remodelled this relationship of *a*- vs. *i*- and *u*-stems by introducing far-reaching agglutinative exponence (= agglutination of significates) in these cases:

	Sg	Acc	dev ã	agg ĩ	bhikkh ũ
		Gen	a ssa	i ssa	u ssa
Short thematic vowel		Abl	a smā	i smā	u smā
		Loc	a smĩ	i smĩ	u smĩ
Long thematic vowel	Pl	Nom	ā	ī	ū
		Instr	ā hi (Mah)	ī hi	ū hi
		Gen, Dat	ā nā	ī nā	ū nā
		Loc	ā su	ī su	ū su

In these data we may observe a trend towards one declension. The thematic vowel (be it *a, i,* or *u*) is followed by a certain suffix for each case without exhibiting 'polymorphy' (or suppletion) as in OIA (where the Gen Sg of *a*-stems was *-asya* but that of *i*-stems *-eḥ*; etc.). The resulting system, however, halted half-way between the fusional and the agglutinative type (as in Turkish). In our MIA data the thematic vowel is long in the plural vs. short in the singular (cf. Turkish *-lar* vs. -ϕ), but the case markers still exhibit polymorphy; contrast, for instance, the following marking for the locative in MIA and Turkish:

	Number Case		Number Case	
Sg Loc	dev-a - ϕ - smĩ	'god'	ev - ϕ - i	'house'
Pl Loc	dev-a - : - su		ev - ler - i	

3.2.1 *a-stems*

The endings of *a* -stems in early (Pāli), middle (AMg) and late (Ap) MIA are given below:

		OIA	Pāli	AMg	Ap
Sg	N	dev aḥ	dev o	dev o, -e	de u
	V	a	a	a	"
	A	am	ã	ã	"
	I	ena, -ā (Ved)	ena, -ā	eṇā	ẽ, -ĩ
	D	āya	assa, -āya		aha, ahu
	G	asya	assa	assa	" "
	Abl	āt	ā, asmā, amhā -ato	ā, -āo[2]	" "
	L	-e	e, -asmĩ, -amhi	e, -āsi,-ammi	ahĩ, -ĩ,-e
Pl	N, V	āḥ	ā	ā	a
	A	ān	e	ā, -e	"
	I	-ebhiḥ (Ved)	ehi (-āhi Mah)	ehĩ	ahĩ, -ehĩ
	Abl		"	ehinto	ahã
	G	ānām	ānã	āṇã	"
	L	-eṣu	esu	esũ	ahĩ, -ehĩ

According to Ghatage (1941:85) AMg prose prefers the form *deve* in the Nom Sg and *devāsi* in the Loc Sg. Other forms are apparently used without any distinction (often side by side). As far as their frequency is concerned, the forms *devo* in the Nom Sg and *devā* in the Acc Pl are frequent in poetry but rare in prose.

Both Pāli and AMg extended the OIA Nom Sg *devo* (used in Sanskrit only before voiced consonants, *y* and *v*) to all environments. The alternative AMg form *deve* is, of course, the typical Mg form which appears in eastern inscriptional Prākrits (cf.1.3).

The OIA Instr *-ena* is continued in both Pāli and AMg. In Pāli, there are also forms in *-enā* and *-ā* (cf. Vedic *devā*). According to Mayrhofer (1951:82) the original form was * *devana* and the form *devenā* (documented in the oldest stages) is a product of analogical levelling along the following lines (= proportional analogy + paradigmatic simplification):

Instr Pl	Abl Pl	Loc Pl	Instr Sg
ātmabhiḥ (< ṇ-bhih)	-abhyaḥ	-asu	-anā
agni-bhiḥ	-ibhyaḥ	-iṣu	-inā
śatru-bhiḥ	-ubhyaḥ	-uṣu	-unā
kartṛ-bhiḥ	-ṛbhyaḥ	-ṛṣu	-ṛṇā
deve-bhiḥ (Ved)	-ebhyaḥ	-eṣu	-enā

The result was a form with long *-ā*, and the form with short *-a* can be explained as a contamination of * *devana* and *devenā*.

The MIA Dat/Gen form *devassa* is from OIA *devasya* (by the assimilation of the glide to the preceding sibilant).

MIA Abl *devā* is from OIA *devāt* (cf. OLat *deiwōd* and OCSl *vlka* 'wolf' < *-ōd).

Pāli Abl Sg forms *devasmā* and *devamhā* are of a pronominal origin -*tasmā* and *tamhā* (cf. OIA *tasmāt*) are Abl forms of the pronoun *ta-* 'that, he'. The second form is derivable from the older *tasmā* by metathesis > * *tamsā* and fricative weakening > *tamhā*. The form *devato* would correspond to OIA * *deva-taḥ* with the suffix *-taḥ* which occurs originally only with adverbs (e.g. *ta-taḥ* 'from there'). *-āo* in AMg *devāo* is apparently a contamination of the nominal *-ā* (< *devāt*) and 'adverbial' *-o* (< *-taḥ*).

Pāli Loc forms *devasmī* and *devamhi* are of a pronominal origin (cf. OIA Loc of *ta-* 'that' *tasmin*). Both Pāli and AMg had forms which underwent metathesis *-sm->-ms-* and then diverged by undergoing different changes of fricative weakening (*s* > *h*) in Pāli and the assimilation of the sibilant by the preceding nasal (*-ms-> -mm-*) in Mah (and also in AMg); the sequence of historical events which produced these forms is sketched in 3.3.2.

The AMg Acc Pl form *devā* continues OIA *devān*. The form *deve* in both Pāli and AMg is of a pronominal origin (OIA distinguished Nom Pl *te* and Acc Pl *tān(s)*, but in MIA times *te* started being used in both cases). Mayrhofer (1951:84) suggested that the starting point could have been syntactic collusions such as * *te devān* > *te deve*; if this were the case, we would be dealing with non-proportional analogy.

The AMg Abl Pl form *devehinto* is a contamination of the Instr Pl *devehī* and the Abl suffix *-to* (< *-taḥ*) of an adverbial origin.

In AMg the original nasalization of the final vowel in the Gen Pl was also extended to the Instr and Loc (thus all trisyllabic forms have alternative forms with or without nasalization of the final vowel: *devehĩ, devāṇã, devesũ*).

Coming to the late period of MIA, the Ap suffix of the Nom Sg in *-u* is explainable by the raising of short mid vowels (2.2.2) from the general Pkt *-ŏ* (which arose by the shortening of OIA *-ō*). As mentioned by Tagare (1948:108), this suffix is older than 500 A.D. as it is found in the Ap illustrations in the *Nāṭyaśāstra* 17 (e.g. *moru* < *mayūraḥ* 'peacock'). Ap shows the single form in *-u* for direct cases (Nom and Acc).[3]

Inst Sg *-ẽ* may be connected with the late MIA Loc Sg *-ahĩ* (> *aĩ* > *ẽ*), as suggested by Grierson, rather than with OIA *-ena* (Bloch). The MIA Loc Sg *-ahĩ* derives clearly from OIA *-asmin* by metathesis and fricative weakening: **-amsin* > *-amhin* > *-āhĩ* > *-ahĩ*.[4]

Loc Sg *-i* is traceable back to OIA *-ē* by shortening and raising: *-ē* > *-e* > *-i*.

The form of the Gen Sg in *-aha* goes back to OIA *-asya* via assimilation, degemination + compensatory lengthening) and fricative weakening (> *-assa* > *-āsa* > *-āha*). The earliest pieces of evidence for fricative weakening in the Gen Sg of *a*-stems appear in the Māgadhī passages of Mṛcchakaṭikā. (The pronominal form *tāha* and nominal *-āha* vs. Mah *tāsa*.) For their alternation with other Prākrits' suffixes (Ś *-assa*, Mg *-aśśa*) cf. 5.4.

The Instr and Loc Pl forms have clearly two sources: *-ehĩ* goes back to the Vedic Instr Pl *-ebhiḥ*, and *-ahĩ* derives from the OIA Loc Sg *-asmin*.

In the case of the Gen/Abl Pl form it is not clear whether we are dealing with an archaism or an innovation of Ap. The suffix *-ahã* might be derived from an undocumented OIA form **āsām* by fricative weakening (**-āsām*>*-āsam*>*-āham*>*-āhã*). Here we might have another piece of evidence for the existence of a non-Sanskritic OIA dialect. The form with *-s-* in the Gen Pl from PIE **-ōsom* (e.g. **putrāsām* vs. Skt *putrāṇām*) would explain MIA *puttāhã* (Mg) and *puttahã* (Ap). The PIE suffix **-ōsom* (and *a*-stem **-āsom*) is established beyond any doubt on the basis of Latin *-ōrum* (and *-ārum*) which show effects of rhotacism. On the other hand, it could also well be that here we are dealing with an innovation of Ap which derived the plural form from its singular counterpart by the nasalization of the ultima (cf. Gen Sg *-aha* vs. Gen Pl *-ahã*).[5]

3.2.2 *ā-stems*

The endings of *ā*-stems in Pāli and AMg are displayed below:

		OIA	Pāli	AMg
Sg	N	tṛṣṇ ā 'thirst'	taṇh ā	māl ā 'garland'
	V	e	e	ā, -e
	A	ām	ā	ā
	I		āya	āe
	D, G	āyāḥ	"	"
	Abl	āyāḥ	"	", -āo
	L	āyām	āyā	āe
Pl	N, V, A	āḥ	ā, -āyo	ā, -āo
	I	ābhiḥ	āhi	āhĩ
	Abl		"	āhinto
	D, G	ānām	ānā	āṇā
	L	āsu	āsu	āsũ

The Instr, Dat, Gen and Abl in Pāli show the syncretized form of the OIA Gen in *-āyāḥ* (the original ending was only *-āḥ*, cf. AGr *khōrās*, Lat (*pater*) *familiās;* this ending was enlarged by *-āy-* taken from the Loc). AMg *-āe* continues, according to Pischel, Bloch and Geiger, the Dat/Gen in *-āyai* of the Brāhmaṇas and Upaniṣads. However, this form could also be a further development of *-āya* found in Pāli. In AMg the Abl Sg in *-āo* is taken from its masculine counterpart. The original form of the Loc Sg was in *-āi* (<* *ā-i*, cf. Lat *Rōmae*), which was enlarged by *-ām* in OIA times. For the Abl Sg in AMg in *-āhinto* cf. under *a*-stems. In Pāli the Nom, Voc, Acc Pl in *-āyo* is an analogical formation with feminine *i*-and *u*-stems (*matiyo, dhenuyo*). The form of the OIA Gen Pl in *-ānām* (vs. PIE *-*ōn*) is an extension from *n*-stems. According to the pattern of

ātma-bhiḥ	(< *ātmn̥-bhiḥ)
ātma-bhyaḥ	(< *ātmn̥-bhyaḥ)
ātma-su	(< *ātmn̥-su)
ātma-nām	(< *ātman-ām)

the Gen Pl form of *ā*-stem forms was created:

tr̥ṣṇā-bhiḥ
-bhyaḥ
-su
-nām

(This was the starting point for the spread of *n*-declension in OIA and MIA.)

In Ap the reduction of length in final vowels has neutralized the distinction between *a*- and *ā*-stems (between Masc/Neuter and Fem nouns). As a result of this phonological neutralization masculine suffixes could appear with feminine nouns (original *ā*-stems). Thus we find *-ẽ* and *-ĩ* in the Instr Sg; *-aha/u* in the Dat, Gen, Abl Sg; *-ahĩ* and *-ĩ* in the Loc Sg as with the Masc/Neuter nouns. Among the relics of *ā*-stems we may mention *-(ā)i* in the Instr Sg (by raising from *-āe* found in Pkts).[6] The Voc in *-e* is a Sanskritism.

3.2.3 *i- and u-stems*

Because of the complete parallelism between *i*-and *u*-stems (3.2) only *i*-stem nouns will be shown in the usual paradigm. The only exception to this parallelism is the Voc Pl of *u*-stems: *bhikkhave* ~ *-o* (vs. *aggayo*). The form *bhikkhave* 'monks' is considered a Magadhism in Buddha's speeches.

(i) Masculine nouns

		OIA	Pāli	AMg	Mah
Sg	N	agniḥ	aggi 'fire'	aggī	paī 'husband'
	V	e	"	i	
	A	im	ī	ī	ī
	I	inā	inā	iṇā	iṇā
	Abl		ismā, -imhā, -inā, -itō	iṇo, -īo	īo
	D, G		issa, -ino	issa, -iṇo	iṇo
	L		ismī, -imhi	īsi, -immi	immi
Pl	N, V, A	ayas	aggayo, -ī	aggiṇo, -īo	iṇo
	I	ibhis	īhi	īhī	īhī
	Ab		"	īhinto	
	D, G	īnām	īnā	īṇā	īṇā
	L	isu	īsu	īsū	īsu

Most of the endings were discussed in 3.2. Among the remaining endings *-ino* (Dat, Gen Sg) was adopted from *in*-stems, and *-inā* in the Abl Sg was borrowed from the Instr. It is worth mentioning that neuters (*akkhi* 'eye', *assu* 'tear') may show up with the nasalized ultima *akkhī, assū* by analogy with *a*-stem neuters (*rūpā*). Plural forms akkhī (~ *akkhīni*), assū (~ *assūni*) are also due to analogy with *a*-stems: *rūpā* (~ *rūpāni*).

The distinction between the Nom and Voc Sg (*agniḥ* vs. *agne*) is lost in Pāli but it appears in AMg (*aggī* vs. *aggi*). The OIA endings reflect PIE qualitative *ablaut* (**-i-s* vs. *-ei*), whereas the AMg distinction *-ī* vs. *-i* is due to merger of *i*- and *ī*-stems:

		OIA		Pāli	AMg
i-stems	Sg	N	agniḥ	aggi	aggī
		V	e		i
		A	im	ī	ī
ī-stems	Sg	N	devī		
		V	i		
		A	im		

(ii) Feminine nouns

		OIA	Pāli	AMg
Sg	N	mati	mati	matī
	V	e	i	i
	A	im	ī	ī
	I	yā	iyā	īe
	Abl		"	īo
	D, G		"	īe
	L	yām	", iyā	", -īsi
Pl	N, V, A		iyo, -ī	ī, -īo
	I	ibhiḥ	īhi	īhĩ
	Abl			īhinto
	D, G	īnām	īnā	īṇā
	L	iṣu	īsu	īsũ

MIA dialects merged several declensional classes of OIA into this one:

(i) Feminine *i*- and *u*-stems (*mati-, dhenu-*)
(ii) Polysyllabic *ī*- and *ū*-stems (*devī-, vadhū-*)
(iii) Monosyllabic feminine *ī*- and *ū*-stems (*dhī-, bhū-*)

The contrast *-ī* vs. *-i* in the Nom vs. Voc in AMg is here extended from *ī*-stems. Even in Pali the Voc ending *-i* is taken from *ī*-stems. The Instr (Abl, Dat, Gen) ending *-iyā* continues probably the monosyllabic *dhiy-ā* or it can be derived from OIA *matyā* with an intrusive vowel *matiyā* (both forms are to be found in Pāli texts: *jātiyā* 'birth' ~ *jaccā* < OIA *jātyā* by palatalization and shortening before CC). The Gen form *matiyā* can be compared with OIA *dhiy-āḥ*. There are also forms without *-i-*, e.g. *pathavyā* < *pṛthivyāḥ* <'earth', *najjā* < *nadyāḥ* 'river' (by palatalization).

The Loc form *matiyā* may be compared with OIA *dhiy-ām*.

In AMg this declension corresponds completely to that of *ā*-stems, with the exception of the Loc form *-īsi*, extended here from its masculine counterpart. Compare:

		ā-stems	*i-stems*
Sg	N	-ā	-ī
	A	-ã	-ĩ

I	-āe	-īe
Abl	", -āo	", -īo
D, G	"	"
L	"	", -īsi

The Nom Pl *matiyo* in Pāli can be compared with OIA *dhiyaḥ*. The oblique forms in AMg show again the optional nasalization of the ultima of the ending.

In Ap the distinction between Masc and Fem *i-* and *u*-stems was almost completely lost. The common set of endings displays some Fem forms (which could be used with both Masc and Fem stems) and some Masc forms (which could be used with Masc *i*-and *u*-stems and Fem *a*-stems). This state of affairs arose as a consequence of the convergence of Masc *a*-stems with *u*-stems (both Masc and Fem), which was caused by the phonological process of the raising of mid short vowels (*o* > *u*).

The following are the endings which are common to Masc and Fem nouns belonging to *i-* and *u*-stems:

Sg	Dir	-ϕ	Pl Dir -ϕ
	I	-e (also with a -stems)	Obl -hĩ
	D,G, Abl	-hi, -he	
	L	-hĩ	

In this set the Instr Sg in *-e* was also used with Fem *a*-stems; the Dat, Gen, Abl, Loc Sg in *-hi* was borrowed from Fem *a*-stems: *-ahĩ* (< *ahẽ* < *āhẽ* < *āsyām*).

Among the suffixes which were common to Masc *i-* and *u*-stems and Fem *a*-stems are: Dat, Gen, Abl Sg *-hu* (in WAp) and Dat, Gen, Abl Pl *-hā̃* (in WAp).

3.2.4 *r-stems*

		OIA	Pāli	AMg
Sg	N	dātā	dātā	dāyā
	V	dātaḥ	a, -e, -ā	"
	A	āram	ārā̃	ārā̃
	I	rā	arā̃, -ārā̃, -unā	āreṇa
	Abl		arā̃, -ārā̃	ārāo

	D, G	uḥ	u, -uno, -ussa	uṇo, -ārassa
	L	ari	ari	āre
Pl	N, V A	āras	dātāro	dāyāro, -ā
	I		ūhi, -ārehi	ārehī
	Abl		" "	ārehinto
	D, G	ṝṇām	ūnā, -ārānā	ārāṇā
	L		usu, -āresu	āresū

The Sg Nom in *-a* in Pāli corresponds to OIA *dātaḥ* (*-r*); or according to Mayrhofer (1951:95), this form could be a result of proportional analogy with Fem *ī*-stems:

$$\frac{\text{devī}}{\text{devi}} = \frac{\text{dātā}}{\text{X}}$$

similarly, the other form in *-e* could be a result of proportional analogy with *ā*-stems:

$$\frac{\text{taṇhā}}{\text{taṇhe}} = \frac{\text{dātā}}{\text{X}}$$

The form in *-ā* in both Pāli and AMg is the Nom. The Sg Instr in *-arā* in Pāli can be explained in two ways: either from OIA *dātrā* with an intrusive vowel *-a-* or from the allomorph *dātar-* which appears in the Loc. The form in *-ārā* is based on the allomorph *dātār-* which appears in the Acc. The form in *-unā* is derivable from the OIA neuter form *dātṛṇā* (where the *-n-* is extended from *n*-stems). The AMg form in *-āreṇa* is a simple extension from *a*-stems. The form of the Abl Sg in Pāli is similarly based on two allomorphs *dātar-* ~ *dātār-* These two were taken as roots and new stems by adding *-a* were formed from them. Thus *dātarā* and *dātārā* are ordinary Abl forms of *a*-stems (similarly Instr Pl *dātārehi*, Gen Pl *dātārāṇā* and Loc Pl *dātāresu*). AMg went even further by forming almost all cases from the *a*-stem *dāyāra*- (with the exception of the Nom Sg and Pl, and Gen Sg). Thus whereas Pāli shows four allomorphs of the stem: *dātar(a)* ~ *dātār(a)* ~ *dātu* ~ *dātū*, AMg has only one *dāyār(a)*.

Pāli preserved the OIA form of the Gen Sg *dātuḥ* > *dātu;* the form in *-uno* (also in AMg) is derivable from the OIA neuter form *dātṛṇaḥ;* the form *dātussa* has the suffix *-ssa* extended here from *a*-stems.

The Pl oblique cases with long *-ū-* in Pāli can be best explained from the OIA Gen Pl *dātṝṇām > dātūnā; -u-* was then extended to other forms. The alternative forms (and the only forms in AMg) are thematic formations from the stem *dātāra-*.

Some other interesting forms appear in the declension of the nouns of relationship.

3.2.5 *Nouns of Relationship*

	OIA	Pāli	AMg	Mah
Sg	N pitā	pitā	piyā	piā
	A pitaram	pitarã	piyarã	piarã
	I pitrā	pitarā	piuṇā	piuṇā
	Abl	" , pitito	piuṇo	
	D, G pituḥ	pitu, -uno, -ussa	" , piusa , piyarassa	piuṇo
	L pitari	pitari	piyari	
Pl	N pitaraḥ	pitaro	piyaro	piaro
	A	pitaro, -e	piyaro, -e	piaro, piuṇo
	I	pitūhi, pitarehi	piīhĩ, piūhĩ	piūhĩ
	Abl	"	piīhĩto, piūhĩto	"
	D, G pitṝṇām	pitūnā, pitunnā, pitarāṇā	piīṇā, piūṇā	piūṇā
	L	pitūsu, pitaresu	piīsũ, piūsũ	piūsũ

First of all, there are only three allomorphs of the stem in Pāli: *pitar(a) ~ pitu ~ pitū* ; similarly AMg shows three *piyar(a) ~ piu ~ piī/ū* (vs. four in OIA).

The Sg Abl *pitito* in Pāli is explainable from OIA *pitṛ-taḥ* with the suffix *-taḥ* with the ablative meaning (see under *a*-stems).

The form of the Pl Gen in Pāli shows nicely the complementarity of vowel and consonant length (V:C ~ VCC).

The AMg forms of the Sg Instr and Gen are, according to Ghatage (1941:144), extended here from the *u*-stem declension (cf. *bhikkhuṇā, bhikkhuṇo* 'monk'); it is possible, however, to explain them as a result of a regular phonological development from OIA neuter forms *dātṛṇā, dātṛṇaḥ* (as above). Compare Pāli *bhātuno* (hapax) 'brothers'< **bhrātṛ-ṇaḥ* for OIA *bhrātaraḥ*.

Of particular interest is the double treatment of OIA *-ṛ-* in AMg: *-ū-* ~ *-ī-* (OIA *pitṝṇām* > *piūṇā̃* ~ *piīṇā̃*). This repeats the development of PIE * *ṝ* (< rH) in OIA; compare Sanskrit *jīrṇa-* 'old' with undocumented OIA * *jūrṇa-*, which gave AMg *juṇṇa;* similarly, Sanskrit *tīrtha-* 'ford' vs. AMg *tūha-* < OIA * *tūrtha-* (cf. Burrow 1955: 45).

The Pāli word *mātā* 'mother' (AMg *māyā*) has been assimilated to *pitā* in the Acc Pl; thus vs. OIA *pitṝn* - *mātṝḥ* we find Pāli *pitaro* - *mātaro* (AMg *piyaro* - *māyaro*). In Pāli there are some forms according to *dhenu*, e.g. Abl Sg *mātarā* ~ *mātuyā* (cf. *dhenuyā*); Gen Sg *mātu* ~ *mātuyā* (cf. *dhenuyā*); Loc Sg *mātari* ~ *mātuyā*, *mātuyā̃* (cf. *dhenuyā*, *dhenuyā̃*).

3.2.6 *an-stems*

		OIA	Pāli	AMg
Sg	N	rājā	rājā	rāyā
	V	rājan	ā, -a	ā, -a, -ā
	A	rājānam	ānā	āṇā, -ā
	I	rājñā	rājinā, raññā	rāiṇā, rāeṇa, rannā (Mg raṇṇā)
	Abl		raññā, rājato	rāiṇo, ranno
	D, G		rañño, rājino	rāiṇo, ranno, rāyassa
	L		rājini	rāyāsi
Pl	N, V	rājānaḥ	rājāno	rāyāṇo, rāiṇo
	A	rājñah	"	rāyāṇo
	I		rājūhi	rāīhī
	Abl		"	rāīhīto
	D, G	rājñām	rājūnā, raññā	rāīṇā, rāyāṇā
	L		rājūsu	rāīsū

Both forms of the Instr Sg in Pāli *rājinā* ~ *raññā*, AMg *rāiṇā* ~ *rannā* (and Mg *raṇṇā*) are regular developments of OIA *rājñā* by retroflexion and assimilation (AMg and Mg forms have to be derived from Proto-Māgadhī * *rājinā*):

	rājñā	rājnā	rājinā	rājinā
retroflexion	-	-	rājiṇā	rājiṇā
syncopation	-	-	rājṇā	-
shortening	rajñā	rajnā	rajṇā	-
assimilation	raññā	rannā	raṇṇā	-
j>y> ϕ	-	-	-	rāiṇā̂

The alternative forms of the Gen Sg (Pāli *rājino~rañño*, AMg (*rāiṇo~ranno*) can be similarly explained from OIA *rājñaḥ*. Note that only one form obtains in the Loc Sg, namely that one which results by the epenthesis of *-i-*: Pāli *rājini* (* *rañña*). AMg displays an *a*-stem formation *rāyāsi*.

The OIA contrast between the Nom and the Acc Pl (*rājānaḥ* vs. *rājñaḥ*) is lost in both Pāli *rājāno* and AMg *rāyāṇo*.

The Instr Pl *rājūhi* was formed by analogy with *r*-stems:

$$\frac{\text{pitā}}{\text{pitūhi}} = \frac{\text{rājā.}}{\text{X}}$$

Similarly in AMg:

$$\frac{\text{piyā}}{\text{piihī}} = \frac{\text{rāyā.}}{\text{X}}$$

In Pāli the Gen Pl *raññā* continues the OIA form *rājñām*. AMg shows a number of thematic formations: Acc Sg *rāyā̃*, Instr Sg *rāeṇa*, Gen Sg *rāyassa*, Loc Sg *rāyāsi*, Gen Pl *rāyāṇā*. This noun was thematized also in Pāli; the starting point, however, was the weak case *rañn-* (< OIA *rājñ-*). Thus we find Nom Sg *rañño*, Gen Sg *raññassa*, etc.

3.2.7 *nt-stems*

	OIA	Pāli	AMg
Sg N, V	bharan	bharā̃	bharā̃to, bharā̃
A	bharantam	bharantā̃	bharantā̃
I	bharatā	bharatā	bharayā, bharanteṇa
Abl	(bharataḥ)	"	bharao
D, G	bharataḥ	bharato	bharao, bharā̃tassa
L	bharati	bharati	barā̃te, bharā̃tā̃si
Pl N, V	bharantaḥ	bharanto	bharanto
A	(bharataḥ)	"	bharante
I	(bharadbhiḥ)	bharantehi	bharantehī̃
Abl	(bharadbhyaḥ)	"	bharantehī̃to
D, G	bharatām	bharatā̃	bharā̃ tāṇā̃
Loc	(bharatsu)	bharantesu	bharā̃tesū̃

OIA shows very nicely the original ablaut relationships (*-ont- ~ *-n̥t- > OIA -ant- ~ -at-, cf. above, whereas AGr extended *-ont-* and Lat *-ent-* (< * -n̥t-) to all cases):

		PIE	OIA	AGr
Sg	N	*bhér-ont-s	bharán	phér-ōn
	A	-ont-m̥	-ant-am	-ont-a
	I	-n̥t-ō	-at-ā	
	G	-n̥t-es	-at-aḥ	-ont-os
	L	-n̥t-i	-at-i	-ont-i (D)
Pl	N	-ont-es	-ant-aḥ	-ont-es
	A	-n̥t-n̥s	-at-aḥ	-ont-as
	I	-n̥t-bhis/-si	-ad-bhiḥ	-ō-si (Attic < *ont-si)
	G	-n̥t-ōm	-at-ām	-ont-ōn

These original ablaut relationships are preserved to a certain degree in Pāli, at least in the singular paradigm. The plural paradigm, however, shows the progressive thematization typical of MIA. The old ablauted Instr (OIA *bharadbhiḥ*) survived only with the participle *sabbhi* 'being, good' (cf. OIA *sadbhiḥ* from *sant-*). Much more common (especially in the later post-canonical literature) are thematic formations from the new *a*-stem *bharanta*. Compare:

		devo 'god' (stem *deva-*)	bharā̃
Pl	I, Abl	devehi	bharantehi (stem *bharanta-*)
	L	devesu	bharantesu

In Pāli, much rarer is thematization by dropping the stem-forming *-nt*, e.g. *passo* (Nom Sg) 'seeing' for *passā̃* (< *passant-*, cf. OIA *paśyant-*).

Both these tendencies increased during the later stages of MIA and the forms such as *bharā̃* (Nom Sg), *bharatā̃* (Instr Sg) etc. became archaisms. AMg shows an almost complete thematization of *nt*-stems (with the exception of the Nom Pl *bharan̆to*):

		a-stems	
Sg	N	devo	bharanto (*bharā̃* is archaic)
	A	devā̃	bharantā̃
	I	deveṇa	bharanteṇa (*bharayā̃* is archaic)
	Abl	devāo	bharāo (stem *bhara* -!)

	G	devassa	bharātassa
	L	deve, devāsi	bharāte, bharātāsi
Pl	A	deve	bharante
	I	devehī	bharantehī
	Abl	devehinto	bharantehīto
	G	devāṇā	bharātāṇā
	L	devesũ	bharātesũ

3.3 Pronouns

A great variety of forms is found in the pronominal system.

3.3.1 *Personal Pronouns*

'I' (orthotonic forms)

	OIA	Pāli	AMg	Mah	Ap
N	aham	ahā	ahā, hā	ahā	haũ
A	mām	mā	mamā, mā	mamā	maī
I	mayā	mayā	mae, mai	mae	maī
Abl	mad	"	mamāo, matto	"	
D	mahyam	mayhā, mamā	majjha, maha,		majjhu, mahu
G	mama	amhā	mama	majjha, mahe, mama	
L	mayi	mayi	mamāsi, mai	mai, mamammi	maī

'I' (clitic forms)

G, D	me	me	me	me	me
A	mā	mā	me		
I	me	me	me		me

The Ap form *haũ* (found in the texts from 500-1200 A.D.) can be traced back to OIA * *aha-ka* (cf. *hage* in Mg) which is documented as *ahaya* in WSAp.

The PIE Acc Sg was reconstructed as * *mē* (cf. Lat *mē*, AGr *me*); the IA languages added the accusative ending *-m* to the original form * *mā* (cf. OIA and OP *mām*, Pāli and AMg *mā*). In AMg a form with reduplication *mamā* appeared.

OIA Instr Sg *mayā* is continued in both Pāli and AMg (*may-ā* > *maï*); *mae* is according to Bloch either a combination of *mayā* and *me* or it has been adopted from the nominal inflection. The OIA form goes back to PIE * *me/ oi-ō* (with the suffix -*ō*).

The AMg Abl Sg form *mamāo* was created by analogy with *devāo* (with the Gen Sg *mama* as the base); similarly, *matto* is from *mama* plus -*taḥ*.

Pāli Gen, Dat Sg *mayhā* developed from OIA *mahyam* by metathesis; AMg and Mah further affricated the palatal glide (*y* > *j*, cf. *yuga* > *juga* 'yoke'): *majjha*. The OIA form *mama* (continued by Pāli and AMg) resulted probably by assimilation from **mana* (cf. AV *mana*, OCSl *mene*, Lithu *manė*). The AMg form *maha* resulted from [*maj:ha*] by simplification of the cluster [j:h].[7]

The OIA and Pali Loc Sg *mayi* (and AMg *maï*) goes back to PIE **me/ oi-i* (with the suffix -*i*). The AMg form *mamāsi* is of a pronominal origin (cf. OIA *tasmin*).

The Ap form *maĩ* shows merger of the Acc and the Instr/Loc cases. Mn Hindi *maĩ* and Marathi *mī* are traceable back to this oblique form of Ap, while Panjabi and Bengali *haũ* goes back to the direct form *ahaya* (< OIA * *ahaka*).

'we' (orthotonic forms)

	OIA	Pāli	AMg	Mah	Ap
N	(vayam)	mayā	amhe	amhe	amhaĩ
A	(asmān)	amhe, asme	"	"	"
I	(asmābhiḥ)	amhehi	amhehī	amhehī	amha(h)ĩ
Abl	(asmabhyam)	"	amhehinto		amhahā̃
D, G	(asmākam)	amhākā̃	asmākā̃	amh(ān)ā̃	amhāṇā̃
L	(asmāsu)	amhesu	amhesũ	amhesu	amha(h)ĩ

'we' (clitic forms)

G, D	naḥ	no	ṇo, ṇe	ṇo
A	"	"	ṇo, ṇe	"
I			ṇe	

The Nom Pl form *mayã* in Pāli shows *m-* adopted from the oblique forms of the Sg.

The Acc Pl forms *amhe* and *asme* in Pāli (*amhe* in AMg) stand for OIA *asmān* as *deve* (Acc Pl) for *devān* (*te* for *tān*). The PIE stem is reconstructible as * *n̥s-me-* (cf. Vedic *asme,* Lesbian *amme* < **as-me*).

The Instr, Abl, and Loc Pl in Pāli (plus Gen Pl in AMg) display thematic forms based on the *a*-stem *amha-* (cf. *deva-*). The Gen Pl in Pāli continues OIA *asmākam* (this form is actually a neuter of the possessive adjective *asmāka-* 'ours').

Already in AMg there was a single direct form *amhe* 'we' in the plural. In Ap this form takes the nominal neuter plural suffix *-aĩ*; in the Instr and Loc there is a form *amha(h)ĩ* whose *-aĩ* might be an extension from the pronominal direct case of the nominal Loc *-ahĩ* (ultimately of a pronominal origin *-asmin*). In the Gen both forms *amhahã* (WAp) and *amhaha* (SAp) appeared at about the same time (*ca.* 1000 A.D. according to Tagare, 1948:210). It would seem that *-ha* (from the singular *ma-ha*?) was added to the stem *amha-* and was nasalized in WAp (an extra-marker for plurality in the case of oblique forms, cf. 3.2.1).

'thou' (orthotonic forms)

	OIA	Pāli	AMg	Māh	Ap
N	t(u)vam	t(u)vã	tumã, tã, tume	tumã	tuhũ
A	tvām	t(u)vã	tumã	"	paĩ
I	tvayā	t(v)ayā	tu(m)e, tumae, tae	tue	paĩ, taĩ
Abl		"	tumão, tumatto		tujjhũ
D	tubhyam	tuyhã, tavã,	tujjha, tu(m)ha,	tujjha, tuha	tujjha
G	tava	tumhã	tava		tuhu
					tuhã
L	tvayi	t(v)ayi	tumãsi, tumammi, tai	tumammi	tai

'thou' (clitic forms)

G, D	te	te	te	te
A	tvā	tã	te	
I			te (Ś)	

In the Nom and Acc AMg and Mah continue the disyllabic Vedic form *tuvaṃ* with *-m-* by analogy with the 1st Pers *mamā̃* (Acc).

The initial consonant cluster *tv-* in Pāli could be simplified either by dropping *-v-* or by adding an epenthetic *-u-*; hence we find Instr *tvayā ~ tayā* or Nom/Acc *tvā̃ ~ tuvā̃.* In Ap *tv* became *p* or was simplified to *t*—hence *paī̃ ~ taī̃* in the Instr.

Pāli Gen, Dat Sg *tuyhā̃* developed from OIA *tubhyam* by metathesis; AMg and Mah further affricated the palatal glide (*y>j*): *tubhyam> tuhyam> tuyhā̃ > tujjha.* Pāli (and AMg) *tumhā̃* was formed from the plural stem *tumh-* (similarly *aṃhā̃*). The simplified form *tuha* in AMg and Mah is formed after the 1st Pers *maha.*

Whereas Pāli continues the OIA Loc *tvayi,* both AMg and Mah adopted here the endings of the 3rd person:

2nd Pers		3rd Pers
tum-āsi	cf.	t-āsi
tum-ammi		t-ammi

In Ap the bases of the 2nd Sg pronoun are *tu-* and *pa-* (both from OIA *tva*). *pa-* developed from *tva-* via *tpa-* (this intermediate stage is documented in Western Aśokan inscriptions, cf. 1.3) through the simplification of a difficult initial cluster. The same processes are observable in the case of *dv- > db- > b-*; cf. OIA *dvādasa* 'twelve', Aśokan (Gi) *dbādasa,* SAp (ca. 1100 A.D.) *bāraha.*

h in Ap *tuhū̃* 'you' is an innovation by analogy with the 1st Pers *aha-* 'I'.[8]

The Instr clitic form *te* is documented in dramatic Pkts; however, in some instances this form may be interpreted as Gen (cf. 4.5).

'you' (orthotonic forms)

	OIA	Pāli	AMg	Māh	Ap
N	(yūyaṃ)	tumhe	tumhe, tujjhe, tubbhe	tumhe	tumhaī̃
A	(yuṣmān)	tumhe,	" " "	"	"
I	(yuṣmābhiḥ)	tumhehi, tumhebhi	tumhehī̃, tujjhehī̃, tubbhe(hī̃)	tumhehī̃	tumhaī̃
Abl	(yuṣmabhyam)		tumhehī̃to, tubbhehī̃to		tumha(hā̃)
D,G	(yuṣmākam)	tumhākā̃, tumhā̃	tumh(āṇ)ā̃, tubbhā̃	tumhāṇā̃	
L	(yuṣmeṣu)	tumhesu	tumhesū̃, tujjhesū̃, tubbhesū̃	tumhesu	

'you' (clitic forms)

G, D	vaḥ	vo	bhe	vo
A	"	"	bhe	"
I			bhe	

OIA possessed two forms in the plural *yū* ~ *yuṣm-*: Nom *yūyam* (after 1st Pers *vay-am*; PIA * *yū-s*, cf. Avestan *yūs*), Acc *yuṣmān* (PIE * *yusme*, cf. Lesbian *umme*). MIA adopted the initial *t-* from its singular counterpart: * *tusme* > * *tumse* (by metathesis) > *tumhe* (by fricative weakening). It may be observed that MIA dialects preserved the PIE ending *-e*, whereas Vedic Sanskrit adopted here the nominal suffix *-ān*. Whereas in Pāli, Mah and Ap only one form *tumh-* is found in all cases, AMg uses three bases: *tumh-*, *tujjh-* and *tubbh-*.

In OIA the only difference between the orthotonic and clitic forms in the accusative in the 1st and 2nd Pers is the feature of nasality *mā̃* vs. *mā*, *tvā̃* vs. *tvā*. Other orthotonic forms were typically disyllabic (or trisyllabic in the case of genitive and dative plural) vs. monosyllabic clitic forms. In Middle Indo-Aryan times the phonological difference between *mā̃* vs. *mā* was lost—thus in Pāli *mā̃* is both an orthotonic and a clitic form. As can be seen from the paradigms only OIA and Pāli show the formal distinction between the direct and the oblique forms in the system of clitics (OIA *me* vs. *mā*). In some dialects this distinction was lost. For instance, in AMg *me* functions as a general oblique case form (i.e., in all grammatical functions with the exception of the subject). The Instr forms are identical with those of the Gen (in AMg in the 1st Pl only *ṇe* is documented as the Instr, whereas both *ṇo* and *ṇe* appear in the Gen and the Acc). A remarkable innovation of AMg is the plural clitic form *bhe* 'you' (by apocopation and aphaeresis from *tubbhehī* > *tubbhe* > *bhe*).[9]

As it may be observed the MIA system of clitics reached the state of affairs found in NIA nominal inflection with its simple dichotomy of one direct and one oblique form (the latter used with postpositions, cf. Hindī *-ā* vs. *-e*).

3.3.2 *Demonstrative Pronouns*

ta 'that, he' (orthotonic forms)

	OIA	Pāli	AMg	Mah	Ap
Sg N	sa(ḥ)	so (sa)	so, se	so	so, su
A	tam	tã	tã	tã	tã
I	tena	tena	teṇa	teṇa	teṇa, tẽ, tĩ
Abl	tasmāt	tasmā, tamhā	tāo		tāsu
D, G	tasya	tassa	tassa	tassa	taho/u
L	tasmin	tasmĩ, tamhi	tāsi, tammi	tammi	tahĩ
Pl N	te	te	te ~ se	te	te
A	(tān)	"	"	"	"
I	tebhiḥ (Ved)	tehi	tehĩ	tehĩ	tehĩ
Abl			tehĩto	"	"
D, G	teṣām	tesã	tesĩ	tāṇã	tāhã
L	teṣu	tesu	tesũ	tesu	

'that, he, she' (clitic forms)

Sg G, D			se	se	
A			se		

As in many other IE languages, the pronominal declension proved to be much more resistant to phonological and analogical changes throughout its history. We may observe that MIA dialects continue the OIA heteroclisis of the stem *sa-* vs. *ta-*, which goes back to PIE times. Old Prākrits (represented by Pāli) continue the OIA forms which were changed only by regular phonological processes (with the loss of the Dat and Abl Pl forms). Thus the Abl Sg *tasmā* shows the loss of the final consonant; *tamhā* is a result of metathesis (< * *tamsā*) and fricative weakening (*s* > *h*).

It was nominal declension which proved to be less resistant and during the development of MIA dialects some of its forms were lost and replaced by their pronominal counterparts. The result was an almost complete identity of nominal and pronominal declension found already in the earliest stage of MIA:

OIA (nominal declension)	Pāli (nominal declension)	Pāli (pronominal declension)

Sg	N	devaḥ	devo	so
	A	devam	devã	tã
	I	devena, devā	devena, devā	tena
	Abl	devāt →	devā ~ devasmā, -mhā ←	tasmā, -mhā
	G	devasya	devassa	tassa
	L	deve →	deve ~ devasmĩ, -mhi ←	tasmĩ, -mhi

Instr Sg *tena* is variously explained. According to Mayrhofer (1951: 108) this form goes back to Proto-Indic * *taina* (also * *tana*) which coexisted with similar nominal instrumentals * *daivā* (> *devā*), * *daivana*, **daivainā*. After the monophthongization of *ai* > *e* (*daivaina*> *devena* and *taina*> *tena*) the alternative forms * *daivana* and * *tana* were lost.

As shown above (2.4.4 and 2.5.2) the great variety of forms found in the Loc Sg is explainable by the assumption of an interplay of several phonological processes (metathesis, progressive and regressive assimilation, fricative weakening, nasalization and denasalization). Starting from the OIA form *tasmin*, the following sequence of historical events may be proposed:

tasmin (OIA)
Nasalization: tasmĩ (Pāli)
Metathesis: *tamsĩ
Assimilation: tassĩ (Ś) — *tammĩ
Fricative Weakening: tamhĩ
Nasalization: *tãhĩ — *tãsĩ
Denasalization: tamhi (Pāli) — tahĩ (Ap) — tãsi (AMg) — tammi (AMg, Mah)

The AMg Abl Sg *tão* (vs. Pāli *tasmā*) is identical with nominal *devāo*, which is explained as a contamination of the Abl Sg *devā* (<*devāt*) and adverbial *-o* (< *-taḥ*).

The Ap Gen Sg shows older forms with *-s-* (*tāsu*) and later forms displaying the result of fricative weakening (*taho/ u*). The earliest pieces of evidence for fricative weakening in the Gen Sg appear in the Mg passages in Mṛcch (*tāha* and nominal *-āha* vs. Mah *tāsa*). For their alternation with other Pkts' suffixes (Ś *-assa* and Mg *-aśśa*) see 5.4.

The Acc Pl in Pāli and AMg is identical with the Nom Pl *te* (vs. OIA *tān* < PIE * *t̥ons*, cf. AGr *tons*). This ending *-e* was extended to the nominal declension (*deve* = Nom and Acc Pl).

The oblique forms in Pāli are derivable from their OIA ancestral forms, whereas AMg developed a new pattern of marking for plurality, namely, the nasalization of the ultima of the ending (*tehĩ, tesĩ, tesũ*). As mentioned above, in AMg this nasalization was only optional in the nominal declension (*-ehĩ, -āṇā̃, -esũ*) but it became obligatory in Ap (*-ahĩ, -ahā̃, -ahũ*). The Gen Pl *tesĩ* is a peculiar innovation of AMg (found also in JMah), the Abl Pl *tehĩto* (vs. Pāli *tehi*) is a contamination of the Instr Pl *tehĩ* and the Abl suffix *-to* (< *-taḥ*).

sā 'that, she' (Feminine)

		OIA	Pāli	AMg	Mah	Ap
Sg	N	sā	sā	sā	sā	sā
	A	tām	tā̃	tā̃	tā̃	"
	I		tāya	tāe, tīe	tīe	tāe, tīe
	Abl		"	tāo	tāe	tāha
	D, G	tasyāḥ	tassā, tissā	tāe, tīe, tīse	tīe	tāhe/i
	L	tasyām	tassā, tissā	tīe, tīse	"	tahĩ
Pl	N, A	tāḥ	tā, teyo	tāo	tāo	tāu
	I	tābhiḥ	tāhi	tāhĩ	tāhĩ	tāhĩ
	Abl		"	tāhĩto	"	tāhā̃
	D, G	tāsām	tāsā̃	tāsĩ	tāṇā̃	"
	L	tāsu	tāsu	tāsũ	tāsu	tāhĩ

The Instr/Abl Sg *tāya* in Pāli is of a nominal origin (similarly the AMg Instr *tāe* and Abl *tāo*). The Dat/Gen and Loc Sg show alternative forms to the older ones with the root *ta-*. These new forms with the root *ti-* are extended here from the pronominal declension of *ka-* 'who' *ki* 'what'. In summary:

OIA	Pāli (nominal declension)	Pronominal declension	Interrogative pronoun
		sā	
		tā̃	
	devāya (extended)	tāya	
	tasyāḥ (continued)	tassā~tissā (extended)	kissa~kassa
	tasyām (")	tassā ~ tissā	

AMg forms show a further development from *tiss* > *tīse* (by compensatory lengthening) > *tīe* (by fricative weakening *-s-* > *-h-* and the loss of intervocalic *-h-* > ϕ).

In Pāli Nom Pl *tāyo* (and AMg *tāo*) is of a nominal origin. *taṇhāyo* is formed analogically with feminine *i*-stems and *u*-stems (*matiyo, dhenuyo*). AMg again shows the typical nasalization of the ultima of the ending in oblique cases as in their masculine counterparts:

tehĩ	tāhĩ
tehĩto	tāhĩto
tesĩ	tāsĩ
tesũ	tāsũ

The Gen Pl with the nasalized ultima is found in JMah and JŚ. In AMg both *tesi* ~ *tesĩ* (and *tāsi* ~ *tāsĩ*) occur.

Ap created a real direct case by extending the Nom Sg form *sā* to the Acc. The suffixes of the Abl, Dat, Gen Sg forms *tāha, tāhe/i* were discussed under nominal *ā*-stems (3.2.1). Loc Sg *tahĩ* is a masculine form.

As mentioned in 1.1, one of the most remarkable archaisms of MIA dialects is the clitic form of the 3rd Pers pronoun (Gen, Dat) *se*. This form continues PIE **swoi* cf. Av *hōi, hē, šē* OP *-šaiy*, AGr *hoi*, Lesbian *woi*. The Gen/Dat clitic form *sē* is not found in Vedic (which, however, possesses clitic forms *sīm* and *īm* in the Acc);[10] neither is *se* found in Pāli and Classical Skt (but it occurs in Buddhist Skt). In MIA the following dialects possess *se*: Mah, AMg, JM, Ś and Mg (*śe*). In AMg (and Buddhist Skt) even the form *si* (with raised ě) has been recorded (cf. Pischel 1900: 299). This form is used without distinction of gender (i.e. the referent might be either male or female). Thus Ś *dehi se āsanam* may be translated—depending on its context—as either 'give him a seat!' or 'give her a seat!'.

With the change of gender, *se* replaced the OIA neuter form *tad* and in AMg spread even to the Pl Nom. An example of orthotonic *se* 'it' from AMg: *se duddiṭṭhā ca bhe* 'it is difficult to see even for you' [Āyār I, 4, 2, 3, 4] (OIA *tad durdṛṣṭaṃ ca vaḥ*).

Demonstrative *ayam* 'this' (Masculine)

		OIA	Pāli	AMg	Ap
Sg	N	ayam	ayā	ayā, ime, iṇamo	āyau, āu
	A	imam	imā	imā	"

	I	anena	anena, iminā	ṇeṇa, imeṇa, imiṇā	(ā)ẽ, (ā)eṇa
	Abl	asmāt	(im)asmā, imamhā	imāo	āyaho
	D, G	asya	(im)assa, imissa	(im)assa	"
	L	asmin	(im)asmī, imamhi	imāsi, assī	āyahī
Pl	N, A	ime	ime	ime	āyaī (Neuter)
	I	ebhiḥ	(im)ehi	imehī	
	Abl	(ebhyaḥ)	"	imehīto	āyahā
	D, G	esām	(im)esā, (im)esānā	(im)esī	"
	L	eṣu	(im)esu	imesū	

The OIA paradigm shows three bases: *a*(*y*)- ~ *i*(*m*)- ~ *a*(*n*)-. The first two continue the PIE pronominal root *ei-* ~ *i-* (ablaut), which was inflected as * *to-*, e.g. Acc Sg *i-m* Neuter *i-d*. The particle * *-em* (OIA *-am*) was added to these forms and the forms *imam*, *idam* resulted. The form *imam* was resegmented as *ima-m* (i.e. *-m* was taken as the suffix of the Acc)—hence a new stem *ima*—which was adopted in all cases during the older and middle stages of MIA (Pāli and AMg Nom Sg *ayā̃* is the only exception). Pāli also continues OIA forms *asmāt* (Abl Sg), *asya* (Gen Sg), *asmin* (Loc Sg), *ebhiḥ* (Instr Pl), *eṣām* (Gen Pl), *eṣu* (Loc Pl). AMg, on the other hand, apart from a few surviving forms, inflects the stem *ima-* identically with *ta-* 'that, he' The forms *iminā* (Instr Sg) and *imissa* (Gen Sg) in Pāli got their *-i-* by an extension from the interrogative pronoun *ka-* 'who' (Gen Sg *kissa*).

During the later stages of MIA (evidence of Ap), however, the whole paradigm could be built around the base *a*(*y*)- (which appears only in the Nom Sg Masc in the previous stages of MIA). Thus the Ap form of the Nom Sg *āyau* goes back to * *aya-ka* and the Instr Sg *-ẽ* (Vikr) arose by contraction from *ā-ẽ* (<*aya-ẽ*); the other forms show the usual suffixes found with nouns and pronouns.

iyam 'this' (Feminine)

		OIA	Pāli	AMg	Ap
Sg	N	iyam	ayā̃	imā, iyā	?
	A	imām	imā	imā	?
	I		imāya	imāe	āyae
	Abl		"	imāo	āyahe
	D,G	asyāḥ	imissā(ya)	imīe, imāe	
			assā(ya)	imīse	

	L	asyām	imissā̃, imissā, imāe, assā	imīse, imāe	?
Pl	N, A		imā, imāyo	imāo	?
	I		imāhi	imāhī	āyahī
	Abl		"	imāhīto	āyahā̃
	D, G		imās(ān)ā, āsā	imāsī	"
	L		imāsu	imāsū̃	āyahī

Pāli lost its gender distinction in the Nom Sg by adopting the masculine form *ayā̃* whereas AMg continues the OIA form *iyam* (or uses *imā* from the stem *ima-*).

In Ap there are quite a few gaps in the paradigm which is built, as its Masc counterpart, on the base * *aya-*. The form of the Gen Pl is adopted from the Masc set of forms.

3.4 Verbs

3.4.1 *Middle Indo-Aryan Verbal System*

The Vedic verbal system, which may serve as a starting point in our discussion, was very rich in its morphology. Its three main sub-systems—that of the Present, Perfect and Aorist—are found in other archaic I-E languages (especially in AGr) and they may be best characterized (with various difficulties) in terms of aspect: 'imperfective', 'perfective' and 'indeterminate' (i.e., unspecified for the contrast of perfectivity). No deeper semantic characterization of OIA aspectual categories will be attempted in this monograph and the reader has to consult enormous literature on this subject. Temporal distinctions are introduced by the system of tense and they may be considered to be of the customary binary nature: past vs. non-past. Their morphological expressions in the sub-system of the Present are imperfect vs. present; in the sub-system of the Perfect pluperfect vs. perfect; and in the (semi-modal) sub-system of the Future conditional vs. future.

The system of mood shows distinct forms of indicative, imperative, subjunctive, optative and injunctive (plus some minor categories which are not relevant to our exposé). The injunctive was an unaugmented secondary tense (imperfect, aorist or pluperfect). It was very common in the Ṛgveda but it has almost disappeared from Brāhmaṇas, except in prohibitive sentences (after the particle *mā́* 'not'). A morphological contrast between the injunctive and subjunctive in the present system was possible only in thematic and some athematic verbs (Classes 2, 3, 7), e.g., *bháras* (Inj Pres) 'may you carry' or *bhárās(i)* (Subj Pres). In other athematic verbs (Class 5 and 9) these two categories were homophonous, e.g., *gṛbhṇā́s* 'may you seize' can be morphologically either the injunctive or the subjunctive. Furthermore, in the 2nd and the 3rd Pers dual, and the 2nd Pers plural the injunctive forms were homophonous with those of the imperative.

Modal forms in the three sub-systems of the Present, Aorist and Perfect are exemplified below:

Chart 3-1. Vedic Sanskrit
Modal Forms in the Present System
(2nd and 3rd Pers Sg of 'make')

	Active	Medio-Passive	Passive
Indicative	kṛṇó-ṣi	kṛṇu-ṣé	kri-y-áse
	-ti	-té	-y-áte
Imperative	kṛṇú-(hí)	kṛṇu-ṣvá	kri-y-ásva
	ó-tu	-tām	-y-átām
Subjunctive	kṛṇáv-as	kṛṇáv-ase	
	-at	-ate	kri-y-ā́te
Optative	kṛṇu-y-ā́s	kṛṇv-ī-thā́s	
	-y-ā́t	-ī-tá	

Chart 3-2. Vedic Sanskrit
Modal Forms in the Aorist System

Indicative	ákar-(as)	ákṛ-thās	
	-(at)	-ta	ákār-i
Imperative	kṛ-dhí	kṛ-ṣvá	
	[kár-tu]	[-tā́m]	
Subjunctive	kár-as(i)	kár-ase	
	-at(i)	-ate	
Optative	[kri-y-ā́s]	[kri-y-ī-thā́s]	
	[-y-ā́t]	[-y-ī-tá]	
Injunctive	kar		[kār-i]

Note: The forms in [ ] are not documented with the root *kṛ*.

Chart 3-3. Vedic Sanskrit
Modal Forms in the Perfect System
(2nd and 3rd Pers Sg of various verbs)

	Active	Medio-Passive
Indicative	cakártha	[cakṛṣé]
	cakára	[cakré]
Imperative	mumugdhí ('release')	vavṛtsva
	mumóktu	
Subjunctive	bubódhas ('wake')	
	tatánat ('stretch')	tatápate ('heat')
Optative	cakriyā́s	vāvṛdhīthā́s ('grow')
	cakriyā́t	vāvṛtītá ('turn')
Injunctive	śaśās ('order')	
	dūdhot ('shake')	tatánanta (Pl)

Modal forms in the Perfect system are of rare occurrence in the *Saṃhitās* (except the RV). Macdonell (1916:155-7) lists seven (or eight) middle forms of the subjunctive (the active ones are more common), a dozen injunctive forms, and about a score of active imperative forms (only two middle ones).

The system of voice was essentially binary: active vs. middle (medio-passive), with distinct passive forms appearing only in the sub-systems of the Present and the Aorist. As mentioned above, medio-passive forms in the sub-system of the Perfect are very rare (the pluperfect does not exhibit them at all). The following chart shows the gaps in the paradigm of Vedic finite forms (organized by aspect and tense):

Vedic finite forms (Aspect-Tense-Voice)

ACTIVE (1st Pers)

	Present	Perfect	Aorist	Future
Non-past	karómi	cakára		kariṣyāmi
Past	ákaravam	ácakram	ákārṣam (ákaram)	ákariṣyam

MEDIO-PASSIVE (1st Pers)

Non-past	kurvé	cakré		kariṣyé
Past	ákurvi		ákrṣi (ákri)	

PASSIVE (3rd Pers)

Non-past	kriyáte		
Past	ákriyata		ákāri

The loss of modal (subjunctive, injunctive) and temporal forms (aorist, perfect) is typical of a subsequent development in MIA. In terms of tense MIA dialects preserved the three-way contrast of referring to the three-time zones: past - present - future.

Coming to the early stage of MIA (represented by Pāli) we note first of all an almost complete loss of the perfect forms (i.e. the aspectual contrast of imperfective versus perfective could not be expressed by finite forms-any more). Pāli, as we know it from the earliest texts, went even further by syncretizing the OIA aorist and imperfect forms into a single past tense (called usually preterite). At this point the OIA synthetic aspecto-temporal system disintegrates and we may represent the new system of early MIA on two levels only (tense and mood). Schematically (using the verb *bhavati* 'to be' instead of *karoti*):

MIDDLE INDO-ARYAN (Pāli) VERB

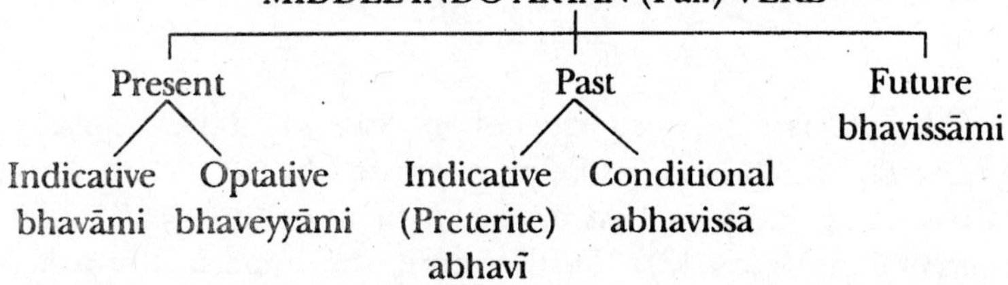

A further simplification took place in Ardha-Māgadhī. The forms of the past started being used without the augment *a-* and as a consequence of this some forms of the conditional became homophonous with those of the future and ultimately the conditional was dropped out from the use. The past indicative had only two forms—one in the singular with the suffix-*itthā* and another one in the plural with *-īsu*.

In the middle stage of MIA (represented by Māhārāṣṭrī) even this simple system was further simplified by a complete loss of the synthetic morphology of the Past. Its place was taken by analytic expressions with the Instrumental of the personal pronoun (noun) and the neuter form of the passive participle, e.g. *mae kaā̃* 'I did' lit. by me (it is) done (cf. 4.4.i).

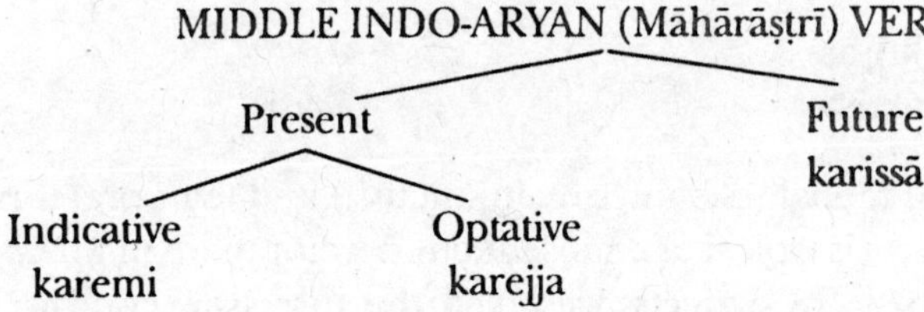

During the final stages of MIA the optative was dropped out from the use (the reason being the homophony of certain forms with the passive, cf. 3.4.7). Thus in Ap the inherited system of the OIA synthetic forms was further reduced to two binary contrasts of voice (active-passive) and experienced time (present - future):

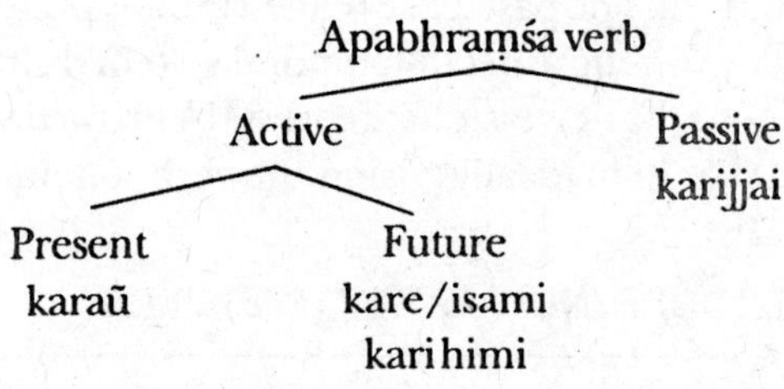

MIA dialects were, of course, not only losers and the contrast of perfectivity which stopped being expressed by finite verb forms started being implemented by means of non-finite (participial) constructions (cf. 4.4.i). Furthermore, the imperfective aspect started being differentiated by means of periphrastic formations and a new sub-category of progressivity made its appearance at the end of the MIA period (cf. 4.4.ii).

3.4.2 *Thematic Conjugation*

OIA possessed two types of conjugation: thematic (with the thematic vowel *a* before personal endings) and athematic (with ϕ before personal endings). Early and middle Middle Indo-Aryan dialects preserved the thematic conjugation of OIA, while the athematic conjugation lost its ablaut and was thematized (for its relics see 3.4.4).

Class I (of OIA)

Sanskrit	Pāli	Ardha-Māgadhī
píbati 'drinks'	pivati	pivai
gácchati 'goes'	gacchati	gacchai
tíṣṭhati (< *tist(h)ati) 'stands'	tiṭṭhati	ciṭṭhai
sī́dati (< *PIE sizdeti) 'sits'	sīdati	sīyai
bhávati 'is'	hoti	bhavai
náyati 'leads'	neti	

The last two examples show the typical contraction *-aya-*, *-ava-* into *-e-*, *-o-* in Pāli.

Class VI (of OIA)

spṛśáti 'touches'	phusati	phusai
diśáti 'shows'	disati	disai
limpáti 'besmears'	limpati	limpai
muñcáti 'liberates'	muñcati	muñcai (also muyai)
kṛntáti 'cuts'	kantati	kantai
iccháti 'wishes'	icchati	icchai

Class IV (of OIA)

In MIA the glide of the suffix *-ya-* palatalizes the final consonant of the root if this ends in a dental (elsewhere it completely assimilates):

nṛtyati 'dances'	naccati	naccai
krudhyati 'is angry'	kujjhati	kujjhai
kupyati 'is angry'	kuppati	kuppai

MIA dialects of the middle stage (AMg and Mah) created a new type of thematic conjugation with the thematic vowel *-e-* which continues the causative marker *-aya-* of OIA. Thus versus Pāli *karoti* 'makes' (= Sanskrit Class VIII) we find AMg *karei* from the causative form *kārayati:*

	OIA	Pāli	AMg
Sg 1	karomi	karomi	karemi
2	ṣi	si	si
3	ti	ti	i
Pl 1	kurumaḥ	ma	mo
2	tha	tha	ha
3	kurvanti	nti	nti

Note that MIA dialects got rid of the OIA ablaut alternation which creates two allomorphs *karo-* (in the Sg) and *kuru-* (in the Pl). AMg created other thematic forms: *kuvvai* from the plural allomorph *kuru-* (< * *kurv-ati*) and completely remodelled *karai* (based on the shape of the root in the singular allomorph). Pāli *kārēti* 'cause X to work' continues the OIA causative *kārayati.*

3.4.3 *Personal Endings*

Personal endings of thematic verbs in early and middle MIA after all the phonological changes described above took place are still very much the same as in OIA:

	OIA	Pāli	Ś	AMg	Mah
Sg 1	-mi	-mi	-mi	-mi	-mi
2	-si	-si	-si	-si	-si
3	-ti	-ti	-di	-i	-i
Pl 1	-maḥ	-ma	-mo	-mo	-mo
2	-tha	-tha	-dha	-ha	-ha
3	-nti	-nti	=ti	-nti	=ti

The early stage of MIA (represented by Pāli) differs from OIA in a single respect, namely, in adopting the secondary ending *-ma* in the 1st Pl (all other MIA dialects show the appropriate reflex *-o* of OIA-*aḥ*). The middle stage shows effects of typical MIA phonological developments: the voicing of inter vocalic voiceless stops *t(h)* > *d(h)*—represented by Śauraseni—and their subsequent reduction to zero *d(h)* > δ (*h*) > ϕ (*h*)—represented by Ardha-Māgadhī and Māhārāṣṭrī. This still rather complicated system finally breaks down during the late stage of MIA (represented by Apabhraṃśa). Here are some data using the verb *pṛcchati* (OIA) 'he asks':

	OIA	Pāli	AMg	Ap
Sg 1	pṛcchāmi	pucchāmi	pucchāmi	pucchaũ
2	asi	asi	asi	ahi, -asi
3	ati	ati	ai	ai
Pl 1	āmaḥ	āma	āmo	ahũ
2	atha	atha	aha	ahu
3	anti	anti	anti	ahĩ

In Ap the 1st Sg *-aũ* can be derived (with Pischel) from the secondary ending *-am* preceded by the stem enlarging suffix *-k-* (i.e., *-ak-am*). According to Sen (1960:150), the ending may have come from the pronominal form *mama* (Gen), and, according to Tagare (1948:287), its source is the pronoun *haũ* 'I'.

In the 2nd Sg *-asi* may be considered a Prākritism[11] while *-ahi* represents a genuine development from Ap. Bloch (1933/1965:244) explains *-ahi* from the imperative suffix * *-dhi.*[12] For reasons given in great detail below, I would prefer to trace it back to *-asi* by the historical process of fricative weakening.

There are various difficulties connected with explaining the origin of the plural suffixes in Ap. *u* in *-ahu* in the 2nd Pers, as suggested by Bloch (1933/1965:244), comes probably from the suffixes of the 3rd Pers: *-a(h)u* (< *-atu*) and *-antu*. *-h-* in *-ahũ* in the 1st Pers may have been extended from the 2nd Pers;[13] in addition, as suggested by Bloch (1933/ 1956:245), *-h-* found in forms such as the pronoun 'we' (Ap *amhaĩ*) and the copula 'we are' (Mah *mho*; not found in Ap) could have reinforced this extension.[14] The 3rd Pers suffix *-ahi* cannot be derived phonologically from *-anti* and we have to take recourse to proportional analogy with the 1st persons (following Bloch 1933/1965:245):

$$\frac{\text{-aũ}}{\text{-ahũ}} = \frac{\text{-ai}}{X} \qquad \text{where } X = \text{-ahĩ}^{15}$$

Personal endings of the imperative are given below:

	OIA	Pāli	Ś	AMg	Mah	Ap
Sg 1	-āni	-ami	-amu	-amu	-amu	
2	-a	-a, -āhi	-asu, -ahi	-asu, -āhi	-asu, -ahi	-(a)hi/u
3	-atu	-atu	-adu	-au	-au	-a(h)u
Pl 1	-āma	-āma	-āmo	-āmo	-āmo	

2	-ata	-atha	-adha	-aha	-aha	-ahu/a
3	-antu	-antu	-ãtu	-antu	-ãtu	-(a)ntu, -ahũ

The 1st Sg *-mi* and the 1st Pl *-ma* in Pāli are obviously extended from the indicative. Similarly in all MIA dialects the 2nd Pl *-tha* (*-dha*, *-ha*) is extended from the indicative. The 1st Sg *-mu* and the 2nd Sg *-su* in middle MIA dialects are formed analogically with the 3rd Persons (indicative versus imperative):

$$\frac{\text{ti}}{\text{tu}} = \frac{\text{nti}}{\text{ntu}} = \frac{\text{mi}}{\text{X}} = \frac{\text{si}}{\text{Y}}$$

where X = *mu* and Y = *su*.

The suffix *-hi* goes back to OIA *-dhi* (note that the thematic vowel is lengthened before this suffix as it is before the suffixes of the 1st person, e.g. AMg *pāsāhi* 'see' (< OIA *paśya*)). In Ap the endings of the 1st persons are not documented. The 2nd Pl *-ha* is extended from the paradigm of the indicative and the form *-hu* can probably be traced back to the middle voice form *-dhvam* (> *dhum* > δ *hum* > *hum* > *hũ* > *hu*). Note that the 2nd Sg *-su* can similarly be derived from the middle voice form *-sva* (as suggested by Alsdorf).

It should be mentioned that Prākrits did away with the phenomenon, found in Sanskrit (in thematic classes I, IV, VI and X) and also in most of the I-E languages, of having no overt indication of person in the 2nd Sg imperative. In Mah the endings of the imperative *-hi* and *-su* spread even to the optative (cf. Jacobi 1886/1967:LXIII).

I would like to return to the problem of the origin of Ap *-ahi* in the 2nd Pers Sg. As mentioned in 2.2.3.iii, the rule of fricative weakening did not operate intervocalically inside the verbal and nominal paradigms. In the paradigm of the future its operation would obliterate the crucial distinction between the 2nd and 3rd Sg (*-asi* vs. *-ati*) or between the present and the future. The paradigms of the latter two in Ś are presented below:

	Present	Future
Sg 1	pucchāmi 'I ask'	pucchissaṃ
2	asi	issasi
3	adi	issadi
Pl 1	āmo	issāmo
2	adha	issadha
3	anti	issanti

At a certain point in time and space the paradigm of the future started being eroded by the operation of the rule of fricative weakening. Thus in AMg we find both *pucchisāmi* (1st Sg), on the one hand, but also *pucchihisi* (2nd Sg) and *pucchihinti* (3rd Pl), on the other hand. Similarly in Mah we find both *pucchissai* (3rd Sg) and *pucchihii* (3rd Sg) coexisting. The starting point could well have been the 2nd Sg with two intervocalic *s*'s (the first one marking the future and the second the category of person/number) and it is easy to think of a dissimilatory process by which the sequence -*VsVsi* became -*VhVsi* in AMg (and Mah). Thus there was apparently a historical stage in the development of Ardha-Māgadhī in which the paradigm of the future looked as shown below:

Sg 1	pucchissāmi	Pl 1	pucchissāmo
2	puchihisi	2	pucchissaha
3	pucchissai	3	pucchissanti

At a certain point in time the dissimilated *-h-* in the 2nd Pers Sg was taken as a future marker and started spreading to other persons, most notably the 3rd Pers of both numbers, where we witness an alternation between the old forms with *-s-* and the new forms with *-h-*: *pucchissai*~*pucchihii* and *pucchissanti*~*pucchihinti*. By then the innovative paradigm in AMg was curiously asymmetric in having half of its forms with *-s-* and half with *-h-*:

Sg 1	pucchissāmi	Pl 1	pucchissāmo
2	pucchihisi	2	pucchissaha
3	pucchihii	3	pucchihinti

What about the three remaining persons with *-s-*? Here the situation is quite complicated because of the lack of these forms in our primary sources and we have to rely on the statements of Prākrit grammarians. *-h-* obviously spread to the 1st Sg since the grammarians know forms in *-ihāmi* and *-ihimi* (Pischel 1900:366 ff.). Thus Hemacandra gives both

(Hc.3,169)	kittaihimi ~ kittaissaṃ (= kīrtayiṣyāmi)
(Hc.3,172)	gacchihāmi, gacchihimi ~ gacchissaṃ

The ending *-himi* is mentioned for the roots in long vowels:

(Hc.3,170)	kāhimi (from *kṛ*)
(Hc.3,170)	dāhimi (from *dā*)
(Hc.3,167)	hohimi (from *bhū*)

Similarly, in the 1st and 2nd Pl the grammarians know the forms with *-h-*. Thus Bhāmaha and Hemacandra give the following future forms of the verb 'laugh':

	with *-s-*	with *-h-*
Pl 1	hasissāmo	hasihimo (Bh.7,15; Hc.3;167)
		hāsihāmo (Bh.7,15)
Pl 2		hasihitthā (Bh.7,15; Hc.3,168)

Hemacandra (3,172) gives the following future forms of the verb 'go':

	with *-s-*	with *-h-*
Pl 1	gacchissāmo	gacchihāmo
		gacchihimo
		gacchimo
Pl 2		gacchihitthā

The future forms of the verb 'be' according to Bhāmaha (7,13 and 15) and Hemacandra (3,168):

	with *-s-*	with *-h-*
Pl 1	hossāmo	hohāmo
		hohimo
Pl 2		hohitthā

There is also a curious form of the 1st Pl in *-ihissā* which combines both the old *-s-* and the new *-h-*:

hasihissā	(Bh.7,15; Hc.3,168)
gacchihissā	(Hc.3,172)
hohissā	(Bh.7,13 and 15; Hc.3,168)
hohissāmo	(Kramadīśvara 4,18)

Kramadīśvara (4,18) gives another curious form for the 2nd Pl, namely *hohitthāmo*, which appears to be based on the recategorization of the suffix *-mo* (1st Pl) as a plural marker:[16]

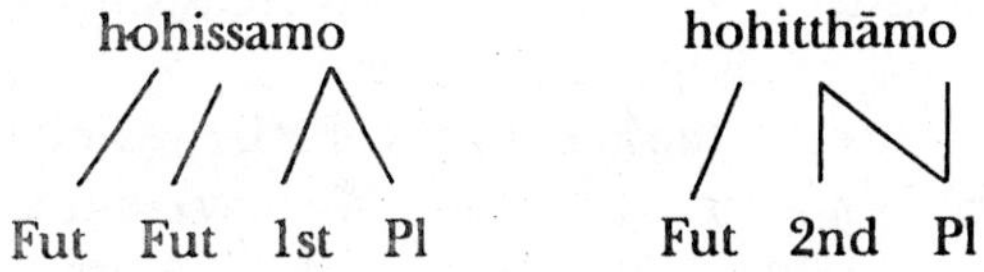

AMg texts present a confusing mixture of both *s-* and *h*-forms. Monosyllabic open roots occur with *-h-*; thus in *Āẏāraṅgasutta* we find the following future forms of *dā-* 'give': *dāhāmi* (1st Sg), *dāhisi* (2nd Sg), *dāhāmo* (1st Pl); *dāhittha* (2nd Pl) occurs in *Uttarajjhayaṇasutta* [359]. On the other hand, verbs such as *bhū* 'be', *gam* 'go', *pṛcch* 'ask' display *s*-forms in the future:

bhavissāmo (1st Pl)	[Āẏār 1, 2, 2, 1]
bhavissaha (2nd Pl)	[Vivāhap 234]
uvāgamissanti (3rd Pl)	[Āẏār 2, 3, 1, 2 ff.]
āgacchissai (3rd Sg)	[Uvās § 188]
puchissamo (1st Pl)	[Āẏār 1, 4, 2, 6]

A major inconvenience appeared in the formation of the future of consonantal roots with the nasal infix. These had consonantal clusters *-psy-*, *-tsy-* and *-kṣy-* in the older stages of their development (Sanskrit):

chid - chetsyāmi
bhid - bhetsyāmi
bhuj - bhokṣyāmi

Clusters *-tsy-* and *-kṣy-* merge into *-cch-* in MIA and the above future forms should look like *chĕcchā, bhĕcchā, bhŏcchā.* These indeed are the forms taught by the grammarians (Hemacandra 3,171). However, our AMg texts do NOT display these forms but rather show *s-* or *h-* future forms with epenthetic *-i-* formed from the present stem: *acchindihinti* [Vivāhap 1277], *bhidissanti* (!) [Āẏār 2, 1, 6, 9], but *bhŏkkhāmi* and *bhŏkkhāmo* [Āẏār 2, 1, 11, 1]. However, *bhuñjihi* is found in JM. It may be argued that the forms with the future marker *-h-* without epenthetic *-i-* come dangerously close to the present ā forms of * *-sk-* verbs, such as *gacchāmi* (< **gwm-sk-ō*), *yacch-āmi* < **ym-sk-ō*), etc.—hence the use of the secondary ending in the 1st Sg in the AMg future form: *dacchā* 'I will see' (< *drakṣyāmi*) *vs.* *gacchāmi* 'I go'. But the situation where the cluster *-cch-* could be interpreted as a part of the stem (*gacch-*) or as a root plus the future marker (*dacc* + *h*) could not be stable. And indeed in the later stages of MIA we find future forms with an extra *-ih-* marking the future. We may contrast AMg *dacchisi* 'you will see' [Uttar 679] with later Mah *dacchihisi* [R 11.93] showing that in the consciousness of speakers of later MIA *dacch* was not understood as a future stem any more.

On the other hand, the old present form such as *gacchāmi* 'I go' could be reinterpreted as a future form *gacchā̃* 'I will go' (i.e. *gacc* + *h* + *ā̃*). This form is known to the grammarians (Vararuci, Hemacandra, Kramadīśvara) and is also found in AMg texts [Thāṇ 156.285].

Middle Indo-Aryan dialects did not weaken *s* to *h* initially while, as we have seen in 2.5, Avestan did. On the other hand, MIA dialects (but not Māgadhī) weakened *s* to *h* before *t* while Avestan did not. Contrast Av *hənti* 'they are' with MIA *santi,* on the one hand, and Av *asti* 'he is' with MIA *atthi,* on the other. The latter form went through all the usual steps *ahti> athi> atthi* in all MIA dialects (AMg, Mah, JMah, Ś) but not in Mg which has *asti.* In the 2nd Sg *asi* 'you are' which has *s* in intervocalic position we never find any example of* *ahi* — *asi* co-occurs with *si* in AMg and *si* is the only form found in other dialects. The whole paradigm of Av and some MIA dialects is presented below:

	Avestan	AMg	Mah	Mg
Sg 1	ahmi	ā̃si, mi	mhi	smi
2	ahi	asi, si	si	si
3	asti	atthi	atthi	asti
Pl 1	mahi	mo, mu	mho, mha	sma
2	sta	ttha	ttha	?
3	hənti	santi	santi	śanti

In 2.2.3 we have seen that the rule of fricative weakening became operative in the environment (i) before and after voiceless stops and (ii) before nasals in all MIA dialects (Ś, Mg, AMg, Mah and JMah).

Its diffusion, however, was considerably delayed in the environment (iii) intervocalically. Thus in Pāli nominal paradigms we find ablative forms *devamhā* 'god' alternating with *devasmā* (where *s* → *h* /-nasal) but intervocalically only *-s-*, e.g. in the Gen Sg *devassa.*

Similarly in verbal paradigms there are alternative forms such as *amhi* 'I am' and *asmi*, *amha* 'we are' and *asma*, but the intervocalic *-s-* in the 2nd Sg never undergoes the change *s*→ *h*—there is only *asi* 'you are' and never * *ahi.*

Similarly, the rule of fricative weakening did not operate intervocalically in Ś and Mg. In AMg, Mah and JMah we find the future in *-h-* alternating with the future in *-s-*. As shown under iii, there are only a few lexical items in Mah showing its incipient diffusion across the lexicon.

When the rule of fricative weakening applied intervocalically across the whole phonological spectrum, i.e., even inside the nominal and verbal paradigms, we witness a major typological change from the stage of Pkts to the later stage of Ap. A glance at MIA dialects (Ś and Mah) reveals that the intervocalic *-s-* in nominal and verbal paradigms (Gen Sg and 2nd Pers Sg) was unaffected by the rule *s*→ *h*, while in Ap there are alternative forms with *s* and *h:*

	Ś, Mah	Ap
Sg Nom	putto 'son'	puttu
Gen	puttassa	puttassu ~ puttahŏ, -a
Sg 1	pucchāmi 'I ask'	pucchaũ
2	pucchasi	pucchasi ~ pucchahi
3	pucchadi (Ś) pucchai (Mah)	pucchai

Later on, after the intervocalic *h* had been reduced to ϕ, the 2nd and the 3rd Sg were conflated. Diphthongal pronunciation *pūchai* is known from some older dialects of NIA (e.g. Braj) and monophthongal pronunciation *pūchē* is typical of a number of NIA languages (e.g. Hindi).

The future tense marker *-h-* proved to be more resistant to complete reduction than *-h-* in the 2nd Pers Sg suffix *-Vhi.* The future marker *-h-* survived until nowadays in some dialects of Hindi, e.g. Avadhi, Bundeli and Braj. It is well-known that the future of some NIA languages derives its marker *gā* from the OIA perfect participle *gata* (> Prakrit *gadō* > *gaō*) and represents thus a participial analytic formation. Avadhi, Bundeli and Braj, on the other hand, continue the old sigmatic future. As was shown above, fricative weakening applied earlier to the future marker *-s* than to the 2nd Sg suffix *-asi,* but later on in Ap *-h-* as a future marker was more stable than *-h-* in the 2nd Sg suffix *-Vhi.* Summarily:

	Pkts		Ap		Bundeli
Sg 1	calissāmi ~	calihimi	calissaũ ~	calihiũ	calahaũ
2	asi	isi	a(h)i	i(h)i	ai
3	ai	ii	a(h)i	i(h)i	ai

It is worth mentioning that even the sigmatic future survives in NIA dialects in Gujarati and Lahnda (Bloch, 1965:247). Gujarati future forms: *calīś, calśe* (2nd and 3rd Sg), *calīśũ, calśo, calśe.*[17]

3.4.4 *Athematic Conjugation*

Class II of OIA included typical athematic verbs. During their PIE ancestral stage the endings were added to the root directly, e.g. * *es-ti* 'is', *ei-ti* 'goes', * *wē-ti* 'blows' (cf. OIA *asti*, Pāli and AMg *atthi*; OIA, Pāli *eti*; OIA, Pāli *vāti*).

In MIA dialects only the roots in *-ā* preserve athematic conjugation, other roots are thematized (but even the roots in *-ā* may optionally be thematized). Thus we find Pāli * *vāti* 'blows' (2nd Sg *vāsi* is documented) but AMg shows the thematic formation *vāyai* (< * *vāy-a-ti*). On the other hand, OIA athematic *ēti* 'goes' is continued by athematic Pāli *yāti* 'goes' and AMg *-yai* (< * *yāti*), both formed from the root *yā-* (OIA < **ei-ti*).

Consonantal roots are usually thematized, e.g., we find Pāli *hanati* 'strikes' and AMg *hanai* versus Sanskrit *hanti.* Pāli *veti* 'knows' is inflected athematically as its Sanskrit counterpart *vetti* (<* *ved-ti*), whereas AMg shows an athematic formation *veyai* (from the causative *vedayati*). The verb *as* 'to be' remained athematic in both Pāli and AMg (Ap forms may be evaluated as Prākritisms):

	OIA	Pāli	AMg	Ap
Sg 1	asmi	asmi, amhi	āsi, mi	mhi
2	asi (< *as-si)	asi	asi, si	
3	asti	atthi	atthi	atthi
Pl 1	smaḥ	asmā, amhā	mo, mu	
2	stha	attha	ttha	
3	santi	santi	santi	

Pāli levelled the paradigm in favor of the strong root *as-*, whereas AMg did it in favor of the weak root *s-* (in the 1st and the 2nd Pers of both Sg and Pl).

Optative forms of the copula in Pāli continue either the weak root *s-* (*syāt* > *siyā*) or show the same generalization of the strong root *as-* throughout the whole paradigm:

	Sanskrit	Pāli
Sg 1	syām	siyā ~ assā (< *asyām)
2	syāḥ	assa
3	syāt	siyā ~ "
Pl 1	syāma	assāma
2	syāta	assatha
3	syuḥ	siyū ~ assu

(Note that Ancient Greek had similarly generalized the strong root *es-* throughout its singular paradigm: *eiēn* < * *esyēm*, etc.)

3.4.5 *Aorist (Preterite)*

As mentioned above, MIA dialects lost the distinction of the OIA Aorist and Imperfect by syncretizing the OIA Aorist and Imperfect into a single Past tense (= Preterite). The Slavic branch of IE developed in a similar way in that Old Slavic languages syncretized the OCSl Aorist and Imperfect into a single Past tense (= Preterite). Formally, the Pāli Preterite looks mostly as the OIA Aorist (i.e. it possesses secondary endings and *s*-suffix). The augment, however, is used only sporadically.

Class I

The first group of 'Aorists' in Pāli corresponds to the OIA root-aorist. See the paradigm of *bhū-* 'to be' (OIA, Pāli *bhavati*, Pāli also *hoti*):

	OIA	Pāli
Sg 1	(bhūvam)	ahū
2	ábhūḥ	ahū
3	ábhūt	ahū
Pl 1	(ábhūma)	(ahumha, according to the grammarians)
2	(ábhūtha)	(ahuttha, according to the grammarians)
3	(ábhūvan)	ahū, ahū

Other examples:

Sg 1	agã 'I went'	OIA ágām
3	agā	ágāt
Sg 3	aṭṭhā 'he stood'	OIA asthāt
Sg 1	adā 'I gave'	ádām
2	ado, -ā	ádāḥ
3	adā	ádāt
Pl 3	adū,	adū
Sg 1	assũ 'I heard'	(á-śrav-am)
2	assu	*á-śro-ḥ
Sg 3	akā 'he made'	ákar (< *ákar-t)

Class II

The second type of Pāli 'Aorists' corresponds to the OIA thematic Aorist and Imperfect (the thematic Aorist was formally the Imperfect of the 6th Class but it was formed from *n*-less Present stems—hence the contrasts such as *ásicat* (Aor) -*ásiñcat* (Impf) 'sprinkle'; *ámucat* (Aor) -*ámuñcat* (Impf) 'release'; *ágamat* (Aor) -*ágacchat* (Impf).

The paradigm of *gam*- 'go':

	OIA	Pāli
Sg 1	agamam	agamā̦
2	agamaḥ	agamā
3	agamat	"
Pl 1	agamāma	agamāma, -amha
2	agamata	agamatha, (-attha)
3	agaman	agamũ

According to our phonological rules the 2nd Pers Sg should be **agamō* (cf. OIA *devaḥ*, Pāli *devō*) and the 3rd Pers Sg **agama* (cf. the OIA aorist *ávocat,* Pāli *avoca*). We have to assume that these phonological rules did not work inside this particular paradigm and that the ending *-ā* was extended here from the root Aorist, where it is phonologically appropriate (OIA *ádāh, ádāt,* Pāli *adā*). This formal identity of the 2nd and 3rd Sg obtains also in the conditional: *abhavissa*, cf. the aorist forms *avoca, adā, agamā* (a typologically similar phenomenon obtains in the OCSl aorist, e.g. 2nd and 3rd Sg *reče* 'said'). The 2nd Pl displays the primary ending *-tha* (vs. OIA secondary *-ta*). For the other endings see under Class III.

The verb 'to be' has another set of forms according to this paradigm: 3rd Sg *ahuvā*, 1st Pl *ahuvāma*, etc. (formed from* *huvati*).

Class III

The third type of Pāli 'Aorists' corresponds to the OIA *s-* (sigmatic) Aorists. The paradigm of *su* 'hear' (OIA *śru-*):

	OIA	Pāli
Sg 1	(áśrau-ṣ-am)	asso-s-ī
2	-īḥ	-ī
3	-īt	
Pl 1	-ṣ-ma	assu-mha
2	-ṭa	-ttha
3	(-uḥ)	asso-s-ū̃

This paradigm continues the paradigm of the OIA sigmatic aorist which exhibited four markers: the augment, ablaut, suffix *-s-* and secondary endings added athematically. Already in OIA times the imperfect endings *-īḥ* and *-īt* of the verbs with 'heavy base' (e.g. *ábravīt, āsīt*) were adopted in this paradigm. In Pāli *-ī-* was further extended to the 1st Sg. The plural forms go back to the ablauted forms *áśrauṣma* and *áśrauṣṭa*. What looks like ablaut Sg *ō* (< *au*) vs. Pl *u* (cf. OIA Sg *tutōda* vs. Pl *tutudimá*) arises as a consequence of the shortening in overweight syllables (2.1.2) and the subsequent raising of short mid vowels (2.1.3). The newly created endings *-mha* (< * *-m-sa* < *-s-ma*) and *-ttha* (< * *-thā* < *- *t(h)-sa* < *-s-t(h)a*) were adopted in other types of the Aorist (cf. *ahumha, agamāma* ~ *agamamha*, etc.). The ending of the 3rd Pers Pl *-ū̃* (found with all aorist types: *ahū̃, agamū̃, assōsū̃, agamisū̃*) is, according to Mayrhofer (1951:154), explainable from the ending of the root aorist of *bhū-* : PIE * *e-bhuv-ent* > OIA *a-bhū-van*. Contrast:

OIA	Sg 3	ánai-ṣ-īt	Pāli	ne-s-i
	Pl 3	(ánai-ṣ-uḥ)		ane-s-ū̃

The *-s-* marker was adopted in many other verbs (especially with stems in *- o*, *-ā* and *-e*). Some alternate forms to the root aorist:

	'give'	'stand'	'be'	'make'
Sg 1	adā-s-ī			
2, 3	adā-s-i	aṭṭhā-s-i	aho-s-i	akā-s-i (<ákār-ṣ-īt)
Pl 1	adā-s-imha			

Similarly, these alternate forms appeared also with the verbs displaying the thematic aorist:

	'go'	'be'
3rd Sg	ágamā-s-i	áhuvā-s-i

Class IV

The fourth type of Pāli 'Aorists' corresponds to the OIA *iṣ*- Aorist. The paradigm of *gam*- 'go':

	OIA	Pāli
Sg 1	áved-iṣ-am	agam-is-ā, -ī
2	-īḥ	-i
3	-īt	"
Pl 1	-iṣ-ma	-imha
2	-iṣ-ṭa	-ittha
3	-iṣ-uḥ	-is-ū, -ī-su

The form of the 1st Sg *agamī* should not be connected with Vedic *akramīm* (Geiger 1916:129); as suggested by Mayrhofer (1951:158), it is an analogical formation to

$$\frac{\text{assosī}}{\text{assosi}} = \frac{\text{X}}{\text{agami}}$$

The forms of the 2nd and 3rd Pers Sg and the 1st and 2nd Pers Pl correspond exactly to Vedic forms. In the 3rd Pers Pl we find the suffix *-ū* after the aorist marker *-is-* (*-is-ū*) or the suffix of the 1st Sg *-ī* followed by *-su*. A similar relationship existed in the conditional:

	Conditional	*iṣ*-Aorist
Sg 1	abhav-iss-ā	agam-ī
Pl 3	-iss-ā-su	ī-su ~ is-ū

The ending *-īsu* was the only ending used in all plural forms in AMg. Similarly there was only one ending *-itthā* used in all singular forms. Contrast Pāli and AMg:

	Pāli	AMg
Sg 1	agamisā 'go'	bhũjitthā 'eat'
2	isi	"
Pl 1	imha	īsu
2	ittha	"
3	īsu ~ isũ	"

The AMg singular ending *-itthā*, according to Ghatage (1941:108), may have come from OIA *-iṣṭa* (= 3rd Pers Sg Middle of the *iṣ*-Aorist). Pischel, however, expressed his doubts about this derivation, since the expected form should be *-iṭṭha* (with retroflexed *ṭ*).

Even this simplified morphology of the Past was lost during the middle and late stages of MIA. Already in Māhārāṣṭrī synthetic morphology of verbs included only Present, Future, Imperative and Optative (rare). The past tense forms had to be formed analytically by means of the past participle: *mae kaā* 'I did' (lit. by me [it is] done). Thus whereas during the early stage of MIA it was still possible to use the synthetic Preterite *agamā* 'I went' (Pāli), later on the only possibility became the nominal analytic phrase *ahā gaa* (Mah, lit. I [am] gone) Similarly in Ap [Vikr] *sā paĩ diṭṭhī* 'did you see her?' (lit. she by you [is] seen). For details cf. 4.5.

3.4.6 *Future*

	OIA	Pāli	AMg
Sg 1	kariṣyāmi	karissāmi, -ā	karissāmi, -ā
2	asi	asi	asi
3	ati	ati	ai
Pl 1	āmaḥ	āma	āmo
2	atha	atha	aha
3	anti	anti	anti

In MIA the future is formed by adding the future marker *-iss-* (corresponding to Skt *-iṣya-*) to the root. As in Skt the *-i-* may be dropped after stems in *-e* and *-o*:

Sanskrit	Pāli	AMg
bhaviṣyāmi 'I will be'	bhavissāmi but also	bhavissāmi
	hessāmi (< *havissāmi)	ho(i)ssāmi
nayiṣyāmi 'I will carry'	nayissāmi	
	nessāmi	ne(i)ssāmi

The derivational base of the future is in many cases identical with that of the present. Thus in Pāli we find *chindissati* 'he will split' (< the root *chid*) vs. Skt *chetsyati* with the root ablauted. (However, the expected form *checchati* also occurs.) Similarly, Pāli *gacchissāmi* 'I will go' vs. Skt *gamiṣyāmi* (AMg shows both *gamissāmi* and *gacchissāmi*). Pāli *suṇissāmi* 'I will hear' (Present *suṇā-mi*), AMg *suṇessāmi* vs. Skt *śroṣyāmi* (< the ablauted root *śru-*), etc. It is remarkable that the future forms which contain consonant clusters with *-s-* undergo fricative weakening (2.2.3) and dental palatalization (2.2.4).

Contrast the following forms:

Sanskrit	Pāli	AMg
śak-ṣyati 'he will be able' (śak)	sakkhati	
chet-syati 'he will split' (chid)	checchati	checchai
lap-syati 'he will obtain' (labh)	lacchati	
vat-syati 'he will live' (vas, -ss- → -ts-)	vacchati	
drak-ṣyati 'he will see' (dṛś)	dakkhati	dacchai

A remarkable phenomenon in MIA dialects is the degemination of *-ss-* in *-s-* (originally after long vowels V:SS > V:S) and a further change of the resulting *-s-* into *-h-* (fricative weakening), cf. 2.1.1.b and 2.2.3.

Sanskrit	Pāli	AMg
hā-syati 'he will give up'	hāhati (< *hās(s)ati)	
bhav-iṣyati 'he will be'	hohiti (< *havis(s)ati)	hohii
*kar-ṣyati 'he will make'	kāhati (< *kās(s)ati)	kāhii

In Ap there are two sets of the future forms: the *s*-type and the *h*-type (for the documented forms cf. Tagare 1948:308-9):

Sg 1	kare/isami	karīhimi
2	ahi	īhisi
3	ai	ihai
Pl 1	ahu	
2		
3	ahī	ihinti

The *s*-type predominates in SAp (cf. *s*-future in Mn Marathi); in WAp both sets are found (among the NIA languages the *s*-type is found in Gujarati and Lahnda, the *h*-type in Marwari, Braj, Avadhi and Bundeli); in EAp no future forms have been documented (hapax [Dks 38] being *basiau* 'you will live, stay' < * *vasiṣyatha*).

Ap *karīsu* 'I will make' may be derived from **kariṣyam* (with the secondary ending) by assimilation in the cluster *sy*, followed by the degemination and compensatory lengthening of the preceding vowel (cf. 2.1.1.b); similarly, *pĕkkhīhimi* 'I will see' from **prēkṣiṣyāmi: īṣy> is> īh* (by fricative weakening).

3.4.7 *Optative*

The marker of the optative in MIA developed from the OIA allomorph *-ey-* (of *-y-*) occurring in Class IV: *-eya-* (OIA) > *-eyya-* (Pāli) > *-ejja-* (AM and Mah). All the forms are listed below (using the verb *paśyati* 'see'):

	OIA	Pāli	AM
Sg 1	paśyeyam	passeyyāmi	pāsejjā (mi)
2	ḥ	āsi	(si) ~ (hi)
3	t	a	
Pl 1	paśyema	āma	ma
2	ta	ātha	ha
3	yuḥ	uḥ	

Pāli possessed also an abbreviated form *passe* which could function as any form in the singular. Similarly in AM *pāsejjā* could function as any form in the singular (and 3rd Pl). Mah forms are almost identical with AMg, but the final vowel in *-ejja* is short.

3.4.8 *Passive*

In MIA the verbs form passive stems by means of the suffix *-ya* ~ *īya* (in Pāli) and later on by means of its reflex -(*i*)*jja* (in AMg, Mah and Ap).

	'make'	'give'
Pāli	karīyati	dīyati
Ardha-Māgadhī		dijjai
Māhārāṣṭrī		dijjai
Apabhraṃśa	karijjai	
Avahaṭṭha	kijjai ~ kīai	

Note that the passive differed from the active only in the stem, e.g. in Pāli active *kar-o-ti* 'he makes' and passive *kar-īya-ti* have the same root *kar-* and the same set of personal endings as the active (*-mi, -si, -ti,* etc.). This represents a considerable simplification against the OIA state of affairs, where the root was ablauted in the passive and the personal endings were those of the middle voice. Contrast Sanskrit *kr-iya-te* 'it is made' with *kar-o-ti* 'he makes'.[18]

The distribution of the later passive marker was *-ijja-* after consonants and *-jja-* after vowels. In Pāli the suffix *-ya-* could be used after consonants but in the case of stems ending in dental consonants these would undergo palatalization or progressive assimilation (cf. 2.2.2 and 4):

'cut'	chid + ya + ti > chijjati
'see'	dis + ya + ti > dissati
'obtain'	labh + ya + ti > labbhati
'kill'	han + ya + ti > hannati

In later times the forms with reduplication (from *-C* + *ya-*) alternate with more distinct forms displaying the suffix *-ijja-*. See some examples from AMg:

śru-	'hear'	suvvai, summai	sunijjai
stu-	'praise'	thuvvai	thuṇijjai
gam-	'go'	gammai	gamijjai, gacchijjai
bhuj-	'enjoy'	bhujjai	bhuñjijjai

– It is of interest to note the loss of optative forms in Ap and Avahaṭṭha. It is likely that these, formed similarly as the passive ones, were not distinct enough and were 'desystematized', and finally dropped completely from the use. Thus the simple system of finite verbal forms in Mah was even more simplified in Ap and Avahaṭṭha with only the Present (active and passive) and the Future ultimately remaining.

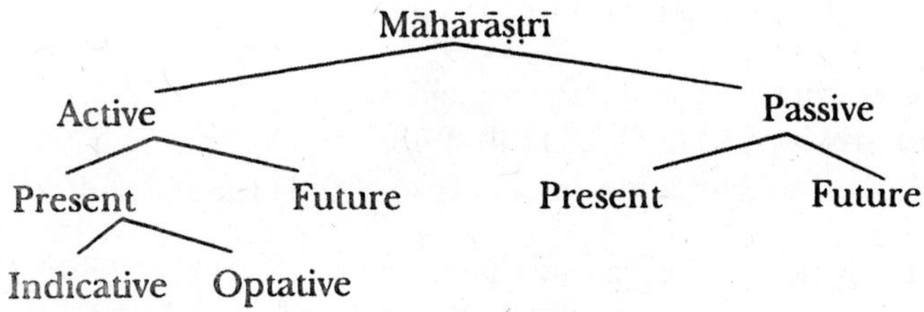

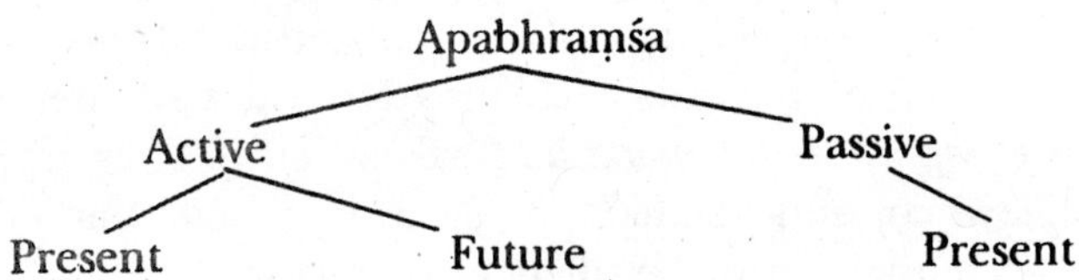

The situation in JM can be surveyed in the following paradigm of the present optative and passive (data from Jacobi 1886/1967: XLVII-III):

	Present Optative	Present Passive
Sg 1	puccheјј ā(mi) 'ask'	pucchijj āmi
2	āsi/su/hi	asi
3	ā	ai
Pl 1	āmo	āmo/imo
2	āha	aha
3	ā	anti

As can be seen certain persons of the optative and the passive came dangerously close to each other, e.g. the 2nd Pl optative *pucchejjaha* 'may you ask' was almost identical with the passive form *pucchijjaha* 'you are asked':

In Ap the marker of the optative was *-e/ijja-* (representing [ɪj: ə], cf. 2.1.3) and that of the passive *-ijja-* or *-ia -* (both from older *-ya*). At this point the single form *pucchijjaha* could express both meanings 'may you ask' and 'you are asked'. As a matter of fact, the passive forms possess quite often a modal meaning:

(1) kijjai vivāhu sukumāra tuha ... [MP 4.6.16]
is-done marriage young-man your
'your marriage, young man, should be done...'

The passive optative forms marked by the sequence of two *-jj*-s are found rarely. An example from JM:

(2) āhāra-virahio sayam eva vivajjejjā [Erz 43.22]
food-deprived self PART fall+PASS+OPT
'he will succumb himself because of the lack of food'

The form *vivajjejjā* was analyzed by Pischel (1900:327) as *vipadyeta*, i.e., as the middle voice optative formed from the passive stem *vipad-y-*. However, it should be analyzed as the optative of the passive causative *vipādyeta* (cf. the indicative of the passive causative *vipādyate* to *vipādayati* 'make X fall'). Thus the first *-jj-* in *vivajjejjā* continues actually the passive causative marker (*-d*) + *y* as in *vāvāijjissai* 'he will be killed' (*vyāpādyiṣyate* ' = future passive causative of *vyā-pad*').

3.4.9 *Causative*

The OIA causative in *-aya* is continued by Pāli and other MIA dialects. The suffix *-aya* developed to *-ē* (through the loss of short *a* and the monophthogization of the diphthong *-ay*). In Pāli the resulting *-ē* is long in open syllables and short in closed syllables, hence the alternation such as *kārēti* (3rd Sg) vs. *kārĕnti* (3rd Pl) 'cause X make Y'. As in OIA, the vowel in the radical syllable is usually lengthened (notice that V: should be shortened before *-aya* according to 2.1.2.b) or ablauted (*vedeti* 'make X know Y', *vid*) or, exceptionally, kept short (e.g. *gămeti* 'make X go, penetrate'). The roots in long *-ā* form their causative, as in OIA, by the suffix *-paya* >*pē*, e.g. *dāpēti* 'make X give Y', *ñāpēti* 'make X know Y', etc. The latter process became a source of numerous formations in MIA; the inherited causatives, such as *dā-pē-ti*, were resegmented into *d-āpē-ti*, and the formative *-āpē* could be used with any verb whose root ended in a consonant: *pac-āpē-ti* 'make X take Y' (vs. OIA *pāc-aya-ti*), *har-āpē-ti* 'make X take Y' (vs. OIA *hār-aya-ti*). The suffix *-āpē* could be added even to a lengthened (or ablauted) root, giving rise to a double causative:

kṛ kār-ē-ti 'cause Y make Z' kār-āpē-ti 'cause X make Y make Z'
han ghāt-ē-ti 'make Y kill Z' ghāt-āpē-ti 'cause X make Y kill Z'
mr mār-ē-ti 'make Y die' mār-āpē-ti 'cause X make Y die'

These formations are already found in Canonic prose and later on became extremely common (for their usage cf. 4.6).

With further phonological changes (*p*> *v* through spirantization and voicing) these formations were continued in later MIA times. Thus we find *kārei* < *kārēti* (Vr., Hc.), AMg *ṭhāvei* 'make X stand' (cf. Pāli *ṭhāpēti* < OIA *sthā-paya-ti*); *jñā* 'know', however, forms the causative from the present stem: JMah *jāṇāvei* 'make X know Y' vs. Pāli *ñāpēti.* Double causatives (with the lengthened radical syllable plus the suffix *-āve*) are also very common; contrast the passive causative participle *jīv-āvi-dā* 'resuscitated' (Ś in Mṛcch) with OIA *jīv-i-tā*; the passive causative *jīv-āv-ī-adi* '(she) is resuscitated' (Mṛcch) with OIA *jīv-y-ate* (*-y-* in the latter example functions as the marker of both the causative and the passive, whereas in MIA they are separated: *-āv-* marks the causative, *-ī-* the passive).

In Ap the markers of the causative are *-a* (and *-āva*) instead of general Pkt *-ē* (and *-āve*). Both Ap *-a* and Pkt *-ē* go back to the same OIA source *-aya*; its bifurcation was caused by a different treatment of *-ay* (after the loss of short *a*): monophthogization in Pkts vs. simplification of the cluster *ay* + C (= initial consonant of the personal suffix), where *a* remained short. Its development in the 3rd Pers Sg:

aya-ti → ăy-ti < -ēti / -ati

Hence the doublets such as:

Ap mārai 'make X die' Mah mārei
Ap karāvai 'cause X make Y' JMah karāvei
Ap jāṇāvai 'make X know Y' JMah jāṇāvei

3.4.10 *Quasinominal Forms*

(a) ***Participles***

The system of Vedic participles, compared with that of finite forms (3.4.1), shows virtually no paradigmatic gaps. The temporal contrast is, of course, irrelevant here, and if we include the gerundive

(=the passive future participle of necessity) under the participial forms in the subsystem of the Future, we obtain the following paradigm (organized according to aspect):

Vedic Participles

	Present	Perfect	Aorist	Future
Active	kurvánt	cakṛvāṃs	kránt	kariṣyánt
Medio-Passive	kurvāṇá	cakrāṇá	krāṇá	kariṣyámāṇa
Passive	kriyámāṇa	kṛtá		kartavyà, -aṇíya kā́rya

The only 'defficiency' of this system is the lack of morphological contrast between the perfect and the aorist in the passive (the rare forms *cakrāṇá* vs. *krāṇá* are medio-passive). The only form found here is the past passive participle in *-tá* (inherited from PIE **-tó*). A glance at Ancient Greek shows how this 'defficiency' could be 'remedied' in the subsystem of the Aorist and the Future (the perfect participle and also the present participle of AGr remained ambiguous, i.e. medio-passive). The system of AGr participles is given below (forms of the verb *poiéō* 'make' where *-thē* is the passive marker):

Ancient Greek Participles

	Present	Perfect	Aorist	Future
Active	poiéōn	pepoiēkṓs	poiḗsās	poiēsōn
Medio-Passive	-ómenos	-ēménos	-sámenos	-sómenos
Passive	"	"	poiētheís	-thēsómenos

(It should be observed that AGr also possessed the past participle in *-tó* and the gerundive in *-téo.*)

In Classical Sanskrit and MIA dialects this rich participial system lost half of its members: the medio-passive forms in *-āna* were seldom used (in the Present in the 2nd conjugation, e.g. *júhvāna* 'sacrifice'; in the Perfect only a few lexicalized forms survived, e.g. *anu-ūc-āna* (*vac*) 'learned', lit. having repeated), and the active forms of the perfect and the aorist participles disappeared at about the same time when their finite counterparts were dropped from the use.

The system found in Pāli displays the dichotomy of active and passive forms with three members in each set: present (imperfective), past (perfective) and future (the future passive participle possesses the modal meaning of necessity and is usually called gerundive). The past passive participle (called also the preterite participle) in *-ta* has the passive meaning with transitive verbs, and the active meaning with intransitive verbs.

Pāli Participles

	Present	Past	Future
Active	-ã/-anto	-ịta-vant	-iss-ā
Passive	-māna, -āna	-(i) ta, -na	-(i) tabba, -anīya, -tāya, -ta/eyya

The present active participle displays two endings in the Nom Sg: *ā* (< OIA *-an)* and *-anto* (thematized *-ant*). The latter form started predominating in postcanonic prose and *-ā* became an archaism.

The suffix of the present (imperfective) passive participle continues the OIA form *-māna.* As mentioned under 1.1, AMg *-mīṇa* represents probably a non-Sanskritic variant of OIA *-māna. -māna* may be added to non-middle verbs and it may compete with the active suffix *-nt.* In AMg the suffix *-māṇa* appears even in the future (*esamāṇā* in *Ṭhāṇaṅgasutta* 178). The suffix *-āna* appears in the language of the *Gāthās* (only rarely in Canonic prose).

Formed from the root *kṛ,* the following forms are documented in Pāli (Geiger, 1916:145-6): *kubbant, kara/ont* (Pres Act Part), *kubbamāna, kurumāna, kubbāna* (< OIA *kurvāṇa*) (Pres Pass Part). The past passive participle shows the suffixes -(*i*) *ta* and *-na.* A great number of the participles formed by these suffixes go back to the OIA period but there are also innovations of Pāli formed by *-ita: jita* 'conquered' (*ji*) vs. *jinita; gata* 'gone' (*gam*) vs. *gacchita*; etc. The form *dinna* 'given' (< **did-na*) vs. Skt *datta* (< * *dad-ta*) was already mentioned (1.1) as a piece of evidence for a non-Sanskritic dialect in OIA times. Other forms which may be mentioned in this context are Pāli (and Mah) *ruṇṇa* 'weeping' (< **rud-na*) vs. Skt *rudita* and (dialectal) *paṭimukka* 'bound to' (< * *muk-na*) vs. Skt *mukta* (cf. Geiger, 1916:148).[19]

The past (perfective) active participle shows a few lexicalized relics from OIA (*avidvā* 'not knowing', *-dassivā* 'seeing' < *darśivān*).

More common (productive ?) was the formation by the suffix *-vant* from the passive participle in *-ta*: *vusitavant* 'who has lived' (*vas*), *bhuttavant* 'who had enjoyed' (regarding formations in *-āvin* cf. 4.4).

Instances of the future active participle are isolated: *marissā* 'who will die' (Geiger, 1916:146). On the other hand, the future passive participle (=gerundive) is extremely common and displays rich morphology inherited from OIA: -(*i*) *tabba* (<-*tavya*), -*anīya*~-*āneyya* (< -*anīya*) and -*ya* (limited to the older period). Here are some examples: *netabba* 'to be led' (< *netavya*), *sotabba* 'to be heard' (<*śrotavya*), etc. The formations in *-anīya* are often lexicalized: *karaṇīya* 'to be done'→ 'duty'. Inovations of Pāli are the gerundival suffixes *-tāya, -tayya* or *-teyya: ñātayya* 'to be recognized', etc.

Several changes took place in the system of participial forms during the middle period of MIA. The most salient one is the formation of the past passive participle from the stem of the present, i.e. not from the special stem as in OIA. Forms such as *gacchita* 'gone' (vs. OIA *gata*) are found already in Pāli and they became even more common during the later period of MIA. Here are some examples from various dialects (data from Pischel, 1900:384-5):

S jaṇida 'born' [Mṛcch] vs. OIA jāta
AMg jaṭṭha 'sacrificed' [Uttar 753] vs. OIA iṣṭa
Mah vāharia 'uttered' [Śak] vs. OIA vyāhṛta
Mg śumalida 'remembered' [Mṛcch] vs. OIA smṛta
JMah vitthariẏa 'strewn' [Erz] vs. OIA vistṛta

The other suffix of the past passive participle, *-na*, is used more frequently than in OIA, (i.e., in more morphological environments). Here are some examples (assembed by Pischel, 1900:385-6):

khaṇṇa 'hole' [Hemacandra] vs. AM, JMah khatta
(cf. also Ś ukkhaṇida)
M, Ś cukka (< * cukna) 'missed, forgotten'

An outcome of these processes, the participial system of Apabhraṃśa, may be outlined as shown below:

Apabhraṃśa Participles

	Active	Passive
Present	-anta	-māṇa
Past		-i (y)a(u)
Future	-iss-anta	-i/evva, -ev(v)a(a)

(The function of the lost past active participle was taken over by the absolutive, cf. 3.4.11.)

Ap continues the Prākrit (and ultimately OIA) present active and passive participles: *-anta* (Fem *-anti*) and *-māṇa* (Fem *-māṇā/ī*). The passive form in *-māṇa* is not found in EAp.

The past active participle in *-ita-vant* (found in Pāli) was lost in Pkts[20] and Ap (its function was taken over by the absolutive). All the suffixes of the past passive participle *-i(y)a(u)* are traceable back to OIA *-(i)ta* (with or without the stem-enlarging *-ka*):

OIA	Pāli	Ap
kṛta 'made'	kata	ka(y)a, kiya
bhūta 'been'	bhūta	hūva(u), hua
kathita 'narrated'		kahi(y)a

As in Prākrits, the future passive participle (gerundive) was very common and its suffixes continue MIA (and ultimately OIA) forms (for details see Tagare, 1948:319-20).

(b) ***Infinitive***

Prākrits preserved the two main infinitival suffixes of OIA: *-tum* (Pāli) and *-tave* < *tavai* (AMg). Pāli *-tũ* continues OIA *-tum* (e.g. *dātũ* 'to give', OIA *dātum*; *ñātũ* 'to kṇow', OIA *jñātum*). This suffix could be added to the present stem (as the past passive participle in *-ta*). The derivation by *-itũ* became extremely productive (cf. the participle in *-ita*). Thus we find

cajitũ 'to abondon'	vs. OIA tyaktum
maritũ 'to die'	martum
pucchitũ 'ask'	praṣṭum

Only in the language of the metrical parts of the Canon one finds relics of the OIA infinitive in *-tave* (*ṇetāve* 'to lead', *dātave* 'to give'). The other two suffixes found in the *Gāthās*, *-tuye* and *-tāye*, are probably innovations of the Gāthic dialect based on the Vedic form(s). In AMg the infinitive in *-tū̃* is relatively rare (e.g. *dāū̃* 'to give', OIA *dātum*; *bhāsiū̃* 'to speak', OIA *bhāṣitum*). Here the common infinitival suffix is *-(i)ttae* which may be connected with Vedic *-tave*. Since the gemination of *t* may be explained by the accent on the ultima (2.1.2.b), the suffix *-(i)ttae* should be traced back to Vedic *-étavái* (which had two accents in Vedic). In AMg the suffix *-(i)ttae* is added above all to the present stem: *hottae* 'to be' ~ *bhavittae* (*bhū*); *sumarittae* 'to remember' (*smṛ*); *gacchittae* 'to go' (*gam*); etc.

A remarkable innovation of Pkts is the passive infinitive which was formed 'agglutinatively' by adding the suffix *-iū̃* (< OIA *-itum*) to the passive stem in *-ijj-*. Contrast the AMg passive form *marijjiū̃* 'to die' (OIA *mriyate* 'he dies') with the general active form *mariū̃* (cf. Ś *maridū̃*); the JM passive infinitive *dijjiū̃* 'to be given' (*dijjai* 'it is given', OIA *dīyate*) with the general active infinitive *dāū̃* 'to give' (JŚ *dādū̃* OIA *dātum*). A remarkable form is Mah *dīsiū̃* 'to be seen' (*dīsai* 'it is seen', OIA *dṛśyate*) which does not show the passive stem marker *-ijj-* [found in *Rāvaṇavaha* 4.51; 8.30].

In Ap a great variety of infinitival suffixes is found. The most important set, from the point of view of subsequent developments, is the set *-aṇa/u*, *-aṇahā̃/ĩ* (in WAp). This *-aṇa* is the primary derivational suffix of deverbative action nouns in OIA (e.g. *darś-ana* 'sight' *dṛś* 'see'). *-anahā̃* is formally the Gen Pl (!) form and *-aṇahĩ* the Loc Sg (or Instr Pl!) form of this action noun. In EAp the suffix *-aṇa* is absent (cf. Mn Bengali which does not possess the infinitive in *-na*). Another characteristic of WAp is the use of the absolutive for the infinitive (this usage is also unknown in EAp). Numerous suffixes of the absolutive, *-ep(p)i(nu)*, *-evi(ṇu)*, will be discussed in 3.4.11. In SAp the commonest suffix of the infinitive was *-hū̃* (probably the source of Mn Marathi *-ū̃*). In EAp *-ai* was used as the suffix of the infinitive (for details and examples see Tagare, 1948:321-4).

3.4.11 *Absolutive*

There are several suffixes of the absolutive in Pāli. *-tvā* is the regular suffix in all periods, while *-tvāna* and *-ya* are found in the earliest portions of the Canon. In the *Gāthās* there are also suffixes *-tūna* and *-yāna* (an innovation on the basis of analogy *-tvā* : *-tvāna* = *-ya*: X). Many absolutives are inherited from OIA, e.g. *ñatvā(na)* 'having known', OIA *jñātvā*; *sutvā* 'having heard', OIA *śrutvā; hutvā* 'having been', OIA *bhūtvā;* etc. Among the absolutives in *-ya* there are: *aññāya* 'having commanded', OIA *-ājñāya; ādāya* 'having placed', OIA *ādāya*; etc.

The suffix *-tvā*, Pkt *-ttā* (*-tā* after nasals) remained the most productive suffix in AMg (less common in JŚ and JMah): *caittā* 'having abandoned' (< OIA *tyajitvā*); *gantā* 'having gone' (cf. Pāli *gantā*) but also *gacchittā* (formed from the present stem). Another AMg suffix of the absolutives is *-thāṇa* (from undocumented OIA **- tvānam*): *bhavittāṇa* 'having been; *caittāṇa* 'having abandoned'; etc.

The commonest suffixes in Mah, JM, JŚ, P (and also in AMg) are: *-tūṇā* and *-ūṇā* (*-tūna* in P, *-dūṇa* in JŚ): *āgantūṇa* 'having come' (but also *gamidūṇa* and *gacchidūṇa*); *pekkhiūṇa* 'having seen'; etc. There are also forms in *-ccā(ṇā)* which arose through the contamination of *-tvā* and *-ya* : AMg *hoccā* 'having been' (OIA *bhūtvā*); AMg *peccā* 'having drunk' (OIA *pītvā*); etc.

Vedic absolutive suffixes *-tvī* and *-tvīnam* are regarded as the source of the Ap suffixes *-ep(p)i, -ep(p)iṇu, -evi, -eviṇu,* which are usually added to the present stem: *gampi* 'having gone' (< OIA *gantvī*, cf. Vedi *gatvī́*) but also *gameppi(ṇu)* (Hc,4,442); *kareppi(nu)* 'having made' < *karevi;* etc.

NOTES

(1) Especially in the Acc Pl. For instance, in Mah, AMg and Ś we find *guṇāī* 'virtues' (OIA *guṇān*); in Mah *gaāī* 'elephants' (OIA *gajān*); etc. As mentioned by Pischel (1900:244), the similarity of the Masc Pl Acc *-ān* and the Neuter Pl Nom/Acc *-āni* could have contributed to this state of affairs.

(2) In Mah, AMg, JMah and JŚ the mid short vowels were raised word-finally in disyllabic suffixes after the long penultima *metri causa* (cf.2.1.3); i.e. /devāo/ could be realized [devāu].

(3) *-u* in the Acc Sg can be explained both morphologically (i.e., by the extension from the Nom) or, less likely, phonologically by raising and denasalization (*õ* > *ũ* > *u*). Bloch (1933/1965:141) prefers the latter solution ('the nasal vowel of the Acc Sg *puttaṃ* closes and

produces puttu') but he offers no explanation for the rounding of the original suffix of the Acc Sg *-ã* (< OIA *-am*).

(4) Bloch (1933/1965:69) keeps the Ap Gen Sg *- āha* and Loc Sg *-ahĩ* distinct from Skt *-asya* and *-asmin* because of 'morphological analogy'. But he mentions that 'the derivation from *s* would be natural in areas, such as Gujarat, where the replacement of *s* by *h* is common'.

(5) Bloch's explanation (1933/1965:143) of these matters is quite different. According to him the expected forms of the Gen Pl would be **puttāṃ* or **puttāã* since *puttena* gave *puttẽ* (like *phalāṇi, phalāiṃ* of Prākrit) and these inconvenient forms were replaced by a double genitive: *puttaha* plus *ã* from *-āṇaṃ*. The Instr suffix *-ẽ* may be derived from the Loc *-asmin* (> *amsin* > *amhin* > *ãhĩ* > *ahĩ* > *aĩ* > *ẽ*). On the other hand, as Bloch put it, 'the nasal of *puttāṇaṃ* had already in Prākrit overflowed to the Instr *puttehĩ* and the Loc *puttesũ*'.

(6) However, according to Tagare (1948:154), the predominance of masculine endings with the original *ā*-stems is so great that 'one is tempted to regard -(*ā*)*i* as a denasalized form of Masc *-iṃ* and *-ĩ* in Ap, instead of taking it to be a weakened form of -*(ā)e* which appears in Pkts and Ap'.

(7) Ghatage (1941:117) traces the AMg form *maha* back to PIE * *megh-ei* (cf. Lat *mihī*).

(8) Tagare (1948:214) proposes complicated proportional analogy of the plural stem of indirect cases with the singular stem of direct cases: *asma-* : *aha-* : : * *tusma* : *tuha-*; the Ap developments of these forms are *amha* : *haũ* : : *tumha* : *tuhũ*. Non-proportional analogy with the 1st Pers *aha-* 'I' would suffice to explain *-h-* in the 2nd Pers *tuhũ*. Analogical remodelling of the 2nd after the 1st Pers is known from elsewhere. For instance, *e-* in *esí* 'you' in Modern Greek is explainable by non-proportional analogy with the 1st Pers *egó* 'I' (vs. AGr *sú* 'you' and *egō* 'I').

(9) *Bhe* Acc [Uttar 363], *bhe* Instr [Āyār 1, 4, 2, 4], *bhe* Gen [Āyār 1, 4, 2, 6].

(10) In RV there are two enclitic pronouns limited to the Acc: *īm* (formed from the pronominal root *i*?) and *sīm* which is ultimately related to Pkt *se* (cf. also Buddhist Skt *se* and *si*); Mayrhofer (1976: 475) explains *sīm* from II **sai* (PIE * *swoi*) by analogy with *īm*. Both forms may be used in referring to male or female beings in any number.

(11) The suffix *-asi* is clearly a Prākritism. In earlier WAp texts *-ahi* predominates but *-asi* is on increase later on under the influence of Skt and Pkt. See the statistics in Tagare (1948:288):

	-ahi	*-asi*
Bhavisatta kahā (1000 A.D.)	47	2
Kumārapāla-pratibodha (1194 A.D.)	7	13

(12) Bloch (1933/1965:244) 'the 2nd person singular... may well come from the imperative; the close relation of the indicative and imperative is, indeed, proved by the 2nd pl. *karahu* (for Pkt. *karaha*) which can only come from the third persons *karau*, pl. *karantu*, supported moreover by 1st pl. * *karamu* or *karahuṃ*, a contingent present naturally adapted to the imperative. But the amphibology, which the facts show to be tolerable in the plural, has, it seems, been found awkward in the singular, in which 2 *karasi* was supported by 1 *karami* and 3 *karai.* The impossible *kara* and the unrythmical *karehi* were replaced in the indicative by *karahi,* which fitted well into the singular system and was in clear opposition to the plural *karahu.* This innovation had the further advantage of keeping *-s-* for the future.'

(13) Cf. footnote (16).

(14) According to Sen (1960:150), if *mama* is the source of the 1st Sg *-aũ* the plural form *mahũ* (< * *mabhyam*) may be the source of the plural ending *-ahũ.*

(15) According to Sen (1960:152), the analogical origin of *-ahĩ* is not tenable since *-ahũ* does not appear as early as *-hĩ.* According to him, the 3rd Pl *-ahĩ* is traceable back to the Instr Pl of a demonstrative pronoun (**ebhim* ~ **ibhim*) represented by the aphetic form *hiṃ,* which was added to the verb stem (in the same way as *-aũ* in the 1st Pers and *-tu* in the 2nd Pers).

(16) The recategorization of the personal suffix as a plural suffix is not unusual. In the Pontic dialects of Modern Greek we find instances of the suffix of the 2nd Pl used in the 1st Pl in the medio-passive conjugation:

Sg	1 kimúme	'I sleep'	Pl 1 kimúmes(tin)
	2 kimáse		2 kimústun ~ ústin(e)

Here *-tin*, originally a part of the 2nd Pl suffix *-stin(e)* appears to be recategorized as a plural marker.

(17) The rule of fricative weakening can be classified as a persistent rule. We still may witness its effects in some modern Hindi dialects, e.g. in the present day Bhōjpurī (Eastern Hindi) where *s*→ *h*/-*t* in recent borrowings from Persian, English and Portuguese (Chatterji 1926/1970:555):

[ahte] 'slowly' < Persian *āhistah*
[dʌhturi] 'customary commission' < Persian *dasturī*
[ihṭisʌn] 'station' < English *station*
[mihtiri] 'mason, artisan' < Portuguese *mestre*

(18) In terms of paradigmatic gaps in the modal system of Vedic Sanskrit,

we may observe that the undocumented present optative passive **kri-y-ī-tá* would be identical with the undocumented aorist optative medio-passive, i.e., 'may it be made' and 'may he have made (it) for himself' or 'may it be made' would be homophonous in Vedic Sanskrit. The reason for this 'leak' in the grammar is the polysemy of the suffix *-y-* (either optative or passive) and the polysemy of the morphological process of zero-grade formation (both aorist and passive):

kri-	*y-*	*ī-tá*	*kri-*	*y-*	*ī-tá*
Voice	Voice	Mood (Voice)	Aspect	Mood	Mood (Voice)

(19) The dialectal Pāli form *paṭimukka* 'bound to' [*Thērīgātha* 500, *Saṃyutta-Nikāya* IV.91.23, 92.1] from OIA **mukna* vs. *mutta* [*Majjhima-Nikāya* III.61.15] from OIA *mukta*. Cf. Geiger (1916:148-9).

(20) Pischel (1900:387) gives some examples of this participle from late authors and uncritical editions.

CHAPTER 4

SYNTAX

The principles of syntax and syntactic change in MIA deserve a monograph of their own. Due to the limits of space only the following major topics will be covered in this study:

(i) Word order
(ii) Cliticization of pronominal objects
(iii) Epistemic and deontic modality
(iv) Evolution of aspect
(v) Passive and the emergence of ergative construction
(vi) Causative constructions

4.1 Word Order in Middle Indo-Aryan

The canonical word order in Classical Sanskrit prose is SOV (cf. Staal 1967). Knowing that Classical Sanskrit is verb—final language we may predict (with Greenberg 1966 and Hawkins 1983) certain other properties of Classical Sanskrit, most notably the use of postpositions and the orders genitive-noun and adjective-noun.

It is generally known that in the previous periods (Brāhmaṇa and Vedic Sanskrit) and in MIA dialects word order was not so rigid as in Classical Sanskrit. VS (verb-initial) and VO (postverbal object) characteristics of Brāhmaṇa Sanskrit were studied by Canedo (1937:28-36) and Gonda (1959:7-69). Their findings may be summarized in the following five points:

(i) The sentence-initial position of the verb is common in narrative passages. The verb in initial position may function as the phonological host to the following clitic (e.g., pronominal object or the adverb):

(1) prakṣyanti mām ime mahāśālā mahāśrotriyāḥ [Ch Up 5.11.3]

ask FUT+3rd Pl me these great-householders great-theologians
'Great householders and theologians will ask me'

(ii) The verb tends to be placed immediately after the sentence initial adverbial expression (an adverb, or its expansions such as the circumstantial clause, or the absolute case):

(2) tád etád út prāvṛ́ṣi jīmū́tāḥ plávante yájante varuṇapraghāsaíḥ [MS I 10.13]
then this rain-season+LOC clouds assemble+3rdPl offer+3rdPl varuṇapraghāsas+INSTR
'as soon as during the rain-season the rain clouds assemble people offer *varuṇapraghāsas*'

(iii) The verb occurs initially in jussive sentences:

(3) dattāsmai bhikṣām [Ch Up IV.3.7]
give=this+DAT food+ACC
'Give food to this (one)'

(iv) In the expressions of volition the dative of purpose and the infinitive (expressing the realization of the wish) appear often postverbally. We may remind ourselves of Greenberg's Universal (15), according to which in expressions of volition and purpose a subordinate verbal form always follows the main verb (except in rigid OV languages).[1] This universal reflects presumably the tendency for language to mirror the temporal order of events. The following examples are from Taittirīya-Saṃhitā:

(4) Agnís tvā hvayati devayajyāyā [TS I 1.12]
Agni you+ACC calls divine-sacrifice+DAT
'Agni calls you to the divine sacrifice'

(5) tám adhriyata hotum [TS VI 5.9]
that decided+3rdSg sacrifice+INF
'he decided to sacrifice that'

(v) In Brāhmaṇa Sanskrit, as in Vedic Sanskrit, Wackernagel's Law may place the verb in second sentential position (e.g., the verb may be cliticized to the sentence-initial preposition)

(6) sáṃ=paśyāmi prajā́ ahám [TS I 5.8]
together see+1stSg posterity I
'I behold the posterity'

Nominal objects in Classical Sanskrit prose appear as a rule to the left of their governing verb; in declarative and jussive sentences the postverbal position is found rarely and it may be explained pragmatically (i.e., by the consideration of the Functional Sentence Perspective). The pronominal objects tend to appear to the left of their governing verb in declarative sentences; in jussive sentences, however, the postverbal position where the pronominal objects are cliticizable to the verb is not uncommon (but less common than in Vedic and Brāhmaṇa Sanskrit).

Sen (1953:355-473) made similar observations about word order in Aśokan inscriptions (representing the oldest stage of MIA). Thus he observed that there was a marked tendency to put the verb before the nominal subject (cf. i):

(7) bahukā hi dosā samājamhi pasati
great+ACC PART fault+ACC samāja+LOC sees
devānāpriyo priyadasi rājā [RE I D; Gi]
gods+GEN beloved Priyadarśin king
'the king Priyadarśin, the beloved of the gods, finds great fault in a *samāja*'

The other versions of this edict [Sh, Ma, Ka] display the finite verb in sentence-final position

(8) bahu[ka] hi [doṣa samajasa devanāpriye] priyadraśi raja [da]kha[ti] [RE I D; Ma]

In Aśokan inscriptions the dative of purpose (cf. iv) generally closes the sentence (so does the adverbial phrase):

(9) pāthesu kūpā ca khānāpitā vrachā ca
roads+LOC wells and dig+CAUS+PASS+PART trees and
ropāpit[ā] paribhogāya pasumanusānā [RE II C; Gi]
plant+CAUS+PASS+PART enjoyment+DAT animals-men+GEN
'on roads wells have been dug and trees planted for the enjoyment of animals and men'

A significant progress in the study of word order in MIA has been achieved by two articles by Andersen (1980, 1982/83) who used in his analysis the Prague school concept of the 'functional sentence perspective'. He has shown that Gonda's (1959) 'amplified sentences' arise through the process of 'commentization' and distinguished three functions related to it:

(i) marking for indefiniteness
(ii) expression of emphasis
(iii) connection of sentences with their textual and situational environment

Under (i), it appears that important new information generally occurs in postverbal position. Those elements which occur after the verb are indefinite and 'new' (mentioned for the very first time in the inscription). Thus the existential statements are typically constructed with the sentence-initial *athi* 'there is/are':

(10) athi pi ca ekatiyā samājā sādhumatā
is also and certain meetings good-considered
devānāpiyasā piyadasine lājine [RE I E]
D.+GEN P.+GEN king+GEN
'but there are also certain festival meetings (which are) considered meritorious by king Devānāpiya Piyadasin'

Locative statements, however, display a definite locative phrase in preverbal position, and the verb *hoti* 'is' stands either at the end of its clause or near the end followed only by 'amplified' elements but never at the beginning of the clause:

(11) ā pi ca aṭavi devanāpiyasa vijitasi hoti [RE XIII M; Er]
also and forest-dweller D.+GEN kingdom+LOC is
'And even the inhabitant of the forest who is in D.'s kingdom, (even him he pacifies ...)'

In Aśokan inscriptions word order functions in distinguishing definite NPs from indefinite NPs: indefinite NPs are placed in comment position after the verb and definite NPs are placed in preverbal position.[2]

As far as MIA narrative passages are concerned, they usually display the verb in final position (SV and SOV); the initial position (VS and VSO) may be exploited for pragmatic and stylistic purposes. However, in some stories VS(O) order appears to be basic (as in OIA). We may examine the story of Double-face [Erz No. V] and the story of beggar-thief Maṇḍio [Erz No. IX] as examples of the narrative prose in JM. Statistically, 71 sentences in each story break down as follows:

	verb-final S(O)V	verb-medial SVO	verb-initial VS(O)
Erz No. V	35	11	44
Erz No. IX	61	1	9

Thus the narrative proceedes 'normally' in S(O)V fashion in the story of Maṇḍio:

(12) Mūladeveṇa bhaniyā: ahā kappadio. teṇa bhaṇṇai: ehi maṇūsā karemi. Mūladevo uṭṭhio. ... [Erz No. IX]
'Mūladeva said: 'I am a pilgrim'. The other said: 'Come, I will make a man of you.' Mūladeva got up. ...'

Maṇḍio and Mūladeva went to a certain man's house where Maṇḍio took a great quantity of plunder and

(13) ... Mūladevassa uvarī caḍāviyā. payaṭṭā ṇayaravāhiriyā. Mūladevo purao, coro asiṇā kaḍḍhieṇa piṭṭhao ei. sāpattā bhūmi-gharā. coro tā davvā ṇihaṇium āraddho. bhaṇiyā ya ṇeṇa bhagiṇī: eyassa pāhuṇayassa pāya soyā dehi! ... [Erz No. IX]
'... piled it upon Mūladeva. They set out for the outskirts of the town. Mūladeva goes in front, the thief comes up behind with a drawn sword. They come to a cellar. The thief set to work to bury the loot, and he said to his sister: Wash the feet of this guest !...'

nayaravāhiriyā 'the outskirts of the town' (in the second sentence) and *bhūmi-gharā* 'cellar' (in the fourth sentence) introduce clearly new information. In terms of pragmatics their postverbal position may be rationalized by the process of commentization. The infinitive of purpose before its verb (against iv) in the following sentence, *ṇihaṇium āraddho* 'set to work to bury', and the whole phrase in sentence-final position may be evaluated as indicating that the SOV order was by now established in MIA (i.e. we do not read *coro tā davvā āraddho ṇihaṇium* or *āraddho coro tā davvā ṇihaṇium*). In the following sentence *bhagiṇī* 'sister' is introduced as a new piece of information into the narrative—hence its sentence-final position.

Here, of course, we may wonder why the author did not construct the sentence with the verb closer to the end, *ṇeṇa ya bhaṇiyā*, i.e. as an SVO sentence. The trend to place the verb as far to the end as possible is observable even in the story of Double-face [Erz No. V] where VSO is more common than SOV. There are instances where the verb intervenes between the argument, which appears in sentence-final position as a result of commentization, and its long attribute:

(14) pañcama-diṇe savva-rayaṇāmao jalaṇo-vva
fifth-day+LOC made-of-all-gems fire-like
teyasā jalanto diṭṭho mahā-mando [Erz No.V]
brilliance+INSTR flashing seen great-diadem
'On the fifth day the workmen found a great diadem of all sorts of gems flashing with brilliance like fire'

This trend, of course, was not an irresistable force as can be seen from the following passage:

(15) theva-kāleṇa vi nimmāyā uttunga-siharā citta-sabhā [Erz No. V]
short-time+INSTR PART completed lofty-pinnacles picture-gallery
'In a very short time a picture gallery with lofty pinacles was completed'

Here *citta-sabhā* 'picture gallery' appears in sentence-final position because it introduces a new piece of information; if the author yielded to pressure to have the verb as far to the end of the sentence as possible (as in an SOV language) we would obtain *theva-kāleṇa vi uttuṅga-siharā nimmāyā citta-sabhā*. A full discussion of these matters would take us far into stylistics (which cannot be attempted in this work). We might be satisfied with observation that the early occurrence of the verb after the adverbial expression in (15) is actually a 'relic' of verb-initial syntax of OIA (cf. ii). The only SVO sentence in our narrative of Maṇḍio was

(16) so vi ṇa sakkai corā geṇhiũ [Erz No. IX]
he also not can thief+ACC catch+INF
'He also is unable to catch the thief'

which displays the infinitival object in sentence-final position. Obviously, we are justified in wondering why not *so vi corā genhiū ṇa sakkai* (with the finite verb form at the end of the sentence). In dramatic Pkts infinitival objects appear in both postverbal and preverbal position (the overall ratio for Mudr, Mṛcch and Vikr is roughly 1:1, cf. 4.2):

(17) icchadi sappā dāsedū [Mudr 2.10.17]
wants snake+ACC see+CAUS+INF
'he wishes to exhibit snakes'

(18) caridā avagāhidū icchasi [Mudr 6.3.7-8]
acting+ACC fathom+INF want+2ndSg
'you wish to fathom the deeds'

The infinitival object is placed behind its governing verb in rigid SOV languages. For instance, in Turkish the sentence such as 'the girl is going out to pick flowers' would be constructed as follows:

(19) kiz cicek dermeğe çıkıyor
girl flower pick+INF+DAT go+PROG+3rdSg

That is in a rigid SOV language the infinitive and its object branch consistently to the left, whereas in non-rigid SOV languages the infinitive may be placed after its governing verb (but the object depending on the infinitive appears before it):

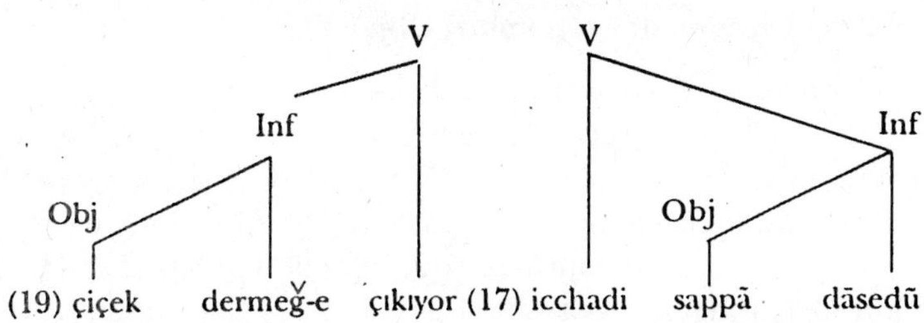

The study of syntactic problems of a dead language cannot be separated from stylistic considerations. It is clear that not all the permutations of word order are to be explained in terms of pragmatics. Thus in

(20) teṇa diṇṇā, vivāhiyā rāiṇā [Erz No. IX]
he+INSTR given married+FEM king+INSTR
'He gave (her), and the king married her'

it is preferable to talk about a conscious effort by the author to write in a 'good' style (using chiasma). But the point remains that non-rigid SOV typology allows for sentences such as (20); or rather, to be even more specific, similar sentences should be statistically more common in non-rigid than in rigid SOV languages.

Finally, it seems to be the case that in Pkts we find instances of genuine linear indeterminacy. The word order in imperative sentences might be mentioned in this context. There is a famous statement by Patañjali à propos this matter, namely, that the command 'fetch the bowl' may be expressed either way in Sanskrit: *āhara pātram* ~ *pātram āhara*.[3] Similar instances of linear indeterminacy in identical pragmatic contexts are plentiful. For instance, Cārudatta (in Mṛcch) commands his servants in Sanskrit in either sequence (VO or OV):

(21) Radanike Maitreyam anugaccha [Mṛcch 1.38.4]
Radanikā Maitreya+ACC follow
'Radanikā, follow Maitreya!'

(22) Maitreya anugaccha tatrabhavatīm [Mṛcch 1.56.33]
Maitreya follow her-ladyship+ACC
'Maitreya, follow her ladyship!'

A statistical study of these matters will be attempted in the next section.

4.2 Cliticization of Pronominal Objects

The study of basic word order brings us to the issue of the position of pronominal objects in Middle Indo-Aryan. My own observations (Bubenik, 1986) based on Prākrit passages in dramas reveal that nominal and pronominal objects may appear in both preverbal and postverbal positions, but in contradistinction with Classical Sanskrit it appears that the postverbal position was the preferred one in jussive sentences. Chart 4-1 surveys the situation in Classical Sanskrit and dramatic Prākrits. Prākrit non-poetic passages in three dramas, *Mṛcchakaṭikā, Mudrārākṣasa* and *Vikramorvaśīya*, were analyzed statistically for the incidence of infinitival, nominal and pronominal objects in declarative and jussive sentences. *Vetālapañcaviṃśatikā* was analyzed in the same fashion as an example of Classical Sanskrit prose.

Chart 4-1. The Incidence of Nominal and Pronominal Objects in Classical Sanskrit and Dramatic Prākrits.

		Declarative Sentences						Jussive Sentences			
		Infinitival Objects		Nominal Objects		Pronominal Objects		Nominal Objects		Pronominal Objects	
		V0	0V	V0	0V	V0	0V	V0	0V	V0	0V
Sanskrit	Vetālapañcaviṃśati	1	68	2	1322	8	303	4	29	4	20
	Ratio					1:37.87		1 : 7.25		1 : 5	
Dramatic Prākrits	Mṛcchakaṭikā	14	17	37	394	23	117	68	56	17	6
	Mudrārākṣasa	8	4	5	54	2	15	10	6	7	2
	Vikramovaraśīya	6	9	3	75	6	23	14	10	8	3
	Total	28	30	45	523	31	155	92	72	32	11
	Ratio	1:1.07		1:11.62		1:5		1.27:1		2.9:1	

In declarative sentences Classical Sanskrit behaves as a rigid OV language. Nominal objects appear in postverbal position only exceptionally (2x) for what appear to be stylistic reasons. For instance, in Vet 18.25-6 the verb intervenes between coordinated objects:

(1) sakhīr ādideśa dauvārikaṃ ca
companions+ACC ordered doorkeeper+ACC and
'she ordered her companions and the doorkeeper'

Similarly, pronominal objects appear in postverbal position only exceptionally. The ratio VO:OV is roughly 1:38 (8:303 instances). For instance, the absolutive 'having heard that' is typically constructed in the OV fashion *etacchrutvā*; however, there are 6 instances of *śrutvaitad*.[4]

In Prākrit declarative sentences the incidence of postverbal nominal objects is ca. 1:11.6. In Mṛcch the ratio VO:OV is 1:10.6 (37:394 instances), in Mudr 1:11 (5:54 instances), and in Vikr 1:25 (3:75 instances).

An example from Chāṇḍālī:

(2) ... āadosi vajjhaṭṭhānā [Mudr 7.3.12]
arrived+2ndSg execution-place+ACC
'you have arrived at the place of execution'

Absolutives occur in both sequences OV and VO:

(3) cāṇakkā nirākaria [Mudr 5.9.67]
Chāṇakya+ACC having-dismissed
'having dismissed Chāṇakya'

(4) nikkāsia rakkhasā [Mudr 6.2.29]
having-discarded Rākṣasa+ACC
'having discarded Rākṣasa'

Infinitival objects in Classical Sanskrit prose appear as a rule in preverbal position. Our statistics for Vet show 68 instances of OV sequence vs. 1 instance of VO sequence:

(5) sakhīr ādideśa ... puradvāram avaroddhum
[Vet 18.25-6]
companions+ACC ordered ... gate+ACC close+INF
'she ordered her companions ... to close the gate'.

In dramatic Prākrits infinitival objects appear in both postverbal and preverbal positions (the postverbal position predominates in Mudr, the preverbal position in Mṛcch and Vikr). The overall ratio is roughly 1:1.

(6) icchadi sappā dāsedũ [Mudr 2.10.17]
want+3rdSg snake+ACC see+CAUS+INF
'he wishes to exhibit snakes'

(7) caridā avagāhidũ icchasi [Mudr 6.3.7-8]
acting fathom+INF want+2ndSg
'you wish to fathom the deeds'

A high incidence of preverbal pronominal objects in Prākrits declarative sentences might be taken as indicating that Prākrits were verb-final languages, i.e. of OV typology:

	VO	OV
Mṛcchakaṭikā	23	117
Mudrārākṣasa	2	15
Vikramorvasīya	6	23

Altogether, in our three dramas, there were 155 examples of the preposed pronominal object in declarative sentences vs. 31 examples of the postposed object. A closer inspection reveals the following points: It is common for focal pronominal objects to be placed in the marked sentence-initial position. Pronominal objects may be cliticized by Wackernagel's Law to sentence-initial adverbs and relative pronouns (especially in interrogative sentences):

(8) kĩ me bhaā dāvesi [Mudr 1.22.22-3]
why me fear show+2ndSg
'why do you seek to intimidate me?'

Furthermore, pronominal objects may be cliticized to the conjunction *jai* (*yadi*), discourse particle *khu* (*khalu*) and the negative particle *ṇa* in any sentential position:

(9) Tā jai me dāsaṇeṇa amacco pasādā ṇa karedi [Mudr 2.10.26-7]
therefore if me audience+INSTR minister favor+ACC not do+3rdSg

'If, therefore, the minister does not wish to favor me with audience.'

(10) kahā paḍivaaṇā vi ṇa me paḍivajjasi [Mudr 7.3.5-6]
how response+ACC even not me give+2ndSg
'how is it that you do not even give me any response?'

Some of the remaining instances of OV typology (i.e., those which cannot be explained functionally or phonologically in terms of enclisis to particles and conjunctions in preverbal position such, as *edā suṇia* 'having heard this' (Mudr 7.16.9)), could perhaps be evaluated as Sanskritisms.

Among the 31 examples of VO there are four of the existential type *atthi-se mokkho*, lit. there is to him a release (i.e., 'he might obtain his release') with the oblique form of the pronoun cliticized to the copula. Seventeen examples display the pronoun cliticized to the verb, as in

(11) asūanti mā pakidīao [Vikr 4.73.2]
be-angry+3rdPl me subjects
'The subjects will be angry at me.'

In five cases there is an adverb intervening between the verb and the pronominal object:

(12) pibaivva mā ṇaaṇehī [Vikr 1.12.2]
drink+3rdSg as-if me eyes+INSTR
'he appears as if drinking me with [his] eyes'.

However, the situation was clearly different in Prākrit jussive sentences. The postverbal position of both nominal and pronominal objects was the preferred one. In the case of nominal objects the ratio of VO to OV is roughly 1.3:1 (92 vs. 72 instances in our three dramas). For the sake of comparison, in *Vetāla* the ratio of VO to OV is 1:7; there are 29 instances of preverbal nominal objects vs. 4 instances of the postverbal position (144.22-3, 150.20, 150.21-2, 154.20). Instances such as *gṛhāṇa balim imam* 'receive this offering!' can perhaps be evaluated as concessions to the colloquial style.

In the case of pronominal objects, VO predominates over OV by the ratio of ca. 2.9:1 in the Prākrit passages in our three dramas (17:6, 7:2, 8:3 instances, respectively), whereas in Classical Sanskrit it is just the opposite: in *Vetāla* OV predominates over VO by the ratio of 5:1

(4:20 instances). These figures indicate that there was a strong tendency to cliticize pronominal objects to their preceding verb in the imperative. In declarative sentences, as shown above, this tendency was much weaker; here the ratio of VO to OV was roughly 1:5.

Virtually, all the VO examples from Prākrit are of the type V + clitic pronominal object, attached immediately to the preceding verb:[5]

(13) ṇedha mā lājamaggam [Mṛcch 2.6.50]
take me king's-highway+ACC
'take me to the king's highway!'

(14) hañje, dehi se āsanam [Mṛcch 2.14.58]
Ceṭī give him seat+ACC
'Ceṭī, give him a seat!'

It is of interest to note that Sanskrit does not have a clitic form in the 3rd Pers pronoun and uses the full forms of the demonstrative pronoun *ayam* (Dat *asmai* or Gen *asya*, as in *dehi asya āsanam*). In my data, there was only one instance of the pronominal object cliticized apparently to the intervening adverb: V Adv-Pron:

(15) moāvehi dāva ṇā [Vikr 1.18.14]
(Skt. mocaya tāvad enam)
disentangle then it
'just disentangle it!'

Altogether, there were 11 examples of the preposed pronominal object in jussive sentences vs. 32 examples of the postposed object. Let us make clear that the preverbal position of the pronominal object does not mean that the pronoun was cliticized to the following verb. First of all, the pronoun can function as a phonological host to the following adverb which may intervene between the pronoun and the verb. The following example which comes from a poetic passage is not included in my statistics:

(16) edā dāva viāraha [Mṛcch 6.12]
this just investigate
'Just investigate this!'

Other instances of the preposed pronominal object may be explained bv the consideration of the Functional Sentence Perspective, whereby the focal object may appear in the marked sentence-initial position. There were 4 cases of the following type:

(17) Muñcadha piavaassā cārudattam. Mā vāvādedha [Mṛcch 10.23.4)
Release dear-friend+ACC Cārudatta+ACC. Me kill.
'Let go [my] dear friend Cārudatta! Kill me!'

There was one instance of what would be called by Givón (1984:137) topic continuity in discourse:

(18) ede khu tiṇṇi alaṅkārasañjoa vikkīandi.
these indeed three ornament-sets sell+PASS+3rdPl
'these three ornaments of a set are offered for a sale
te paccakkhīharedu amacco [Mudr 2.22.72-3]
them examines+IMP minister
[and] you should examine them yourself!'

In this example, the pronominal form *te* 'them' topicalizes the known information from the preceding discourse. If *te* were cliticized to the imperative *paccakkhīkaredu* 'may he examine' the 'thread of discourse' would be disrupted.

Finally, the non-focal pronoun may be cliticized to another argument by Wackernagel's Law, as in the following example:

(19) Aṇṇāṇioeṇa mā ajjo aṇugehṇadu [Mudr 1.5.2]
command-entrusting+INSTR me lord favors+IMP
'May the lord favor me with (his) command!'

There were three examples of prohibitive sentences with the personal pronoun apparently cliticized to the confirmatory particle *khu* (Skt *khalu*) 'indeed' in preverbal position:

(20) sahi mā khu mā visumarehi [Vikr 3.18.3]
friend not indeed me forget+IMP
'Friend, please, do not forget me!'

In *Vetāla* the ratio of VO to OV in jussive sentences is 1:5 (4:20 instances), excluding 8 instances of jussive sentences with relative-correlative pronouns *yat-tat* (the type *yat kiṃ cin nigadāmi tac chrṇu,*[6] lit. whatever I have to say that hear), the ratio would be 1 : 3 (4 : 12 instances). Broadly speaking, this is the opposite ratio of what we saw above for our dramatic Prākrits. Several questions must arise: How to evaluate those 4 instances of VO in *Vetāla*? *praveśaya tam* (8.4) 'bring him in!' *bhajasva mām* (32.1) 'give me the favor of your love!'[7] and *rakṣa mām* (84.30 and 138.4) 'protect me!' Should they be viewed as a concession to a colloquial register? (Or perhaps, a lower class dialect?) Is the source of OV word order in jussive sentences modelled on the pattern of sentences with relative-correlative pronouns *yat-tat*? Also the preceding absolutive (which is almost always constructed as OV) could provide the model:

(21) tāṃ niścitya māṃ jñāpaya [Vet 42.17-18]
her having-discerned me inform
'Find out who she is and inform me!'

No attempt has been made to collect and systematically study numerous instances of zero anaphora in both Classical Sanskrit and Prākrits. Thus in dialogue it is quite common to say 'Tell for what reason!' instead of 'Tell me for what reason!' as in (22):

(22) Kathaya kasmin nimitte [Mudr 1.5.8]

As noted earlier, Classical Sanskrit did not use the clitic form of the 3rd Pers Sg *se* which is common in Prākrits. We find *vada me* 'tell me' but not **vada se* 'tell him' where the full form *asmai* would be used. Here it may be observed that the active imperative **vada se* would be homophonous with the mediopassive indicative *vadase* 'you speak (for yourself)'. Zero anaphora are typically used with passive imperatives when the recipient is obvious from the extralinguistic context:

(23) Dīyatām eṣā [Mudr 2.22.38]
is-given+IMP she
'Give it (to him)!'

(*eṣā* refers to the 'ring' *mudrā*).

In causative constructions the pronominal Causee Agent and the Goal are often not grammaticalized, as in

(24) Mudrāṃ paripālayan udghāṭya darśaya [Mudr 5.9.13]
seal+ACC preserving having-opened see+CAUS+IMP
'Open (the letter) preserving the seal and show (it to me)!'

Similar examples are available from Prākrit passages:

(25) jadā me paoaṇā tadā gehnissā [Mudr 2.22.21]
when me occasion then take+FUT+1stSg
'I will take (them) away when there is an occasion for me.'

Finally, a few words on the pragmatic flexibility of word order in Prākrits vis-à-vis that of Classical Sanskrit. Both Classical Sanskrit and Prākrits may place the focal argument in sentence-initial position. The focal argument may be reinforced by the enclitic particle of emphasis *eva* (*jjeva* in Prākrits) 'in fact, really'. However, rigid OV languages are at odds with the requirement of the Functional Sentence Perspective to place objects (which usually convey new information) in postverbal position in jussive sentences. Prākrits, on the other hand, favored strongly the postverbal position for both nominal and pronominal objects in jussive sentences.

Furthermore, Classical Sanskrit as an OV language is at odds with postverbal enclisis of non-focal objects. In other words, Sanskrit and Prākrits differed in the way they expressed non-contrastive *kíll=him* (but not in expressing contrastive *kill HÍM*):

	Classical Sanskrit	Prākrits
kíll=him	tam māraya	mārehi=ṇa
kill HÍM	tam=eva māraya	tā=jjeva mārehi

The difference between non-contrastive *kíll=him* and contrastive *kill HÍM* was shown solely by the emphatic particle *eva* in Sanskrit, whereas Prākrits reinforced this contrast by different word order: the focal object appeared in sentence initial position as a phonological host for the emphatic particle *jjeva* (as in Sanskrit).

How, then, is Cārudatta's VO Sanskrit in jussive contexts to be evaluated?

(26) Dehi me prativacanam [Mṛcch 10.57.4-7]
give me reply+ACC
'Give me a reply!'

A rigid SOV language would not allow both cliticization of the pronominal recipient and postverbal position of the object.[8] We saw above that in Classical Sanskrit this two-argument imperative would be typically constructed as a single-argument imperative in the passive: *prativacanaṃ dīyatām* lit. may the reply be given. On the other hand, we also saw that in Brāhmaṇa Sanskrit two-argument imperatives with cliticized pronouns were common (cf. the example (3) in 4.1). VO sequences in Classical Sanskrit imperatives can thus be evaluated as either archaisms or concessions to the colloquial style. It should be observed in this respect that dramatic Sanskrit, which presumably reflects a colloquial form of Classical Sanskrit, appears to be typologically in an intermediate position between Classical Sanskrit prose and the Prākrits of drama. Thus in Sanskrit passages of Vikr (Chart 4-2) VO sequences in both declarative and jussive sentences are, on the one hand, more common than in *Vetāla* but, on the other hand, less common than in Prākrit passages of the same drama (as in Chart 4-1, the Sanskrit poetic passages have been excluded from the statistics).

Chart 4-2 shows the intermediate position of Sanskrit prosaic passages of *Vikramorvaśīya* in the incidence of postverbal infinitival and pronominal objects in declarative sentences; the incidence of postverbal nominal objects in Sanskrit passages of Vikr is even higher than that found in the Prākrit passages of the same drama. In jussive sentences, the incidence of the postverbal nominal object in Sanskrit passages of Vikr shows an intermediate value between that found in prosaic Sanskrit (*Vetāla*) and in Prākrit passages of the same drama.

Measured against the colloquial registers, it would seem that the strong verb-final rule of Classical Sanskrit prose texts (categorial in case of declarative sentences with infinitival and nominal objects) may be largely a matter of literary style. Chart 4-3 places the dramatic Prākrits in a broader perspective of Old and Middle Indo-Aryan. Vedic and Brāhmaṇa Sanskrit, and Prākrits share the trend to place the verb immediately after the initial scene setting adverbial expression (ii) and to open the jussive sentence with verb (iii). Similarly these three diachronic stages of Indo-Aryan show a predilection for postverbal enclisis of pronominal objects in declarative and jussive sentences (iv and v). It may be said that word order in Vedic and Brāhmaṇa Sanskrit, and in Prākrits is governed pragmatically, i.e., it is subservient to the purposes of Functional Sentence Perspective. For instance, we have seen above that the unmarked position of the pronominal object in jussive sentences in Prākrit was

Chart 4-2. The Incidence of Nominal and Pronominal Objects in Sanskrit and Prākrit Passages of Vikramorvaśīya

		Declarative Sentences						Jussive Sentences			
		Infinitival Objects		Nominal Objects		Pronominal Objects		Nominal Objects		Pronominal Objects	
		V0	0V	V0	0V	V0	0V	V0	0V	V0	0V
Prosaic Sanskrit		1	68	2	1322	8	303	4	29	4	20
(Vetāla)	Ratio					1:37.87		1 : 7.25		1 : 5	
Dramatic Sanskrit		1	5	8	51	1	20	7	12	ϕ	4
(Vikr)	Ratio			1:6.37				1:1.71			
Dramatic Prākrits		6	9	3	75	6	23	14	10	8	3
(Vikr)	Ratio	1:1.5		1:25		1:3.83		1.4:1		2.66:1	

postverbal. The preverbal position was marked and could be exploited for the purposes of the FSP (focal objects may be preposed in 'emotive order' and topical objects may be preposed to maintain topic continuity). If, on the other hand, the basic word order is fixed by a syntactic rule of placing the verb in sentence-final position and the object in preverbal position, then the verb stands outside of this perspective. This, of course, was the case of Classical Sanskrit, as known to us from late prose texts.[9]

In 4.4 it will be shown that the 'auxiliaries' of aspect appear in both postverbal (as in SOV languages) and preverbal positions (as in VSO and SVO languages). The ambivalent syntactic typology of older MIA is also reflected in the use of postpositions and prepositions. Contrast Pāli *bhikkhūhi saddhī* 'with the monks' [Vin 3.42.5] with *saddhī bhikkhusāghena* 'with an assembly of monks' [Vin 4.74.16]. Postpositions predominate in Ap (Tagare 1948:192-7) but no statistical accounts are available for middle MIA dialects.[10]

Chart 4-3. Word Order in Old and Middle Indo-Aryan

	Vedic Sanskrit	Brāhmaṇa Sanskrit	Dramatic Prākrits	Late Sanskrit Prose
(i) V cliticized to sentence initial adverbial preposition	+	+		
(ii) V after initial scene-setting adverbial expression	+	+	+	
(iii) V-1 in jussive sentences	+	+	+	-
(iv) postverbal enclisis of pronominal objects in declarative sentences	+	+	+	-
(v) postverbal enclisis of pronominal objects in jussive sentences	+	+	+	-

(vi)	VO in expressions of volition (O = infinitive)	+	+	+	-
(vii)	zero anaphora	rare	rare	rare	common

4.3 Epistemic and Deontic Modality

In this section various interactions between mood, modality and agentivity in MIA jussive sentences will be examined. I would like to maintain certain terminological distinctions, most notably 'statement' and 'command' for utterances with a particular illocutionary force, and 'declarative' and 'jussive' for sentences with a particular grammatical structure. 'Statements' are unqualified in terms of possibility and necessity whereas 'commands' are qualified. Three kinds of possibility and necessity are recognized—namely, alethic, epistemic and deontic (cf. Lyons 1977:793-808, 823-831). The epistemic mode evaluates the actuality of an event, while deontic mode expresses the imposition of actuality.

In MIA the class of jussive sentences (i.e., the sentences that are characteristically used to issue commands, demands, requests, entreaties, and make deontic statements, etc.) included imperative, optative and gerundive sentences. In OIA this class was larger and included also injunctive, subjunctive, desiderative and infinitive sentences. OIA morphology of the imperative, subjunctive, optative and injunctive in three aspectual subsystems (Present, Aorist and Perfect) was surveyed in 3.4.1.

In the indicative, subjunctive and optative we have a classical triad of factivity, non-factivity and contra-factivity (cf. Lyons, 1977:816). More specifically, from the point of view of epistemic modality, the indicative was the mood of factivity and a categorical assertion; the subjunctive was the mood of non-factivity and less remote possibility; and the optative was the mood of contra-factivity and remote possibility.

The optative (and the imperative) in the 2nd and 3rd person are used in utterances which impose, or propose, some course of action and indicate that it should be carried out. These utterances are governed by the general addressee based condition that the speaker must believe that the addressee is able to comply with the directive (i.e., one cannot command, request, advise or exhort someone to perform an action which one knows he is incapable of performing). On the morphological side, we have to distinguish between the imperative and optative sentences in MIA. The Vedic subjunctive did not survive into MIA[11] and the previous three-way morphological system used in active jussive sentences was reduced to a two-way system of the imperative and the optative. Both of them could be used to issue what is called 'mands' or 'directives'.[12]

Let us assume that the difference between imperative and optative sentences was primarily the difference between commanding and requesting and only secondarily that between intimacy and deference. Primarily, by the imperative the speaker commands the addressee to realize the event whereas by the optative the speaker only desires an event of some participant.

The following minimal pair of sentences may be used to establish this distinction:

(1) Kaṭaṃ kuru 'Make the mat'
mat+ACC make+IMP+2ndSg

(2) Kaṭaṃ kuryāḥ 'Make the mat, please'
mat+ACC make+OPT+2ndSg

Leaving the semantic difference between commanding and requesting aside, it would seem that the crucial difference between (1) and (2) is that in the optative sentence (i.e., the request) the speaker leaves the addressee the option of refusal to comply with the command, whereas the command does not. It would seem that this option of refusal could be encoded in MIA by the optative morphology. Thus when the deontic mode is applied to primary events (those expressed by syntactically independent clauses) a number of distinct senses can be distinguished depending on the strength of modality. Imperative and optative are probably the most common ones (there are others such as cohortative, desiderative, obligative, permissive, etc.). The imperative encodes the quintessential form of the deontic mode: the speaker is the source that imposes an event on the addressee. Even the optative may be used to express commands, but with a weaker degree of strength of imposition. An example from Ap:

(3) pacchai cintijjahu paramu dhammu [BhK 55.9]
afterwards think+OPT+2ndSg paramadharma

'Afterwards, please, think of the *paramadharma*' (or 'may you think ...').

Imperative *cintehi* 'think!' would leave the addressee with no option of refusal; optative *cintijjahu* in its desiderative sense 'may you think', 'please, think' represents a weaker imposition on the freedom of the addressee to act. A stronger form of imposition is represented by the obligative optative seen in the following example from Ap:

(4) tā sayalu khamejjahi [Pc 19.14.4]
that all pardon+OPT+2ndSg
'You should pardon all that!' (or 'pardon all that!')

Weaker prohibitions are realized by the optative preceded by the negative particle *ṇa(u)* in MIA. An example from Ap:

(5) ahavai eu vi ṇau bujjhijjai [Pc 47.3.3]
otherwise this PART not understand+PASS+OPT+3rdSg
'Otherwise this should not be understood'

Strong (categoric) prohibitions are introduced by the prohibitive particle *mā*. As is well-known, in OIA the injunctive was the only mood which could be used in prohibitive sentences introduced by this particle. In later development in MIA *mā* could be used also with the imperative and the optative.[13] Thus to issue a prohibition such as 'Don't be afraid' we have to use the injunctive of *bhī* 'fear': *mā́ bhḗs* (or *mā́ bhaiṣīs*) in Vedic Skt, whereas in MIA the imperative would be used. An example from Ap:

(6) mā bībhasu kaṇṇe [Jc 1.15.5]
not be-afraid+IMP+2ndSg girl
'Girl, don't be afraid!'

If used with the imperative in the third person, the prohibition is again weakened (or made more polite) as in the following Ap example:

(7) tā sesā mā bhaṇijjantu [SR 17]
then other not tell+OPT+3rdPl
'then the others should not tell'

The aspectual contrast of perfectivity was possible with the imperative in OIA (*śṛṇudhí* (Pres) 'hear!' vs. *śrudhí* (Aor) 'have heard!') but not in Pkts. The only distinction of time we might expect to find grammaticalized in the imperative are distinctions of more immediate and more remote futurity. The future imperative is found in OIA (it is also known from Latin and Hindi). The suffix of the future imperative *-tāt* was limited in Classical Skt to the 3rd Sg in polite requests. Summarily:

Chart 4-4. Imperative Morphology in Some I-E Languages

	OIA	Pkts	AGr	Latin	Hindi
2nd person	+	+	+	+	+
3rd person	+	+	+	+	
Future	+		+	+	+
Aspectual contrasts	+		+		
Passive	+	+	+		

The imperative is universally connected with the verb in the 2nd person and the addressee in the vocative. It is implicit in the very notion of commanding and requesting that the command or request is addressed to the person who is expected to carry it out. Logicians assume that 'the subject of imperative sentence will necessarily refer to the addressee' (the participant in the discourse who is typically in the same space, ignoring commanding over the telephone), cf. Lyons (1977:747). However, this statement has to be modified in several respects. There is no apriori reason that the subject of a command or a request must be the participant in the discourse which should be grammaticalized by the second-person pronoun. We can transmit a command or a request indirectly through an intermediary. This is done commonly in IA languages by means of the causative imperative:

(8) Praveśaya tam
enter+CAUS+IMP+2ndSg him
'Make him enter!'

Here the immediary could be grammaticalized by the second-person pronoun (*Tvaṃ taṃ praveśaya*). Normally, however, there would be no overt indication of person (the imperative singular has a zero-suffix while the indicative is marked for person). The ultimate receiver and the potential performer of the command (i.e., the Causee) is grammaticalized by the pronoun in the third-person which, furthermore, has to be put in the accusative. If the construction is passivized then the Causee will appear as the subject in the 3rd person: *Praveśyatām* 'May he be made to enter.'

Of equal importance, in the polite style in Classical Skt and Pkts we can refer to an addressee in the 3rd person. Classical Skt and Pkts thus have a true third-person imperative. In Classical Skt the addressee in the polite style is typically grammaticalized by *bhavān* and *bhavatī* (Fem) and there are various forms in Pkts: *bhavã, bhante* (Mg) and *bhotī, hodī* (Fem)

(9) Mantram ekaṃ mahyaṃ dadātu bhavān [Vet 92.17]
charm one I+DAT give+IMP+3rdSg sir
'Give me a charm!'

The same, of course, can be done in requesting, i.e., we refer to an addressee in the 3rd person. Thus, at least morphologically, we obtain a double binary system of intimate and polite command and request:

Imperative		Optative	
2nd person	3rd person	2nd person	3rd person
Intimate	Polite	Intimate	Polite
command	command	request	request

(10) kaṭaṃ kuru 'make the mat!'
kaṭaṃ bhavān karotu 'make the mat, please!'
kaṭaṃ kuryāḥ (lit.) may you make the mat 'please, make the mat!'
kaṭaṃ bhavān kuryāt (lit.) may the lord make the mat 'please, make the mat!'

A further option is introduced by the combining of the third-person imperative with the addressee in either the nominative or vocative. The latter option was probably felt as a more honorific mode of address than the combination of the third-person imperative with the nominative. Superficially, it looks like a contamination of the second-person imperative and the vocative with the third-person imperative and nominative. The following examples are taken from *Vetāla*:

(11)

vada deva	2nd Pers	Vocative
'tell(me), your majesty!'	Imperative	
vadatu devaḥ	3rd Pers	Nominative
'let your majesty speak'	Imperative	
vadatu deva	3rd Pers	Vocative[14]
'let your majesty speak'	Imperative	

The above mentioned assumption of modern logicians that 'the subject of an imperative sentence will necessarily refer to the addressee' may be furthermore discredited by the passive imperative in OIA and MIA. As their non-modal counterparts, these constructions grammaticalize the semantic notion of Goal as the subject, but limit their predicate to the 3rd person (of any number):

(12) Mahyam imā dīyantām
I+DAT those+NOM give+PASS+IMP+3rdPl
'Give them to me!'
(lit. let them be given to me)

An example from Ap:

(13) appijjau gehini Rāmaho [Pc 49.3.10]
give+PASS+IMP+3rdSg Rāma+GEN
'Give the wife to Rāma!'
(lit. may the wife be given to Rāma)

Their addressee may be grammaticalized by the agentive phrase in the instrumental:

(14) Iyaṃ niḥsāryatāṃ bhavatībhiḥ [Vet 20.1-2]
she+NOM go-forth+CAUS+PASS+IMP+3rdSg ladies + INSTR
'Ladies, send her forth!'
(lit. may she be sent forth by the ladies)

In the case of intransitive verbs it is common to encounter impersonal constructions (with the predicate limited to the 3rd person singular) or the gerundive:

(15) Atra upaviśyatām
here it-is-seated+IMP
'Be seated here!'

As in the personal constructions, the addressee may be grammaticalized by the agentive phrase in the instrumental:

(16) Bhavatyā matsamīpam āgantavyam
lady+INSTR my-proximity+ACC it-is-gone+GERUNDIVE
'Lady, you must come to me!'
(lit. by the lady it is to be gone to my proximity)

Three aspects of the passivization in jussive sentences have to be considered: pragmatic, semantic and honorific. Jussive contexts presuppose dialogues and the participants in the dialogue are always 'given' (or 'topical'); what is typically focal is the Goal or the beneficiary of the action or the action itself. The passivization can thus be seen as the option left to the interlocutor in the dialogue of not grammaticalizing the non-focal addressee as the subject of the sentence (or, positively, as the option of grammaticalizing the focal Goal of the action as the subject). Since, as mentioned above, the second-person singular imperative does not grammaticalize the category of person, this statement is more meaningful in the plural imperative which grammaticalizes the second person plural by *-ta*:

(17) Mahyam imān datta
I+DAT these+ACC give+IMP+2ndPl
'Give them to me!'

(18) Mahyam imā dīyantām
I+DAT these+NOM give+PASS+IMP+3rdPl
'May they be given to me' or
'Let them be given to me'

In both (17) and (18) the beneficiary of the action is in the focus. However, only the active imperative sentence (17) grammaticalizes the addressee of the command. Semantically, the passivized imperatives can be classified as demands, i.e., they differ crucially from commands and requests (realized typically by the imperative and optative in the active voice) in that they are not necessarily addressed to those upon whom the obligation of fulfilment is imposed.[15] Thus the passive imperative in

(19) Deva, kumārī dīyatām
your majesty girl+NOM give+PASS+IMP+3rdSg
'Your majesty, let this girl be given to me'

would be appropriate in the context when the suitor asks the king to intercede on his behalf at the girl's father. The active counterpart

(20) kumārīṃ dadātu bhavān
girl+ACC give+IMP+3rdSg sir
'Sir, please, give me the girl'

would be uttered directly by the suitor to the girl's father. If, however, the instrumental grammaticalizes the addressee, as in (16), we are dealing with the polite request NOT the demand.

It has already been mentioned that the participant-roles in Sanskrit discourse are grammaticalized and lexicalized in terms of social status. The perusal of Ancient Indian literature shows that in most cases of social interaction it was clear to any pair of participants whether they were of equal social status or not. It would be inappropriate for me to venture into an analysis of social superiority in Ancient India which depended on at least three variables of social role, sex and age. For linguistic purposes it is enough to assume the existence of two poles of *superior* and *inferior*. We saw above that the feature 'superior' may be lexicalized by *bhavān* 'sir' and *bhavatī* 'lady' or grammaticalized by the use of the 3rd person imperative in passive contexts. But, obviously, we have to assume a number of possible positions along the continuum of deference when addressing superior and inferior interlocutors. As we saw above, the passivization in the jussive context (with the addressee realized by the instrumental) supplied the speakers of Sanskrit with another possible position on the scale of politeness. In most cases, it seems to me, the passive construction is more respectful than the polite request grammaticalized typically by the active third-person imperative (+ *bhavān*). Of course, any limitation to three positions (such as intimate - polite - respectful) on the scale would be totally arbitrary; further nuances could be provided by additional lexical material as in the following context of requesting somebody to take a seat:

(21) upaviśa — 'sit down'
upaviśatu bhavān — 'sir, please, sit down'
upaviśyatām (bhavatā) — (lit.) may-it-be-seated (by the sir)
idam āsanam alaṃkuryāt bhavān — 'sir, please, decorate this chair'
idam āsanam alaṃkriyatām (bhavatā) — (lit.) may this seat be decorated (by the sir)
idam āsanam anugṛhyatām (bhavatā) — (lit.) may this seat by favored (by the sir)

The gerundive is found typically in contexts of deontic modality, i.e., the modality which is concerned with the necessity or possibility of acts performed by morally responsible agents. Clearly, when we impose upon someone the obligation to perform or to refrain from performing a particular act, we are not describing either his present or further performance of that act. One of the salient characteristics of deontically modalized utterances is that deontic necessity typically derives from some source or cause such as the notions of moral obligation and right conduct. I will not be concerned with drawing a distinction between morality and legality but rather with establishing the fact that the use of Skt and Pkt gerundive may reflect some universally valid notion of obligation (which can be lexicalized by a variety of distinctions such as *adharmya* 'wrong', *anāyya* 'illegal', *anarha* 'improper', *duṣta* 'immoral', etc.). Let us establish the difference between a directive, the utterance of which brings into existence a certain obligation, and a deontic statement to the effect that the obligation exists. We may think of several bad characters trying to kill a brahmin who are admonished to refrain from their action by a third party. This witness has an option of issuing a direct prohibition *Pāpāḥ mā hata imaṃ brāhmaṇam* 'Villains, don't kill this brahmin' or he may modalize his prohibition deontically by using the gerundive (which has to agree with the subject):

(22) Nanu pāpāḥ na hantavyo brāhmaṇaḥ [Das 24.14]
'Forbear, you villains, a brahmin must not be killed!'

It may be noted that the word *brāhmaṇaḥ* in (22) has a generic reference (i.e., no brahmin is ever to be killed); it would be rather inappropriate to use the demonstrative pronoun as in (23)

(23) na hantavyo yaṃ brāhmaṇaḥ
'This brahmin is not to be killed'

since it would imply that other brahmins could be killed. (23) is an example of restricted obligation whereas (22) is an example of an unrestricted (generic) obligation: the prohibition on murdering a brahmin is absolute in the sense that it holds at all times and in all possible worlds. The validity of this obligation is analogous with the truth-value of logically necessary propositions (= apodeictic judgements). However, whatever view we take of the logical status of unrestricted obligations, it is arguable that our understanding of their force is based upon our understanding of the way in which directives function in everyday social interaction.

The same is, of course, true about imposing a restricted obligation as in (24)

(24) Idānīm aparakanyā tava putrāya dātavyā [Vet 84.27]
now another-girl+NOM your son+DAT she-is-given+GERUNDIVE
'Now give another girl to your son!'

whose understanding may be said to be based upon the understanding of a simple directive

...aparakanyāṃ tava putrāya dehi.

A crude schema of the discussed correlations between modality, mood and agentivity in MIA syntax is presented in Chart 4-5.

Chart 4-5. Jussive Sentences in Middle Indo-Aryan.

Modality		*Mood*	*Addressee*
Command	Intimate	Active imperative (2nd pers)	Vocative
	Polite	Active imperative (3rd pers)	Vocative ~ Nominative
Wish, request	Intimate	Optative (2nd pers)	Vocative
	Polite	Optative (3rd pers)	Vocative Nominative ~
Demand	Polite	Passive imperative (3rd pers)	Vocative ~ Instrumental
Statements of epistemic and	Gerundive	(3rd pers)	Instrumental

deontic necessity (institutionalized authority, etc.)	Infinitive (only in Vedic[16] and Brāhmaṇa Sanskrit)	Instrumental

The Skt and Pkt gerundive can be used as the inferential mode in which the event is characterized as inferred from evidence. (It should be noted that the inferential is only one of the submodes of the epistemological mode which evaluates the actuality of an event with respect to a source. Another submode found in the IA language is the quotative, marked by the particle *iti*, in which, the event is reported from another source). The gerundive used as the inferential mode must be put in the neuter singular (impersonal construction)[17] with the agentive phrase in the instrumental:

(25) asmin latāmaṇḍape bhavitavyaṃ Śakuntalayā [Śak 3.6.1]
this+LOC creeper-bower+LOC it-is+GERUNDIVE Śakuntalā+INSTR
'Śakuntalā must be in this bower of creepers'

An example from Mg:

(26) tadhā takkemi śāpadā ajjaāe ālūdhāe hodavvam [Mṛcch 6.4.14]
so infer+1stSg now lady+INSTR ascended+INSTR it-is+GERUNDIVE
'So, I infer Madam must have by now mounted up'

An example from Mah [Jacobi, 1886/1967:LXV]:

(27) hoyavvam ettha mayakariṇā
it-is+GERUNDIVE here mad-elephant+INSTR
'A mad elephant must have been here'

Inferential statements[18] do not have to be grammaticalized by the gerundive (i.e., by the passive voice). As in many other languages, the future tense in the active voice may be used as the inferential mode. Thus the inferred event grammaticalized by the gerundive in (27) can also be expressed by the future tense:

(28) mayakarī ettha bhavissai
mad-elephant here be+FUT+3rdSg
'A mad elephant must have been here'

4.4 Evolution of Aspect

Further evolution of the perfective and progressive aspect is typical of MIA.

(i) The finite way of expressing perfectivity (by the perfect forms inflected for person in OIA) gave way to analytic non-finite constructions in MIA. There are only a handful of relics of OIA perfect in Pāli (most notably, *āha* 'he has said', *vidu* 'they knew/have known'). The new way of expressing perfectivity was by means of the past passive participle + copula (in the 3rd Pers *atthi* 'is' (OIA *asti*) is regularly and *hoti* (OIA *bhavati*) often omitted). With intransitive verbs the meaning of the periphrastic perfect is active:

(1) āgato 'mhi 'I (male) have come'
come I-am

This participle has, of course, to agree with its subject in gender and number:

(2) āgatā 'mhi 'I (female) have come'

With transitive verbs the meaning of the periphrastic perfect is passive:

(3) mutt' amhi (=muttā amhi) 'I (female) have been liberated'

(4) nimantit' amha (=nimantitā amha) 'We have been invited'

With certain transitive verbs, however, the periphrastic perfect has both the active and the passive meaning; e.g. *patto* (< OIA *prāpto*) means both 'obtained' (Pass) and 'having reached' (Act):

(5) patto 'si nibbāṇa 'you have reached the nirvāṇa'
reached you-are nirvāṇa+ACC

This polysemy could be eliminated by the activization of the past passive participle by the suffix *-vant*:

prāpta 'obtained' (Pass) ~ (having) reached' (Act) → *prāpta-vant* 'having reached' (Act). But similar formations are rare in Pāli and they tend to be lexicalized: *bhutta* 'eaten' → *bhuttavant* 'having eaten, one who has eaten'. An innovation of Pāli is the activizing suffix *-āvin*: *bhuttāvin* 'having eaten, one who has had a meal'; *vijita* 'conquered' → *vijitāvin* 'victorious'; *kata* 'done' → *katāvin* 'one who has done'. In this fashion it was possible to form even the periphrastic pluperfect and the future perfect:

(6) patto abhavissā 'I had reached'
(lit.) reached I-was

(7) gato bhavissati 'He will have gone'
(lit.) gone he-will-be

The combinations of the absolutive with the verb *tiṭṭhati* 'stands' and *viharati* 'dwells' possess inchoative meaning (setting oneself into the state of what is expressed by the verb in the absolutive):

(8) ekasmī gumbe laggitvā aṭṭhāsi [S IV.60.15]
one+LOC bush+LOC stick+ABS stood
'remained stuck on a bush'

(9) paṭhamajjhānā upasāpajja viharati [D I.37.3]
first-trans put-himself+ABS dwells
'he put himself into the first stadium of trans (and remains in it)'

Also the combination of the present (active or passive) participle with the verb *tiṣṭhati* in the past may have inchoactive meaning:

(10) atha kho āyasmā Ānando .....rodamāno aṭṭhāsi [D II.143]
then PART venerable Ānanda...weeping stood
'then the venerable Ānanda...burst into tears'

i.e. the meaning is not 'Ānanda stood weeping' but 'became weeping' (= 'burst into tears').

Past perfective events were expressed during the whole MIA period as in Pāli, i.e. by combining the past passive participle with the copula. With intransitive verbs the meaning of the periphrastic perfect is active; (11) is an example from Ś, (12) from Dhakkī:

(11) tumā mae saha...gadā āsi [Mṛcch 28.14]
you me with gone you-were
'You had come with me'

With transitive verbs the meaning is passive:

(12) tassa jūdialassa...ṇāsikkā bhaggā āsi [Mṛcch 36.18]
this+GEN player+GEN... nose broken was
'The nose of this player was broken'

With the *verba dicendi et sentiendi* expressions of perfectivity necessitate the use of the impersonal construction (cf. 4.5) with the past passive participle in the neuter singular. An example from JM:

(13) pacchā rannā cintiyā [Av 32.19]
later king+INSTR thought+NEUT
'The king thought later'

At the end of the MIA period the expressions of the perfective aspect were systematized in the following fashion in Ap:

Present perfect	=	past participle + copula *acch-* in the present
Past perfect	=	past participle + copula *acch-* in the past (*āsi*)
		past participle + 'auxiliary' *thiu-* (<past participle *sthita* of *sthā* 'stand')

Some examples from Ap:

(14) acchai āsaṇapaṭṭi ṇisaṇṇau [Bh K 74.2]
is seat-slab+LOC seated
'He is seated on the seat'

(15) gayau āsi [Pc 36.4.6]
gone was
'He had gone'

(ii) Progressive aspect could be expressed in Pāli by the combinations of the present participle with the verb *tiṣṭhati* 'stands' or (*vi*) *carati* 'walks'.[19] These are rather rare constructions:

(16) te aññam-aññam patvā sarīrāni lehentā aṭṭāsu [JāCo II.31.18]
they other-other reach+ABS bodies+ACC licking they-stood
'they were licking each other'

(17) Bodhisatto ekā upamā upadhārento vicarati [JāCo III.102.16]
Bodhisatva one+ACC simile+ACC inventing he-walks
'Bodhisatva was inventing a simile'

Lasting and ongoing actions in the future may be expressed by the combination of the gerundive or the past passive participle with the copula in the future tense:

(18) aṭṭha guṇe samādiyitvā tapo caritabbo bhavissati
eight virtues+ACC undertake+ABS penance practice + GERUNDIVE will-be
'I shall be doing penance practising the eight virtues'

The combination of the absolutive with the verb *vattati* 'becomes' may express habitual aspect:

(19) Gotamo ime dhamme anavasesā samādāya vattati [D I. 164.5]
Gotamo these+ACC rules+ACC restlessly undertake+ABS becomes
'Gotamo follows restlessly these rules'

These rare formations employed to express ongoing and habitual actions were continued and further developed during MIA. At the end of the MIA period they were systematized in the following manner in Ap:

Present progressive	=	(a) present participle + *acchai* (copula in the present)
		(b) absolutive + *acchai*
Present habitual	=	(a) present participle + *thakkai* ('stands')
		(b) absolutive + *thakkai*
Past progressive	=	(a) present participle + *acchiu* (past participle of the copula) or + *thiu* (past participle of *thā* 'stand')
		(b) absolutive + *thiu*

Some Ap examples for the present progressive:

(20) acchai duri bhamantu [Pd 4.17.2]
he-is far wander+PRES PART
'He is wandering far away'

(21) vollau savvu haseppinu acchami [Pc 38.19.2]
said all laugh+ABS I-am
'I am laughing at all (that has been) said'

Present habitual:

(22) khaṇe khaṇe dukkhanti ṇa thakkai [Pc 39.4.9]
moment+LOC moment+LOC give-pain+PRES PART not stands
'It does not continue giving pain each moment'

(23) thiru hoviṇu thakkai [BhK 269.9]
steady be+ABS stands
'He remains steady'

Past progressive:

(24) bhavakaddami haũ hiṇḍantu acchiu [Jc 4.17.2]
world-mud+LOC I wander+PRES PART be+PAST PART
'I was wandering in the mud of the world'

(25) vaṇe vijjau ārāhanta thiu [Pc 9.8.9]
forest+LOC *vidyā* worship+PRES PART stand+PAST PART
'He was worshipping *vidyā* in the forest'

(26) jaṇēri ṣiri karapallava dharivi thiya [BhK 164.9]
mother head+LOC hand hold+ABS stand+PAST PART
'The mother was keeping the hand on the head'

The combinations of the passive participle of transitive verbs with the copula or the 'auxiliary' 'stand' have, of course, passive meaning (cf. 4.5).

Summing up, at the end of the MIA period we encounter a rich system of periphrastic formations which could express adequately aspectual contrasts of perfectivity and progressivity. The following 'auxiliary' verbs were used in Ap:

acchai 'is'	(present of the copula)
acchiu 'was'	(past participle of the copula)
āsi 'was'	(preterite of the copula)
thakkai 'stands'	(present of *thā* 'stand')
thiu 'stood'	(past participle of *thā*)

It should be pointed out, however, that the full fledged analytic system of NIA has not yet been reached in Ap. Most noticeably, the 'auxiliaries' (the copula and the forms of the verb *thā* 'stand') can appear both before and after the main verb (contrast 20 and 24) and they may be separated from it by other words (e.g. by the adverb in 20).

The reduced system of inherited synthetic forms in Ap (as sketched in 3.4.1) has to be completed by the system of periphrastic formations expressing aspectual contrasts of perfectivity and progressivity as shown in the following diagram:

Aspect in Apabhraṃśa

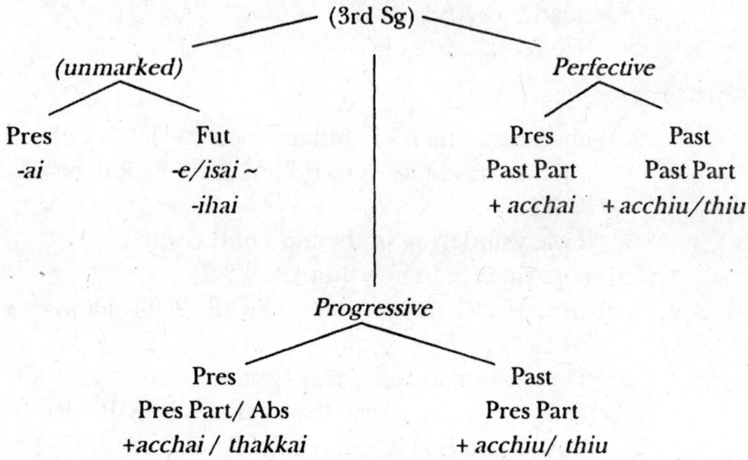

4.5 Passive and the Emergence of Ergative Construction

In the passive construction the notional object (Goal) is assigned subject function (Dik 1989). In OIA there were two morphological strategies by which this task could be accomplished:

(i) the finite construction in *-ya* and (ii) the non-finite (participial) construction.

The finite passive form was inflected for person and number and was limited to the imperfective aspect (the Present system, cf. 3.4.1).

2nd Sg kriyase	'you are (being) made'
3rd Sg kriyate	'he is (being) made'
3rd Pl kriyante	'they are (being) made'

Outside the Present system the passive could not be formed. The only exception was the aorist (which did not participate in the opposition of perfectivity). In the aorist we find mediopassive forms limited to the 3rd person singular whose characteristic was the strengthened root (cf. 3.4.1):

kṛ	'do'	ákāri	'was made' (3rd Sg)
dṛś	'see'	ádarśi	'was seen' (3rd Sg)

(1) práti divó adarśi duhitā́ [RV iv.52.1]
against heaven+GEN see+AOR+PASS+3rdSg daughter+NOM
'the daughter of heaven has appeared'

(ii) The non-finite way of expressing the passive was not aspectually restricted since the mediopassive participles were available for aspectual contrasts: the imperfective aspect was expressed by the present *kurvāṇa*, the perfective aspect by the perfect (*cakrāṇa*); and there was the aspectually unmarked aorist (*krāṇa*). In addition, there was the passive imperfective participle in *-māna* (*kriyámāṇa*) and the perfective passive participle in *-tá* (*kṛtá*). Morphology of all these forms is surveyed in 3.4.10. (a).

The imperfective mediopassive participles (and their active counterparts) could co-occur with verbs such as *i* 'go', *car* 'move', *ās* 'remain', *sthā* 'stand' to express habitual actions or durative events:

(2) tè sya gṛhāḥ paśáva upamūryámāṇā īyuḥ [ŚB]
these his houses cattle crush+PRES+PASS+PART go+OPT+3rdPl
'his house and cattle would go on being destroyed'

These are not particularly frequent constructions; on the other hand the perfective passive participle in *-tá* could be used more frequently in the meaning of the completed past event whose results were relevant in the present:

(3) tatáṃ me ápas tád u tāyate púnaḥ [RV i.110.1]
done me work it and is-done again
'my work is done and it is being done again'

Statistically speaking (i.e. disregarding pragmatics), in Vedic Sanskrit the active constructions for the expression of past events in both aspects predominate. The speaker of Vedic would use the active imperfect and the active perfect and aorist for the narration of past imperfective and perfective events. Statistically, the most 'natural' way to say the sentence such as 'he said it' would be to use the active aorist:

(4) tad avocat
it+ACC said+3rdSg
'he said it'

Passive constructions in OIA are typically agentless:

(5) yuktás te astu dákṣiṇaḥ [RV i.82.5]
yoked you be+IMP right
'Let thy right (steed) by yoked'

If the agent is to be expressed it can be done by the agentive phrase (instrumental):

(6) tvám̥ nṛ́bhir hávyo viśvádhā asi [RV vii.22.7]
you men+INSTR invoke+GERUNDIVE always you-are
'you are always to be invoked by men'

The agentive phrase may also be realized by the genitive. However, the genitive agents are limited to certain verbs, most notably those of perception, consumption and enjoyment (cf. Jamison 1981:322):

(7) tád vā ṛ́ṣīṇām ánuśrutam āsa [ŚB]
that or seers+GEN heard was
'That was heard by the seers'

In similar instances we are dealing rather with the experiencer than the agent. In the case of the participle of necessity (gerundive) the agentive phrase may also be realized by the dative:

(8) sákhā sákhibhya īḍyaḥ [RV i.75.4]
friend friends+DAT praise+GERUNDIVE
'A friend to be praised by friends'

In the case of ditransitive verbs ('give' etc.) the dative can be interpreted only as the recipient (i.e. *not* the agent). Thus

(9) tasmai deyam [ŚB]
he+DAT give+GERUNDIVE

can mean only 'to him (gifts) should be given'. If we want to say 'He has to give it to him' the agentive phrase has to be realized by the instrumental:

(10) Idam tasmai tena deyam
it he+DAT he+INSTR give+GERUNDIVE
'It has to be given to him by him' or
'He has to give it to him'.

Potential ambiguites arise with clitics. In (5) *te* 'you' was cliticized to the first word by Wackernagel's Law but it is clearly a possessive pronoun determining the last word in the sentence. However, in the following example matters are not so clear:

(11) tatáṃ me ápas tád u tāyate punaḥ [RV i.110.1]
done me work it and is-done again
'my work is done and it is being done again'

Here, *me*, the clitic form of 'I' in the genitive case, could be understood as a possessive pronoun determining the following word inspite of being cliticized by Wackernagel's Law to the first word in the sentence. In this case the structural dependency of the possessive pronoun on its head-noun is interrupted (the phonological host of *me* and its head-noun do not coincide).

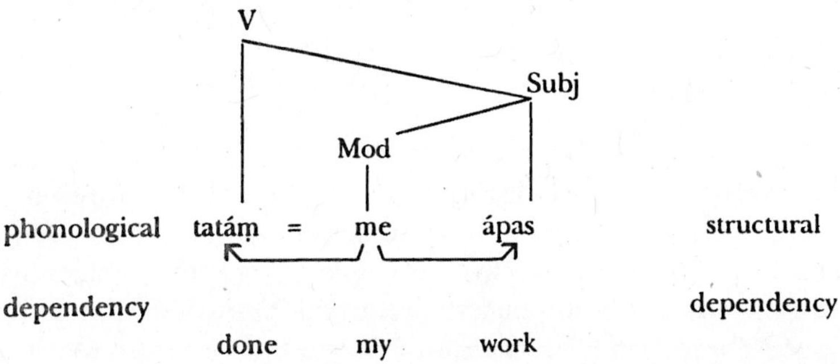

Alternatively, we might prefer to understand *me* as the agentive phrase 'by me'. In this case there would be no disruption of the structural dependency of the agentive phrase 'by me' by Wackernagel's Law (the phonological host of *me* and its head coincide):

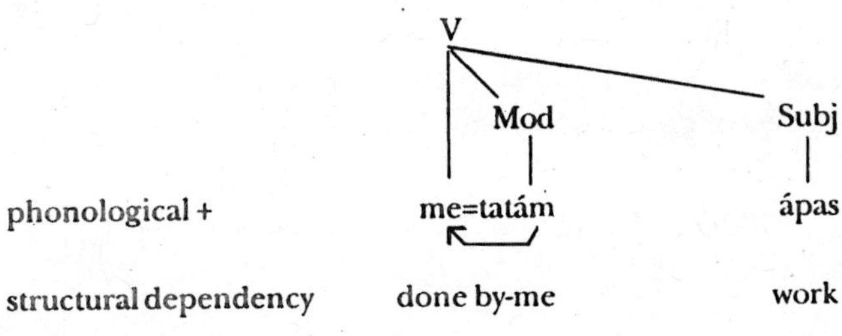

The translation *tatáṃ=me ápas* '(my) work is done by me' is certainly plausible. The problem, of course, is the form *me* which could be taken for either Gen or Dat (cf. 3.3.1). *me* in (11) is an atypical agentive phrase which cannot be understood as an experiencer. But we might be willing to entertain a hypothesis of syntactic analogy with sentences such as (8) where *sakhibhya* 'friends + DAT' is clearly an agentive phrase inspite of being realized by the dative.

As is well known one of the salient differences between Old and Middle Indo-Aryan syntax was the predilection of the latter period for the use of the passive construction. Statistically, in Vedic Sanskrit the active constructions predominate wheras in Classical Sanskrit and MIA dialects the passive constructions are more common. Thus in MIA the most 'natural' way to say (4) would not be by the finite form (Aorist or Perfect) as in Vedic but by the use of a non-finite construction with the passive participle in *-ta*. The agent of this act has to be expressed by the agentive phrase (instrumental):

(12) tat tena uktam
it+NOM he+INSTR said+NEUT+SG+NOM
'he said it'

With the gradual loss of the finite active forms for the expression of perfectivity (cf. 3.4.1) the non-finite way of expressing past events (i.e., by the passive perfective participle in *-ta* with the agentive phrase) became the only means for the realization of the perfective aspect. The intermediate state of affairs is found in old MIA (Aśokan inscriptions, Pāli) where in addition to the inherited finite passive in *-ya* (imperfective aspect) and the non-finite construction with the passive participle (perfective aspect) we still find the relics of the old aorist. However, as shown by Andersen (1986:88), the opposition of voice with the aorist in Aśokan inscriptions was reinterpreted in terms of aspect (i.e., the active aorist expressed the imperfective and the passive aorist the perfective aspect); contrast

devānāpiyā ...*nikhamisu* (Active Aorist)
'the 'beloved of gods' used to go' [RE VIII A]

with

se ..lājā ... nikhamitha (Mediopassive Aorist)
'the king went' [RE VII C]

In MIA the agentive phrase in the passive construction may be expressed either by the instrumental or by the genitive. An example for the instrumental in Aśokan inscriptions:

(13) iyā dhāmalipi devānāpiyena
this dhamma-inscription+NOM devānāpiya+INSTR
piyadasinā lājinā likhāpitā [RE I A]
piyadasin+INSTR king+INSTR write+CAUS+PASS+PART
'This dhamma-inscription was caused to be written by king Devānāpiya Piyadasin'

(13) is a passivized causative construction, the king is the Causer and the Causee—one of the stone—masons—is not specified (cf. 4.4). An example of the genitive:

(14) athi pi cu ekatiyā samājā sādhumatā devānāpiyasa
is also and certain meetings good-considered D.+GEN
piyadasine lājine [RE I E]
P.+GEN king+GEN
'But there are also certain festival meetings (which are) considered meritorious by king Devānāpiya Piyadasin'

The passive participle of the verb *mannati* 'consider' as a verb of perception governs rather an experiencer than the agent (Gen and Dat merged quite early in MIA, cf. 3.1).

But in Aśokan inscriptions there are also contexts where the genitive realizes clearly the agentive phrase as in the following example:

(15) ...ḍevānāpiyasa piyadasine lājine kaligā vijitā [RE XIII A]
...D.+GEN P.+GEN king+GEN Kalingas+NOM conquered
'... king Devānāpiya Piyadasin conquered the Kalingas'

Andersen (1986:81) has shown that the genitival agent in (15) and similar instances conveys old information (and thus it is definite) whereas the goal conveys new information. On the other hand, the instrumental agent in (13) conveys new information and the goal which has been assigned subject function conveys old information. Furthermore, the instrumental agent can be both animate and inanimate whereas the genitival agent can be only animate. Hinuber (1968:239) gives examples from Vinaya-Piṭaka [4.2.17 and 21] which show this clearly: *diṭṭhā me* (Gen) 'seen by me' vs. *cakkhunā* (Instr) *diṭṭhā* 'seen by the eye'.[20] We may conclude with Andersen (1986:83) that here we are dealing with two different constructions: the ergative construction whose genitival agentive phrase conveys old information but whose patient (goal) conveys new information; in the passive construction, on the other hand, the instrumental agentive phrase conveys new information. Furthermore, the agentive phrase in the ergative construction is limited to the animate nouns. Using fictive MIA examples, we find the following three constructions:

Active construction (past event unmarked for perfectivity):

(16) putto kaññā adassa
boy+NOM girl+ACC saw
'The boy saw a girl'

Ergative construction (past perfective event; the agent is known from the preceding context and the goal is a new piece of information):

(17) puttassa kaññā diṭṭhī
boy+GEN girl+NOM seen+FEM
'The boy has seen a girl'

Passive construction (past perfective event with the agent being a new piece of information):

(18) puttena kaññā diṭṭhī
boy+INSTR girl+NOM seen+FEM
'The girl was seen by a boy'

In the case of the pronominal agentive phrase we would expect the anaphoric pronoun (conveying old information) to be realized by its clitic form. And indeed sentences of this type are readily available:

(19) duvāḍasavasābhisitena me iyā ānapayite [RE III B]
twelve-year-anointed+INSTR me this ordered
'This has been ordered by me after I had been anointed for twelve years'

According to Pischel (1900:292) and Sen (1960:198) *me* can be either Instr or Gen. For the former case speaks the agreement of the appositional modifier (*duvāḍasavasabhisitena*) which is in the instrumental; paradoxically, or rather by Wackernagel's Law, this modifier functions also as the phonological host to the head of the phrase (clitic *me*): 'by me, (the one) who had been anointed...'. Andersen (1986:84-5) considers *me* in this and several other instances Gen, or rather the ergative case, because it conveys old information, and claims that (19) is the parallel case to (15), which displays the nominal genitival agent conveying old information. It would seem to me that the case of personal pronouns is different since the speaker and the addressee are always given ('old' information) in the context of the dialogue (or the speaker in the context of the narrative). One would thus expect the contrast of the type clitic form of the personal pronoun vs. its orthotonic form to be used in the context dependent statements such as the following pair of sentences: 'I HEARD it' vs. 'It was heard by ME' (i.e., not by someone else). In MIA:

(20) imā = me sudā
this I+GEN heard
'I HEARD it'

(21) imā mae sudā
this I+INSTR heard
'It was heard by ME'

Our evidence suggests rather an indiscriminate usage of the orthotonic Instr form and the ambiguous clitic Gen/Instr form. Thus in the following Ś example we would expect the clitic form *me* after the particle *khu* 'indeed' (OIA *khalu*):

(22) sudā khu mae tāda Kaṇṇassa muhādo [Śak 14.12]
heard indeed I+INSTR father Kanva+GEN mouth+ABL
'I have indeed heard (so) from father Kanva's mouth'

Orthotonic *mae* in (22) is unambiguously Instr whereas clitic *me* in (23) can be interpreted as either Gen/Dat or Instr (an example from AMg):

(23) Suẏā me āusā teṇa bhagavaẏā evam akkhāẏā [Āẏār I.1,1,1]
heard I+GEN longlived that+INSTR lord+INSTR thus

spoken+NEUTER
'I heard, long-lived one, that the Lord had spoken thus'

Here the argument for the interpretation of *me* as an experiencer (Gen/Dat) is not particularly strong because the use of the orthotonic Instr *mae* would result in morphological doubling (*...mae... tena...*).

The following two examples in Ś are taken from the same context (Vasantasenā tells her maid that she (=maid) understood her behavior well):

(24) suṭṭhu de jāṇidā [Mṛcch 2.75]
well you+GEN/INSTR known

(25) suṭṭhu tue jāṇidā [Mṛcch 2.57]
well you+INSTR known

In (25) Instr *tue* is to be taken as an agentive phrase 'It was recognised well by you', whereas in (24) we may entertain the idea that *de* (Gen/Dat) expresses the experiencer (lit. it was known well to you) 'You understood it well'. In other instances the agentive interpretation of the clitic form is warranted by the agreement with a noun or a participle in the Instr:

(26) ṇa khu te... sāhasā karanteṇa... ācaridam [Mrcch 4.5.8-9] not indeed you+INSTR daring+ACC doing+INSTR acted+NEUTER
'you have not done well by acting daringly'

Verba *dicendi et sentiendi* may also be passivized. The use of the finite form in the present is rare. An example from JM:

(27) teṇa bhaṇṇai [Erz IX.10]
he+INSTR say+PASS+3rdSg
'He says' (lit. it is being said by him)

To express the past perfective event the verb has to be put in the past participle in the neuter singular (=impersonal construction):

(28) Mūladeveṇa bhaṇiyā: ahā kappaḍio [Erz IX.10]
Mūladeva+INSTR said+NEUTER I pilgrim+NOM
Mūladeva said: 'I am a pilgrim'

Notionally, this impersonal construction possesses a sentential subject and the neuter singular of the passive participle *bhaniyā̃* is the only agreement marker available. As long as the question of agreement arises we cannot talk about a real ergative construction. That is the ergative interpretation is not available for sentences such as (Ap) *maĩ naru diṭṭha* 'I saw the man' (lit. I+INSTR man+NOM seen) vs. *maĩ kanna diṭṭhī* (lit. I+INSTR girl+NOM seen) 'I saw the girl'. Here the Goal which was assigned Subject function governs the shape of the passive participle (Masc vs. Fem). Only when there is no choice in the agreement marker (with human definite objects) come we closer to the ergativity as known from NIA languages. As we saw above (28), the question of choice in the agreement marker does not arise with sentential subjects (here the neuter form is the only one available and as such cannot be considered a real agreement marker). A further condition for the emergence of the ergative construction arose in Ap when the absolute case appeared (Nom = Acc, e.g. *deu* 'god', cf. 3.2.1). This means that the same nominal form would be used as an intransitive subject and transitive object: *naru carai* 'the man walks' and *naru dekkhami* 'I see the man'. At this point it is arguable that the sentence such as 'I saw the man' (lit. the man seen by me) may be given rather the ergative than the passive interpretation:

(29) maĩ naru diṭṭha
I+INSTR man+NOM see+PASS PART (passive interpretation)
I+ERG man+ABS see+PASS PART (ergative interpretation)

The following example with a sentence-initial agent from JM [KI 22] may be analyzed as either a passive or rather an ergative construction:

(30) teṇa siri-kakkueṇā ... kāraviā ... imā bhavaṇā
this+INSTR illustrious-Kakkuka+INSTR make+CAUS+CAUS+PASS+PART
(passive interpretation) this+NOM temple+NOM
this+ERG illustrious-Kakkuka+ERG make+CAUS+CAUS+PASS+PART
(ergative interpretation) this+ABS temple+ABS
'This illustrious Kakkuka has caused this temple to be built.'

On the other hand, sequences with the agent in marked post-verbal position can be interpreted passively (cf. Bubenik, 1989 for a functional account of these matters).[21] Only when another postposition is used in the agentive phrase of the passive construction (such as *se* in Hindi) do we reach full-fledged ergative typology. It may be mentioned in this context that the ergative postposition of Mn Hindi, *ne*, has probably arisen from the participal form *lāgi* (*lag* 'adhere, stick, attach oneself to') and that it was originally used as a dative postposition (OH *nai*).[22]

The OIA finite construction in *-ya* survived through the MIA period until Ap. As shown in 3.4.8, in MIA the verbs form their passive stem with the suffix *-(ī)ya* (Pāli) and later on with its reflex *-(i)jja* (in AM, Mah and Ap), e.g., *hammai* ~ *haṇijjai* 'he is killed' (OIA *hanyate*). As in OIA, even intransitive verbs may be passivized:

(31) siddhimahāpuri jāiyai [Pd 132]
siddhi-big-city go+PASS+3rdSg
'the big city of *siddhi* is gone to'

In MIA there arose a need to create a new passive construction. This need may be understood as a direct consequence of the incorporation into the inflectional paradigm of MIA dialects of the passive participle as the ergative construction. Also the indistinctiveness of the passive forms inherited from OIA (e.g., *hammai* < *hanyate* is (being) killed) and the polysemy of some forms of the passive forms with *-ijja* (cf. 3.4.8) contributed undoubtedly to the appearance of periphrastic passive formations. In Ap we find several 'auxiliaries' combined with the passive participle used as new passive formations. The following verbs could be used as the passive 'auxiliaries' in Ap:

acch- 'be', *thā-* 'stand' and *jā* 'go'.

(32) acchami baddhau dīhẽ ḍorẽ [Ja 3.3.11]
I-am tied long+INSTR rope+INSTR
'I am tied by a long rope' (or 'I have been tied....')

(33) ṇāĩ daveṇa daḍḍhu thiu mahiharu [Pc 29.2.7]
as if fire+INSTR burnt stood mountain
'As if the mountain was burnt by the forest-fire'

Such analytic passive formations of Ap as *acchami baddhau* 'I am tied' and *daḍḍhu thiu* 'was burnt' (*thiu* = past participle of *thā* 'stand') would correspond to synthetic forms in earlier MIA (cf. Pāli *bajjhati* 'is tied' and *ḍayhati* 'is burnt'). It was, however, the third option which became an ancestor of the *jānā-* passive of NIA languages. Periphrastic constructions with the 'auxiliary' *jā-* 'go' (OIA *yā-*) plus the abstract noun, infinitive, absolutive or the past participle in *-ta* occur in Classical and Buddhist Skt, and all MIA dialects. Their agentive phrase is expressed either by the Instr or the Gen. See some Ap examples: Abstract noun + *jā-*:

(34) sãdesaḍau savittharau, para mai kahaṇu na jāi[23]
message long but I+INSTR telling not go+3rdSg
'The message is long, but I cannot tell it' (lit. but it cannot be told by me)

Infinitive + *jā-* (in the passive!):

(35) bahiṭṭhiyāṇā kī jāyai ajjhāiũ[24]
outsiders+GEN what go+PASS+3rdSg study+INF
'What can be studied by outsiders?'

The construction of the passive participle with *jā-* appears to have been rare (it has not been reported for Classical Skt). An example from Mah [R XV.44]:

(36) diṭṭhīhi a bāṇehi a tūliā jāi lahuā pavāgamaseṇṇā
looks+INSTR and arrows+INSTR and made-equal go+3rdSg
easily monkey-army
'Now the monkey-army has been easily matched by (his) looks and arrows.'

Summing up, in MIA there appeared a 'proto-ergative' construction anticipating that of NIA languages. Typologically, we have to do with the so-called split ergativity (limited to the perfective aspect). As we saw above, MIA in its last stages moved some way towards creating an absolute case and reducing the agreement. The related problems of definiteness and animacy are yet to be explored in more detail. Contrasting the MIA 'proto-ergative' construction with the real ergative construction found in Mn Hindi we see the difference immediately. In Hindi the Goal in the ergative construction has to be definite (marked with *ko*) and is typically high on the scale of animacy.

(37) maĩ ne laṛkī ko dekhā
I+ERG girl+*ko* saw
'I saw the girl'

If the Goal is indefinite the 'semi-ergative' construction has to be used:

(38) maĩ ne laṛkī dekhī
I+ERG girl seen+FEM
'I saw a girl'

In both (37) and (38) the ergative case (marked by the postposition *ne*) is used; if the Goal is definite, however, there is no agreement between it and the (originally) non-finite participial form *dekhā*; the latter form in its lack of agreement with the Goal resembles thus ordinary finite verb forms. On the other hand if the object is indefinite as in (38), the construction in spite of displaying the ergative case preserves the essential feature of the passive construction, that is the agreement between the grammatical subject and the passive participle—hence we may label it 'semi-ergative' (or 'semi-passive'). The real passive construction would be used in contexts when the identity of the agent is irrelevant (taken for granted vel sim.); its auxiliary in Mn Hindi is *jānā* 'go':

(39) laṛkī dekhī gaī
girl seen gone+FEM
'The girl was seen'

There are no aspectual restrictions on the use of passive (both perfective and progressive forms are available: *kitāb likhī gaī* 'the book was written', *kitāb likhī gaī rahī* 'the book was being written'). If the speaker wishes to express the agent he may do so by using the agentive phrase marked by postposition *se*. The subject of the passive sentence is definite and the agent may be emphasized by being moved towards the end of the sentence. Contrast:

(40) mujh se kitāb likhī gaī
I+AGNT book written gone+FEM
'The book was written by me'

(41) kitāb mujh se likhī gaī

book I+AGNT written gone+FEM
'The book was written by ME'

4.6 Causative Constructions

Two aspects of the causativization in MIA will be considered: the passivization of causative constructions in the context of increased passive orientation of MIA, and the doubling of active and passive causatives.

The causativization (=causative predicate formation) may be understood as an extension of the valency of the input predicate-frame by an extra Causer argument. If the causative construction is to be passivized, this extra argument supplies the speaker with an additional candidate (to the Causee) for the assignment of Subject function.

Using the terminology of Functional Grammar (Dik 1989), we may account for the syntactic and semantic properties of causative constructions in Classical Sanskrit and Prākrits by assuming the following special rules regarding the subject and object assignment to apply:

(R1) The Causee Agent may be assigned Object function (morphological accusative) for contactive causation, or it may be realized in the form of the agentive phrase (morphological instrumental) for non-contactive causation.

(R2) The Causer Agent is assigned Subject function in the active causative construction.

(R3) The Causee Agent or the Goal of the action is assigned Subj function in the passive causative construction.

(R4) If the Goal is assigned Subj function both the Causer and the Causee may be expressed by the agentive phrase (instrumental).

(R5) If the Causee Agent is assigned Subj function the Causer Agent may be expressed by the agentive phrase and the third argument (Goal, Recipient) remains in the original case.

The semantic parameter of the degree of control retained by the Causee in the causative construction interrelates closely with the formal expression of the Causee.

It is intuitively satisfactory to assume that in the case of inanimate

Causee this Causee has no potential for exercising any control over the situation. Where, however, the Causee is animate as in our examples (1) and (2), there is the potential for a continuum of degree of control retained by that Causee:

(1) dāsaṃ bhāraṃ hārayati
servant+ACC burden+ACC carry+CAUS+3rdSg
'he has a servant carry the burden'

(2) dāsena bhāraṃ hārayati
servant+INSTR burden+ACC carry+CAUS+3rdSg
'he has the burden carried by a servant'

Example (1) with the Causee in the accusative implies low retention of control on the side of the servant (it would be appropriate for a situation where the grudging servant was compelled or forced physically to carry the burden). Sentence (2) with the Causee in the instrumental leaves greater control in the hands of the Causee, where the event of his carrying the burden was not preceded by any physical or psychological coercion. Here the servant is simply performing his duty by serving his master without being directly affected. Even clearer examples were discussed by Patañjali in Bhāṣya 13 (on p. 1.4.52), namely, *vāhayati bhāraṃ Devadattena* 'he has D. carry a load' (with an instrumental Causee) vs. *vāhayanti balīvardān yavān* 'they have bullocks carry the barley' (with an accusative Causee). The non-human animate Causee in the latter example has very little potential for exercising any control over the situation, whereas the human instrumental Causee is left with a greater control over the situation (i.e., the bullocks cannot refuse but Devadatta can refuse to act). Examples in Bhāṣya 14 are similar: *bhakṣayati piṇḍīm Devadattena* 'he has D. eat a sweetmeat' (with a human indirectly affected Causee grammaticalized by the instrumental) vs. *bhakṣayanti balīvardān yavān* 'they make the bullocks eat barley' (with a non-human directly affected Causee in the accusative).[25]

According to (R3) the Causer Agent in Sanskrit does not necessarily have to be assigned Subj function (in contradistinction to many modern languages where it has to be). Since in (R1) the Causee Agent may be assigned Obj function (for contactive causation), there are two candidates for the subjecthood in the passivized version of the causative construction: either the Causee Agent or the Goal of the action. According to (R4) the passivization on the Goal may result in syntactic doubling (with both the Causer and the Causee grammaticalized by the instrumental). The passivization on the Causee Agent (R5) results in a construction with an agentive phrase expressing the Causer Agent; the Goal and other arguments of the action remain in the original case (accusative, dative, locative).

My small corpus of 97 active and 96 passive causative constructions is taken from the late drama *Mudrārākṣasa* (written not later than about 800 A.D. by a certain Viśākhadatta. This corpus is based on the Sanskrit and Prākrit prose passages (i.e., the passages of poetry have been excluded). In terms of frequency it may be observed that the passive constructions are on a par with the active ones.

The statistical breakdown for passive causatives is given below:

Passive causative constructions
(Mudrārākṣasa)

	Passivized on the Goal	Passivized on the Causee Agent
Sanskrit	22	43
Prākrits	15	16
	37	**59**

The passivization on the Causee Agent appears to be more common than that on the Goal.

Assigning Subj function to the Goal will result in a construction with two agentive phrases (one expressing the Causer Agent and the other the Causee Agent).

(3) viṣakanyayā rākṣasena ... ghātitas
poison-girl+INSTR R.+INSTR kill+CAUS+PASS+PART
tapasvī parvatakaḥ [Mudr 1.14.4-5]
unfortunate P.+NOM
'unfortunate Parvataka ... has been killed by Rākṣasa by means of a poison-girl'

For obvious reasons these constructions are difficult to process and out of their linguistic context they could be interpreted in two ways.

The Causer Agent, of course, does not have to be expressed by the agentive phrase (in the instrumental); it may be grammaticalized by an adverbial phrase, or the syntactic doubling may be avoided by compounding. The latter option is seen in the following example:

(4) yuṣmatprayuktayā viṣakanyakayā
you-employed+INSTR poison-girl+INSTR

ghātite tapasvini parvateśvare [Mudr 2.18.7]
kill+CAUS+PASS+PART+LOC unfortunate+LOC P.+LOC

'when unfortunate Parvateśvara was killed by the poison-girl employed by you'

The compound *yuṣmat-prayuktā* 'employed by you' helps to avoid a sequence of two instrumentals (that of the Causer Agent and that of the Causee Agent).

In the following example the Causer Agent has been realized by the adverbial phrase *ājñaptyā* 'by the order' of the Causer Agent:

(5) so kkhu ... ajjacāṇakkassa āṇattīe
he indeed ... noble-C.+GEN command+INSTR
duvehī amhehī ... vāvādaidavvo [Mudr 6.3.30-1]
two+INSTR we+INSTR ... perish+CAUS+GERUNDIVE
'By the order of His Honour Chāṇakya we two have to kill him'

The following example avoids the syntactic doubling by realizing the Causee Agent as the adverbial phrase (absolutive):

(6) tahī avasale lakkhasena gūḍham
that+LOC time+LOC R.+INSTR mysterious+ACC
visakannaāpaoā uppādia ghādide ... pavvadīsale
poison-girl-means+ACC having employed kill+CAUS+PASS+PART P.+NOM [Mudr 5.5.41-2]
'At that time Rākṣasa killed Parvateśvara by the mysterious means of a poison-girl'

In both narrative passages and dialogues it is quite common to leave the Causee Agent unexpressed. This is statistically the most common option (14 among the 37 instances of the passivization on the Goal). In most cases the identity of the Causee Agent is not relevant to the discourse; in some cases the Causee Agent is not realized to avoid syntactic doubling. In the following instance with the instrumental of manner the realization of the Causee Agent would result in a morphological triplication:

(7) cāṇakyahatakena vicitravadhena vyāpāditaḥ [Mudr 2.15.66-7]
C.-wretched+INSTR variegated-death+INSTR perish+CAUS +PASS+PART
'that wretched Chāṇakya ordered him to be killed in a fearful way'

Put differently, this sentence conveys the information about the manner of this causative action but not about its intermediary.

It is of interest to notice that the other option, i.e., that of realizing the Causee Agent but not that of the Causer Agent, is found only in dialogues (jussive or interrogative sentences) where the Causer Agent is always obvious from the extralinguistic context:

(8) itarau tu hastibalakāmukau
other two then elephant-force-wishing+NOM
hastinā eva ghātyetām [Mudr 6.21.14]
elephant+INSTR indeed KILL+CAUS+PASS+IMP
'the other two who wish to have elephants should be killed by means of an elephant'

In the passive jussive sentence it is clearly redundant for the interlocutor receiving the command to be realized by the agentive phrase *tvayā* 'by you'. Here the Causer Agent coincides with the interlocutor receiving the command.

Most typical instances of passivized jussive causative sentences involve the verb *vedaya-* 'inform, tell to' (causative of *vid-* 'know'). With this verb the Causee Agent appears in the guise of Recipient (indirect object) grammaticalized by the dative:

(9) Bhadramukhe, nivedyatām ... Cāṇakyāya [Mudr 7.4.5-6]
Friend+VOC know+CAUS+PASS+IMP C.+DAT
'Friend, tell the wicked Chāṇakya'

The Causer Agent does not have to be realized by the agentive phrase, because it coincides with the addressee of the command (i.e., *tvayā* 'by you' is redundant in this context). The whole construction may be understood as the impersonal one ('may it be told to Chāṇakya'). Its personal counterpart would involve passivization on the Recipient: **nivedyatāṃ cāṇakyaḥ* 'may Chāṇakya be told' which is disallowed in Classical Skt (but it appears in late MIA dialects).[26]

Equally common, in both narrative passages and dialogues, is to leave both the Causer Agent and the Causee Agent unexpressed (there are 12 among the 37 instances of the passivization on the Goal). The identity of both the Causer and the Causee can be inferred from the linguistic and/or extralinguistic context. The following instance is typical of narrative passages:

(10) Ajja dāva vāvādīadi [Mudr 6.17.21]
today then perish+CAUS+PASS+3rd Sg
'he will be executed today'

In jussive contexts the passive imperative or the gerundive may be used:

(11) nivedyatāṃ yathā avasthitam [Mudr 5.9.53]
know+CAUS+PASS+IMP as happened
'Tell everything as it happened'

In (11) it would be possible to add both the Recipient (*mahyam* 'to me') and even the Causer Agent (*tvayā* 'by you') but it is clearly redundant to do so, since the Causer Agent coincides with the addressee of the command, and the Recipient with the addresser.

The use of the causative gerundive in jussive contexts is rare:

(12) bho bhoḥ śūlāyatanāḥ na khalu vyāpādayitavyaś candanadāsaḥ [Mudr 7.3.65-6]
oh oh hangmen not indeed perish+CAUS+GERUNDIVE Ch.
'Oh hangmen, don't kill Chandanadāsa!'

In this case it is redundant to realize the Causee Agent by the agentive phrase (*yuvābhyām* 'by you'), since it is expressed by the addressee of the command ('hangmen').

The agentive phrase is seen in the following case:

(13) mahābhāgena ... eteṣāṃ prathamabhaṇito
magnanimous+INSTR their first-said
'rthah saṃpādayitavyaḥ [Mudr 5.9.63-4]
matter arise+CAUS+GERUNDIVE
'the magnanimous one ... should please them by granting them the aforesaid things'

Assigning Subj function to the Causee Agent will result in a construction with an agentive phrase expressing the Causer Agent. The Goal of the action remains in the accusative or dative (or local cases, such as locative or ablative); after the passive causative verb *jñāpya* 'be ordered' (lit. to be caused to know), the Goal of the action is typically realized by direct (reported) speech. In contradistinction to the passivisation on the Goal, the passivisation on the Causee Agent does not result in morphological doubling. This is why it is quite common to find both the Causer Agent and the Goal of the action expressed (in 26 among 51 instances). Typical instances in narrative passages involve causative passive participles such as *grāhitaḥ* 'caused to take', *śrāvitaḥ* 'caused to hear', *lekhitaḥ* 'caused to write', *praveśitah* 'caused to enter', *prāpitaḥ* 'caused to attain', *preṣitaḥ* 'caused to send out'. See some examples:

(14) sa mayā ... sakhyaṃ grāhitaḥ [Mudr 1.15.16-8]
he I+INSTR ... friendship+ACC take+CAUS+PASS+PART
'That person was made by me to form friendship ...'

(15) Tado mae ... suṇāvido amaccasandesā
Then I+INSTR hear+CAUS+PASS+PART minister-message + ACC
veālio tthaṇakalaso [Mudr 4.8.20-1]
minstrel+NOM S.+NOM
'Then I ... communicated Your Honour's message to the minstrel Stanakalaśa'

(16) ahā khu amaccarakkhaseṇa
I indeed minister-Rākṣasa+INSTR
candauttasaāsā pesido [Mudr 5.9.55-6]
Chandragupta-presence+ACC send+CAUS+PASS+PART
'the minister Rākṣasa ... sent me to Chandragupta'

The Goal of the action with the participle *preṣitaḥ* 'caused to send out/caused to be sent out' may also be grammaticalized by the dative:

(17) kumāreṇai 'tan mahyam anupreṣitam [Mudr 5.13.38]
prince+INSTR this+NOM I+DAT send+CAUS+PASS+PART
'This was sent to me by you'

The Goal of the action is typically realized by direct speech after the passive causative participle *ājñāpitah/ vijñāpitah* 'ordered' (lit. caused to know):

(18) dāva ahā amaccena āṇṇatto jaha
then I minister+INSTR know+CAUS+PASS+PART thus
karabhaa kusumapurā gaccha ... [Mudr 4.8.11-2]
Karabhaka Kusumapura+ACC go
'I was ordered by Your Excellency thus:
'Karabhaka, go to Kusumapura ...'.'

In jussive contexts, either the Goal or the Causer Agent may remain unexpressed. The order 'let him come in' or 'bring him in' may be grammaticalized by either the active or the passive causative of the verb *praviś-* 'enter':

(19) praveśaya [Mudr 5.5.11]
you enter+CAUS+IMP
'let him come in!'

(20) sa tvayā praveśayitavyaḥ [Mudr 5.3.6]
he you+INSTR enter+CAUS+GERUNDIVE
'bring him in!'

The active causative imperative grammaticalizes the Causer Agent but not the Causee (which is obvious from the extralinguistic context). On the other hand, the causative gerundive (used here in the meaning of the passive causative imperative) grammaticalizes the Causee and (optionally) the Causer Agent. However, neither of the above constructions grammaticalizes the Recipient which coincides with the addresser of the command ('to me').

Following are the examples of the passive causative constructions used in jussive contexts without grammaticalizing the Causer Agent (but expressing the Goal of the action):

(21) yo 'yam aparaḥ ... śūlam āropyatām [Mudr 1.20.35-7]
who that other stake+ACC ascend+CAUS+PASS+IMP
'and that other man ... should also be impaled'[27]

Quite rarely, the causative gerundive may be found in jussive contexts (without grammaticalizing the Causer Agent):

(22) ghātakāḥ ... saṃjñāṃ grāhayitavyās [Mudr 1.20.22-3]
executioners ... sign+ACC take+CAUS+GERUNDIVE
'make the executioners understand the sign!'

To express the Causer by the agentive phrase (*tvayā* 'by you') is clearly redundant in the jussive context, since the Causer coincides with the addressee of the command. Finally, there were isolated instances when neither the Causer Agent nor the Goal were expressed. The following instance of the passive causative imperative is typical:

(23) samarpyatāṃ rākṣasagṛhajanaḥ [Mudr 1.22.12]
move+CAUS+PASS+IMP Rākṣasa-family
'surrender the family of Rākṣasa'

Semantically, the verbs whose causatives may be passivized fall neatly into two groups. Those verbs which allow the passivization on the Causee Agent include the following three subcategories:

(i) 'to order someone': *ā/vijñāp* (causative of *jñā* 'know')
(ii) transitive verbs such as *grah* 'take', *śru* 'hear', *pā* 'drink', *likh* 'write', *āp* 'obtain', *viś* 'enter', etc.
(iii) verbs of motion (which keep their spatial satellites grammaticalized by various cases) *iṣ* 'set in motion', *bhraṃś* 'fall down', *vah* 'carry', *ṛ* 'move', *ruh* 'ascend', *pad* 'fall', etc.

Those verbs which allow the passivization on the Goal include the following two subcategories:

(i) verbs of 'killing': *ghātaya* 'make Y kill Z' (causative of *han* 'kill'), *vyāpādaya* 'make Z perish' (*vyāpad* 'perish')
(ii) verbs with the Causee in the dative: *nivedaya* 'tell' (causative of *vid* 'know'), *darśaya* 'show' (*dṛś* 'see')

The only verb whose passivized causative was found to occur in both types of constructions (i.e., those involving passivization on the

Goal and on the Causee Agent) was *likh* 'write'. That means that the passive causative participle *lekhitaḥ* is two-way ambiguous:

(i) 'someone who is caused to write'
(ii) 'something which is caused to be written'
Both instances are found in Mudrārākṣasa:

(24) śakaṭadāso 'pi tapasvī taṃ tādṛśaṃ
Śakaṭadāsa+NOM also poor+NOM that+ACC such+ACC
kapaṭalekham ... mayā lekhitaḥ [Mudr 7.8.6-7]
forged-letter+ACC ... I+INSTR write+CAUS+PASS+PART
'Poor Śakaṭadāsa, also, was made by me to write that forged letter'

(25) āryacāṇakyena ... lekhito[28] ... lekhas [Mudr 5.1.3-4]
minister-Chāṇakya+INSTR ... write+CAUS+PASS+PART ... letter
'the letter ... which was caused to be written by his Honour Chāṇakya'

This certainly was not an ideal situation. We saw above that the passive causative participle *vyāpāditaḥ* was used in Mudr only in the meaning of 'caused to be killed', but—theoretically, at least—it could also be understood as 'caused to kill (someone else)'. However, Sanskrit could avoid this unpleasant ambiguity by the activation of the causative passive participle (by the suffix *-vant*) seen in the following example:

(26) eṣa rākṣasaprayuktayā viṣakanyayā
he Rākṣasa-employed+INSTR poison-girl+INSTR
parvateśvaraṃ vyāpāditavān [Mudr 2.18.10]
Parvateśvara+ACC perish+CAUS+PASS+PART+ACT
'He (=the Jaina mendicant Jīvasiddhi) killed Parvateśvara through the agency of the poison-girl employed by you (= minister Rākṣasa)'

In this case there are actually two Causee Agents: the first Causee is the Jaina mendicant Jīvasiddhi who entrusted the second Causee, the poison-girl, to kill Parvateśvara. Both Jīvasiddhi and the poison-girl were employed by minister Rākṣasa (who is the ultimate Causer Agent).

As we saw above, the majority of our examples of the passive causative involve the past passive participle in *-ta* used typically in the narration of past events. About 25% of the passive causatives were found in jussive contexts (imperative and gerundive). The passive causative is used rarely in the present indicative, where the active causative is preferred. The statistical breakdown for Mudr is given below:

Passive causatives		Active causatives	
Pres Ind	4	Pres Ind	62
Imp (3rd Pers)	15	Imp (2nd & 3rd Pers)	16
Pass Part in *-ta*	68	Pres Part	1
Gerundive	9	Absolutive	5
		Infinitive	13

Further observations on the use of the passive causative are in order. Finite forms are almost always in the 3rd Pers (of both imperative and indicative). An isolated example of the passive causative in the 2nd Pers involves the verb (*pra*) *viś* 'enter':

(27) mā gummāhiāriehī ... rāakulā pavesīasi [Mudr 5.2.31-2]
lest troop-officers+INSTR ... king-tent+ACC enter + CAUS + PASS + 2nd Sg
'lest you might be taken to the King's tent by the officers of the company'

Here, the passive causative form *pavesīasi* (Skt. *praveśyase*) could easily be replaced by the active form (with the Causee grammaticalized by the accusative).

Among the 68 participial constructions there was a single example of the imperfective passive form in *-māṇa:*

(28) adhikāraśca tādṛśeṣu ... punar āropyamāṇaḥ [Mudr 3.2.4.40-2]
office+NOM and such+LOC ... again rise+CAUS+PASS+PART
'and if such people ... are restored to office'

Another peculiarity here is the inanimate Causee (*adhikāraḥ* 'office') which is 'caused to ascend' to the animate Goal ('people').

As shown above, the causative gerundives are used in jussive contexts where the focus is on the Goal of the action. Here the gerundives compete with passive imperatives. In other modal contexts (such as the statements of necessity) we observe the use of the causative infinitive and the modal verb:

(29) sa khalu ... vṛṣalasya sācivyaṃ grāhayituṃ na śakyate [Mudr 1.13.3-4]
he indeed ... Vṛṣala+GEN ministership+ACC take+CAUS+INF not is possible
'he cannot, indeed, be made to accept the ministership of Vṛṣala'

As far as morphology is concerned, most of Sanskrit and Prākrit causatives are of a morphological nature. In a morphological causative the predicate describing a certain non-causative situation undergoes some derivational process in order to express causativity. In Sanskrit the so-called 10th conjugation includes these derivatives (e.g., *bhar-* 'carry' → causative *bhār-aya-*). In a lexial causative a completely different lexical item is used as a causative counterpart of the non-causative verb. Notorious examples in English are the verbs *to die* and *to kill* (= make someone die). In Sanskrit the pair *paś-* 'see' and *darś-aya-* 'show' (= make someone see something) comes close to this type (notice, however, the causative suffix *-aya* attached to the root). It should also be observed that lexicalized causatives in Sanskrit and Prākrits exhibit various syntactic idiosyncrasies. According to (R1) we would expect the Causee Agent of *darś-aya* 'show' to be assigned Obj function (= morphological accusative). This indeed happens. However, the Causee may also quite commonly be realized by an indirect (dative or genitive) or an oblique (locative) case.[29] The following is a Prākrit example of the Causee in the indirect case (clitic *me* is both dative and genitive):

(30) Ajja, kĩ me bhaã dāvesi [Mudr 1.22.24-5]
sir why me+DAT fear+ACC see+CAUS+2nd Sg
'Sir, why do you seek to intimidate me?'

The following is a Sanskrit example of the Causee in the locative (instead of the expected dative); furthermore, this construction has been passivized on the Goal:

(31) darśitaś candraguptena rākṣase bhaktipakṣapātaḥ [Mudr 4.10.7-8]
see+CAUS+PASS+PART C.+INSTR R.+LOC affection-

leaning+NOM
'Chandragupta has shown his leaning through affection towards Rākṣasa.'

As we saw in (9), another verb whose Causee appears in the guise of the Recipient (=indirect object grammaticalized by the dative) in Classical Sanskrit is *nivedaya* 'tell to X'. Here we may assume that the causative analysis 'make X know Y' was not available to the speakers of MIA and that this causative was lexicalized. In Pkts we find the Causee of this verb grammaticalized by the genitive as in the following example from Mg:

(32) mama āgamana ajjacāludattaśśa nivedehi [Mrcch 5.11.1-2]
I+GEN arrival+ACC noble-Carudatta+GEN tell
'Inform the noble Carudatta of my arrival!'

Summing up, the causative constructions of Classical Sanskrit and Prākrits are passivizable to a larger degree than in OIA. This fact has to do with the increased passive orientation of MIA (cf. 4.5). Taking our data at their face value it appears that the active causative was used in the present indicative and the imperative; the passive causative was used in the past indicative and also in the imperative and the gerundive to issue more polite directives (cf. 4.3). Syntactically, the Causer Agent in MIA does not necessarily have to be assigned Subj function.[30] Since the Causee Agent may be assigned Obj function there are two candidates for the subjecthood in the passivized version of the causative construction: either the Causee Agent or the Goal of the action. According to (R4) the passivization on the Goal may result in syntactic doubling (with both the Causer and the Causee grammaticalized by the instrumental). These valency changes in a monotransitive verb can be summarized in the following diagram:

Active Causative — *Passive Causative*

SUBJ — SUBJ (Causer) — Agentive phrase — SUBJ
DO — DO (Goal)
DO (Causee) — Agentive phrase

The passivization on the Causee Agent (R5) results in a construction with an agentive phrase expressing the Causer Agent; the Goal of the action remains in the original case (accusative, dative, locative). These valency changes can be summarized in the following diagram:

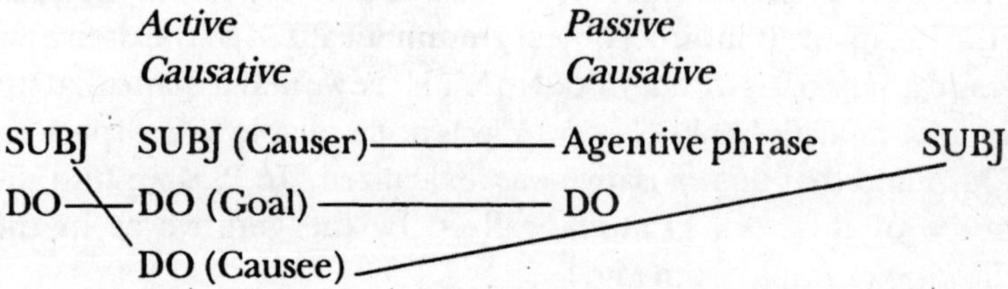

In MIA, as in NIA languages, it was possible to form double causatives from certain verbs. Their morphology has been surveyed in 3.4.9. While the act of causation in a 'single' causative is carried out through one intermediary (Causee), the act of causation in a double causative is carried out through two intermediaries. The first Causee functions as the Causer for the second Causee who performs the Goal. Theoretically, double-causativization should result in morphological doubling or even triplication. Let us examplify these complicated matters in (33)-(35):

(33) Agent Goal
Viṣakanyā Parvateśvaram hanti
'The poison-girl kills Parvateśvara'

(34) Causer Causee Goal
Rāksaso viṣakanyāṃ Parvateśvaraṃ ghātayati
'Rākṣasa makes the poison-girl kill Parvateśvara'

(35) Causer Causee 1 Causee 2 Goal
Rākṣaso Jīvasiddhiṃ viṣakanyāṃ Parvateśvaraṃ ghātāpayati
'Rākṣasa entrusts to Jīvasiddhi to make the poison-girl kill Parvateśvara'

The causativization in (34) involves morphological doubling (for contactive causation); we saw in (3) that this was tolerated (in the passive version) or that it could be avoided (4). The double-causativization in (35) could result in morphological triplication (of the accusative) which was definitely avoided (as in 26). A similar problem of morphological triplication (of the instrumental) would arise if (35) were passivized on the Goal:

(36) Rākṣasena Jīvasiddhinā viṣakanyayā Parvateśvaraḥ ghātāpitaḥ

The commonest solution of this problem was to omit both Causees in the active (35) and the passive double causative (36). Thus *Rākṣasaḥ Parvateśvaraṃ ghātāpayati* or *Rākṣaśena Parvateśvaraḥ ghātāpitaḥ* would be understood as 'Rākṣasa has/had Parvateśvara murdered 'through the agency of two intermediaries' vs. *Rākṣasaḥ Parvateśvaraṃ ghātayati* or *Rākṣasena Parvateśvaraḥ ghātitaḥ* where only one intermediary was involved.

Examples of double causatives are surprisingly common in MIA. The following is an example of a double active causative from JM [Erz No. IX]:

(37) tao ... savvā davvā davāveūna Maṇḍio sūlāe ārovio
then... all+ACC wealth+ACC give+CAUS+CAUS+ABS M.+NOM stake+LOC ascend+CAUS+PASS+PART
'after that—having made (him) to give away all his wealth—Maṇḍio was impaled'
(or 'after Maṇḍio had been made to give away all his wealth, he was impaled')

In (37) the king is the Causer, the judge (vel sim.) is the first Causee, Maṇḍio is the second Causee and his wealth is the Goal; *davāveūna* is the absolutive of the double causative *davāvei* (there is no OIA counterpart to this form; theoretically, it would be **dā-pā-paya-ti* cf. 3.4.9). The following is an example of a double passive causative from the inscription of Kakkuka [KI 22]:

(38) teṇa siri-kakkuena ... kāraviā acalam ima bhavaṇā
this+INSTR illustrious-Kakkuka+INSTR make + CAUS + CAUS + PASS + NEUT imperishable this temple
'This illustrious Kakkuka has caused this imperishable temple to be made' (or simply 'K. made this temple')

Here Kakkuka is the Causer, his architect(s) the first Causee, the workers the second Causee, and the temple is the Goal; both Causees go unmentioned (the kings, of course, do not build temples with their own hands). There might be some doubt, however, whether the opposition between *kāriā* (< OIA *kāritam*) and *kāraviā* (<**kārāpitam*) was indeed understood as that between a single and a double causative (because of the indistinctiveness of *kāriā* with its lengthened root, *kāraviā* could be understood as a double-marked single causative). A more convincing example of a double passive causative (marked by double *-v-*) is found in the story of Maṇḍio [Erz No. IX]:

(39) eeṇa pagāreṇa savvā davvā dāvāvio
this+INSTR manner+INSTR all+ACC wealth+ACC
give+CAUS+CAUS+PASS+PART
'In this manner he was made to give all (his) wealth away'

While (38) was passivized on the Goal, (39) is an example of the passivization on the second Causee (the first Causee is inferrable from the extralinguistic and the Causer from the linguistic context).

In practice one would expect various cases of 'disagreement' of the type: two Causees but the verb in a 'single' causative, or one Causee but the verb in a double causative (or even non-causative). These indeed can be documented from Aśokan inscriptions which show a bewildering variety of non-causative, causative and double causative passive participles with the verb *likh* 'write':

RE I.A	[lekhit]ā	Ka	causative (gradation in the root)
	likhapitu	Sh	causative (*-p-*)
	likhāpitā	Jg	causative (*-p-*)
	lekhāpitā	Gi	double causative (gradation + *-p-*)
RE IV.K	likh[i]te	Er	non-causative
	likhite	Dh	non-causative
	lekhitā	Ka	causative (gradation in the root)
	likhapite	Ma	causative (*-p-*)
	lekhāpitaṃ	Gi	double causative (gradation + *-p-*)

The alternation between *likhite* 'incised', *likhāpitā* and *lekhāpitā* 'caused to be incised' should not be taken literally as implying that Aśoka himself incised some of the inscriptions and had the others executed through his stone-masons who were commanded to do so by him directly or through an intermediary (in the case of a double causative). The conclusion is rather that the 'agreement' (1 Causee—causative, 2 Causees—double causative) was far from being of a categorial nature in the colloquial language.

NOTES

(1) Thus in Turkish (a rigid SOV language) we may find the infinitive of purpose before its governing verb:

kIz, çiçek dermeg-e çIkIyor
girl flower picking+DAT goes+PROGR
'the girl is going out to pick flowers'

(2) Typologically similar marking for definiteness is found in articleless languages. Thus Hindi places indefinite NPs in comment position which is as close to the end of the sentence as possible (the sentence final position is, of course, occupied by the verb since Hindi is a rigid SOV language), and definite NPs in sentence-initial topic position. We may contrast (1) with (2):

(1) mez par kitāb hai
table on book is
'On the table (there) is a book'

(2) kitāb mez par hai
book table on is
'The book is on the table'

(3) Cf. the explicit statement by Patañjali: *saṁskṛtya saṁskrtya padāny utsṛjyante teṣām yatheṣṭam abhisaṁbandho bhavati tad yathā āhara pātram pātram āhareti* (ed. Kielhorn, I.39,11.18-9) 'words are generated in accordance with grammatical rules, but their order [abhisaṁbandha] is free, as in *āhara pātram* and *pātram āhara* 'fetch the bowl'.

(4) Manuscript P (Bengali recension) corrected several of these to (*e*) *tat śrutvā* (Vet. 8.30; 10.28).

(5) I cannot find any clear examples of synenclisis (of the type *dehi se ṇā* 'give him it!') but it is very likely that they existed in MIA. For instance, Bloomfield-Edgerton (1930:99) list Atharvavedic variants such as the following:

indo marutvān dadātu tan me
dadād idaṃ me

'may Indra, accompanied by Maruts, give me that/this'

The first variant may be evaluated as an example of synenclisis: *dadātu=tan=me.*

(6) But there are also instances of postposed clausal objects:

brūhi yad abhimataṃ bhavataḥ [Vet 10.14]
say what desire lord+GEN
'Say what you desire!'

Which of the two constructions, the above or that with relative-correlative *yad abhimataṃ bhavataḥ tad brūhi* (i.e., VO or OV) is more basic?

(7) *bhajasva mām* (32.1) appears with the preposed object in manuscript P (Bengali recension): *māṃ bhajasva.*

(8) Colloquial Turkish may place the nominal object and the focal pronominal recipient in postverbal position: *ver şu kitabi bana* 'give that book to ME' (Mardin 1961:38).

(9) It should be borne in mind that rigid SOV languages can achieve the same pragmatic effects of the focalization and backgrounding of information by the use of the particles, e.g., in Hindi we may say *Rām ne kavitā hī paṛhī* 'Ram read the POEM' (with the exclusive particle *hī* in SOV sentences). In Prākrit or Brāhmaṇa Sanskrit the same would be achieved by placing the object sentence-initially (or finally): *kāvyaṃ paṭhitaṃ Rāmeṇa (Rāmeṇa paṭhitaṃ kāvyam).* In addition, the emphatic particle *eva* could be cliticized to the focal object in sentence initial position: *kāvyam=eva Rāmeṇa paṭhitam* 'It was the POEM Ram read.'

(10) The situation in Pkts is complicated by the fact that instead of certain postpositions adjectives (or participles) in the respective case are used. Thus in JM commitative 'with' may be expressed by postpositions (or prepositions) *saddhi, sama, samāṇa, saha* or by the participle *sahiya, sameya.* 'accompanied' in the instrumental. The latter forms always precede their head-nouns (AN).

(11) The subjunctive in the 2nd person was used exhortatively and it could replace the rightmost imperative in the sequence of two imperatives:

Agne śṛṇuhi; devébhyo bravasi (RV i.139.7)
Agni hear+IMP gods+DAT you-say+SUBJ
'Hear, O Agni, do you say to the gods!'

(12) Their relatively complete list is found in Pāṇini 3.3.161-2. It includes terms such as *vidhi* 'command', *nimantraṇa* 'summons', *āmantraṇa* 'invitation', *adhīṣṭa* 'respectful command', *saṃpraśna* 'request' and *prārthanā* 'urging'. Under all these meaning conditions Pāṇini states that either the L-suffix *liṅ* (i.e., optative) or the L-suffix *loṭ* (i.e., imperative) is introduced.

This schema was criticized by several scholars (cf. Cardona, 1976:225-27). For instance, the question arises whether it would be as well to consider four of these as mere varieties of one meaning, namely, prompting someone to action (*pravartanā*). Further, the question arises, what precisely is meant by the term *vidhi,* translatable alternatively as 'injunction, command, order, grammatical rule', etc.

(13) Ancient Greek shows similar development to the aspectually unmarked prohibitive expressed by the subjunctive of the aorist. Its use, however, complements that of the imperative of the present for its imperfective counterpart (a well-known syntactic rule of Ancient Greek disallows the use of the prohibitive particles *mē* 'not' with the imperative of the aorist):

Mē poíei (cf. Latin nōlī facere)
not make+IMP
'Don't make!'
Mē poiḗsēis (cf. Latin nē fēceris)

not have-made+SUBJ
'Don't have made!'

(14) It would seem that the suffix *-tu* (3rd Sg Act Imp) has been recategorized as a honorific particle. Vedic *-tāt,* originally a marker of the future imperative, has probably developed in the same fashion to the honorific particle.

(15) Passive voice is used in demands also in other languages. For instance, Classical Arabic uses the passive jussive (*apocopatus*) (= *jazm* in Arabic linguistic terminology) with the particle *li. Li-yuqtal* 'let him be killed' could be typically uttered to the intermediary to bring the victim to the executioner who, in his turn, could be commanded in the active imperative *? uqtul-hū* 'kill him!' In Latin the passive subjunctive (*occīdātur* 'let him be killed') and in Ancient Greek the passive imperative or subjunctive (*phoneuthḗtō* or *phoneuthêi*) would be used in demands.

(16) In Vedic Sanskrit in contexts of deontic modality there also occurs the so-called dative infinitive. The agent of the action expressed by the infinitive (i.e., the person upon whom the obligation or prohibition is imposed) may be grammaticalized by the instrumental:

ná anyéna stomo vasiṣṭhā ánvetave vaḥ [RV vii.33.8]
not another+INSTR laudation V.-s [is] to-be-equalled your
'Your laudation, Vasiṣṭhas, is not to be equalled by another.'

In contradistinction to the gerundive which cannot be used impersonally there are examples of the impersonal use of the infinitive (such as the following one from Maitrāyaṇī Saṃhitā):

ná purá sū́ryasyaúdetor mánthitavā́i
not before sun+GEN rise+GEN [is] to-be-rubbed
'One should not rub fire before sunrise'

(17) In contradistinction to Greek and Latin the gerundive cannot be used impersonally in the cohortative sense of the deontic mode. That is we cannot use the IA gerundive to exhort the addressee to participate in realizing the event along with the speaker as in

Diōktéon toùs polemíous (AGr)
persecute+PASS+GER+NEUTER the+ACC enemies+ACC
'We have to persecute the enemies'

(18) It is not clear to me whether the Sanskrit gerundive can also be used in contexts of hearsay (as the Turkish inferential mode can be). Given the perfective nature of the Sanskrit gerundive the answer might be no, but more data have to be examined. In any case, subjectively modalized sentences (25)-(27) are not acts of telling and their illocutionary force is rather similar to that of questions, which are also non-factive. Thus in (25) the speaker actually had a choice of asking a question *Api Śakuntalā asmin latāmaṇḍape asti* 'Is Śakuntalā in this bower of creepers?'

(19) In OIA the imperfective active and mediopassive participles could co-occur

with verbs *sthā* 'stand', *i* 'go' and *car* 'move' to express habitual actions or durative events (cf. 4.5).

(20) Sometimes the pronominal genitival agent is determined by the adjective in the instrumental:

mūḷhena me etaṃ kataṃ [Vin 2.81.3]
confused+INSTR me+GEN it done
'This was done by me, the confused one'
('Das ist von mir als einem Verwirrten getan')

(21) These matters will be analysed in great detail in my forthcoming monograph *Historical Syntax of Apabhraṃśa and Early New Indo-Aryan Languages.*

(22) The same is true of Gujarati and Nepali (cf. Beames II 1875:262 ff)

	Instr	Dat
Hindi	ne	naī (OH)
Panjabi	nai	
Gujarati	e	nẽ
Nepali	le	lai
Marathi	nẽ	

The use of dative *naī* as a marker of the ergative case is a later phenomenon dating back only to the 17th c. Old Hindi poets use the ergative construction without the postposition *ne* with the agent in the oblique or even in the direct case. Both are seen in the following verses from Chand [PrR i.49]

jihi hatyo śrapp ~ jo hatyo śrapp
who+OBL killed snake who killed snake
'He who killed the snake'

Ergative constructions with the agent in the direct case are well documented in Ap:

tuha kahiyaī naravai kim [Kc 1.10.6]
you+GEN told+NEUT king+NOM what
'What did the king tell you'

A real ergative case would be *naravaī* or *naravaiṇa* (Instr).

(23) Saṃdeśa Rāsaka 71 a (quoted according to Schokker 1969-70:6).

(24) Devendra's Sukhabodhā (in manuscript form) on Uttarādhyayanasūtra II,13 (quoted according to Schokker 1969-70:4).

(25) There have been several papers approaching the causative constructions semantically—most notably that by Saksena (1983) for Hindi and by Hock (1981) for Sanskrit. According to Hock the semantic notion of 'reduced agency' accounts for the difference between instrumental and accusative causatives. In Saksena's terminology (1983:80) for typologically similar Hindi causative, the causative marker *-koo* (corresponding to the Sanskrit accusative) signals an 'affected' Causee, while the causative marker *-see* (corresponding to the Sanskrit instrumental) signals 'non-affected' Causee:

(4) mai-nee raam-koo paaṭh paṛh-aa-yaa

I-Ag° Ram-Ag' lesson study-CAUS-PAST
'I taught Ram the lesson'
(5) mai-nee raam-see kaam kar-aa-yaa
I-Ag° Ram-Ag' work do-CAUS-PAST
'I had Ram do work'

Semantically, affected Causees share the property of being recipients of the verb activity—they are often affected by it physically or psychologically.

In fact the issue of 'decreased agency' or 'non-affected' Causee has been handled as far back as 1886 by Speijer in his Sanskrit Syntax (pp. 36-7):

'If one wants to say 'he causes me to do something, it is by his impulse I act', there is room for the accusative case, but if it be meant 'he gets something done by me, I am only the agent or instrument through which he acts' the instrumental is in its place...'

(26) An example from JM [Erz No.V]
dīsanti diṭṭhi-mohaṇāī indayālāī, indayāliṇo ya dijjanti tambolāī
'dazzling illusions are shown, and the magicians are given betel'

Here the Recipient *indayāliṇo* 'magicians' was assigned Subj function in the second sentence; it appears as a first argument in the sentence since it represents known information (by the linear progression of discourse). An example from Ap:

tiha hũtau haũ ikki ṇa lehā pesiyau [Saṃdeśa Rāsaka]
'from there (or 'by him') I have not been sent a single letter'

(27) The Goal of the action of 'impaling' may also be expressed by the locative or even by the instrumental. Both examples are found in Vet [148:14]:

Tair eva daṇḍapāśikaiḥ śūlena samāropitaḥ
they+INSTR really policemen+INSTR stake+INSTR ascend + CAUS + PASS + PART
'I was impaled on a stake by the police.'
The Bengali recension (Manuscript V) shows the locative *śūle* 'on the stake'

(28) It is of interest to observe that the Prākrit version shows only the simple passive participle (i.e., the non-causative one):

ajjacāṇakkeṇa ... lihido ... leho.

(29) In late Skt prose the usage vacillates between the direct case (Acc) and the indirect case (Gen or Loc) as in the following example from Vet 82: *taṃ bhaṭṭaputram aham ānīya tava darśayiṣyāmi* 'I shall bring that bard's son and show him to you'. The author of the manuscript V (Bengali recension) constructs the causative verb *darśayati* with the accusative form *tvāṃ*. The Causee Agent appears in the locative in Vet 152.1: *tena tvayi rahasyaṃ jñāpayāmi* 'I will tell you a secret', but the author of the manuscript P constructs the causative verb *jñāpayati* with the accusative form *tvāṃ*.

(30) In modern languages passive causatives seem to appear only marginally. Thus in Turkish it is possible to say *köprü tamir et-tir-il-iyor* (repair +

CAUS + PASS + PROG) 'the repair of the bridge is being carried out' with the passive causative of *tamir etmek* (Lewis, 1967:155). Zimmer (1976) gives an example of the passivization on the Goal with both the Causer and the Causee retained acceptable:

Bu is Hasan-a Ahmet taraflndan yap-tIr-Il-dI
this job H.+DAT A. by do+CAUS+PASS+PAST
'This job was caused by Ahmet to be done by Hasan.'

Some French speakers will find the following passive causative construction (passivized on the goal) acceptable:

Une lettre lui a été fait écrire par son pere
a letter him has been made write + INF by his father
'His father made him write a letter.'

CHAPTER 5

SOCIOLINGUISTIC CONTEXT OF ANCIENT INDIA

5.1 Linguistic Attitudes of Pāṇini and Pāṇinīyas

I have followed Deshpande (1979) in outlining the brahmanical puritanism in Ancient India on the following two pages.

Pāṇini, an educated brahmin born in North-Western India, called the language spoken by himself and his social class which was the topmost in the Indian echelon, *bhāṣā* 'language'. Deshpande demonstrated that we do not find in Pāṇini's work any attempt to show that this current Aryan language is identical with the 'Divine Language' of the Vedic texts. It is clear that when Pāṇini says *bhāṣā* 'language', he in fact refers to the *spoken dialect of the upper classes* (i.e. brahmins). What can we infer about the varieties spoken by the lower classes, i.e., kṣatriyas, vaiṣyas and śūdras? We may safely assume that other social varieties of Indo-Aryan were viewed as 'substandard' languages as their speakers were placed in the lower classes of the social hierarchy. As far as the non-Aryan languages are concerned, we have texts which explicitly prohibit an Aryan from learning a non-Aryan language. In what regards the social and regional dialects of Sanskrit, there are a few rules in Pāṇini's grammar describing the latter ones. Otherwise, Pāṇini with the linguistic intuition of a native speaker described his native upper class brahmanic dialect and also the older Vedic dialect (about one-third of rules). We know that Pāṇini was born in the north-western corner of India (in Śalātura, identified with present day Lahore in Pakistan) which had sizable Sanskrit speaking communities as far west as Gāndhāra. Thus Pāṇini probably had no access to the eastern varieties of Indo-Aryan spoken by kṣatriyas—and even if he had, he certainly was not interested in describing them, since these varieties are not mentioned in his *Aṣṭādhyāyī*. Here I am alluding to the speech of two great contemporaries(?) of Pāṇini: Buddha (+486) and Mahāvīra (+468). As is well-known, the 5th century B.C. saw the rise of Buddhism and Jainism, and the insistence of these two new faiths on using the local Indo-Aryan languages in preference to Sanskrit. Buddha and Mahāvīra were born in the eastern kṣatriya clans which lie outside the Brahmanical region of Āryāvartta.

In the Mauryan period (321-185) the royal family showed distinct preference for Buddhism and Jainism. As discussed in 1.2, all the inscriptions of Aśoka are in non-Sanskrit dialects and there seems to be very little encouragement for Sanskrit studies during this period. From Pāṇini's commentators Kātyāyana (about 300 B.C.) and Patañjali (about 100 B.C.) we may infer that the Prākrit languages started moving gradually up on the scale of social prestige. During the 3rd-2nd B.C. this upward movement of the Prākrit languages reached the topmost stratum of Indian society—that is, even the Brahmins started using Prākrits as their first languages, retaining Vedic Sanskrit for the ritual and scholastic purposes. Linguistically, the upper classes were 'Prākritized' and this brought them into contact with larger segments of the population.

The reaction of the topmost social class of Ancient Indian in this case is well known: the Brahmins linked officially the use of the Sanskrit language with their own conception of Dharma, whereas the use of non-Sanskrit languages (= Prākrits) by Buddhists and Jainas was directly associated with their opposition to it. Symptomatic is a statement by Kātyāyana that only the use of Sanskrit leads to Dharma, while the use of 'subnormal' languages leads to Adharma. We may infer from this statement that Brahmins did use non-Sanskrit languages in their everyday life (and some of them were tempted to use them even during ritual and teaching). Deshpande (1979:18) quotes an interesting comment by Patañjali (MB, Vol.1, pp.19 and 21) who says that a Brahmin woman could not speak the Sanskrit word *ṛtaka* in the proper way, mispronouncing it *ḷtaka*. This is perhaps the oldest observation which shows that even the upper-class women were using Prākrits and did not speak Sanskrit. The most probable cause of this phenomenon would seem to be that Brahmins of the post-Vedic period were marrying women from the lower ranks of society. The form *ḷtaka* may be evaluated as a Māgadhism (as shown in 1.4, in Māgadhī the two liquids of OIA merged into *l*).

5.2 Linguistic Attitudes of Nāṭyaśāstra

At this point we may look at the famous treatise of dramaturgy *Bhāratīya Nāṭyaśāstra* (the present text of which existed in the 2nd century A.D. but which is a compilation from previous works going back to a period as early as 100 B.C.). This treatise considers Prākrit to be disfigured in comparison with Sanskrit and lacking in the proper grammatical processes and qualities. In Chapter XVII, stanzas 25 to 56, seven *bhāṣās* 'major dialects' and their users are mentioned; but no explanation of a principle regarding the divergent use of Sanskrit and different *bhāṣās* in the same play is given.

> māgadhy avantijā prācyā śauraseny ardhamāgadhī
> bāhlīkā dākṣinātyā ca sapta bhāṣāḥ prakīrtitāh
> [Nāṭyaṣāstra XVII (XVIII) 47]

Let us examine some of the elaborate rules for the use of languages by the characters as given in the *Nāṭyaśāstra.*

(i) *Sanskrit.* The use of Sanskrit is proper in the case of kings, brahmins, generals, ministers, learned persons. The chief queen and minister's daughters are assigned Sanskrit but this rule is not in practice observed (they speak Prākrit everywhere). On the other hand, Sanskrit is occasionally used by Buddhist nuns, hetaerae and artists (cf. 5.4).

(ii) *Prākrit.* The use of Prākrit is the general rule for women and persons of inferior rank.

Complicated is the case of hetaerae—it was usually assumed that they were for obvious reasons well versed in both Sanskrit and Prākrit. We learn that in order to become a fully qualified hetaera the candidate must be adept in 64 arts, be endowed with all the 64 kinds of accomplishments, and be conversant with the 18 popular languages *aṭṭhārasa-desī-bhāsā-visāroyā* (Nāyā-dhamma-kahā 480). In the *Kāmasūtra* (33,9) only the *deśa-bhāṣās* in general are referred to.

Here are some of the symptomatic contemporary statements regarding the use of the language by females:

In Kumārasambhava (7.90) the priest Sarasvatī praises the married pair, Śiva and Pārvatī, in two languages: Śiva in Sanskrit and Pārvatī in Prākrit.

In Mṛcch [44,1 ff] the Vidūṣaka says that two things make him laugh: one is a Sanskrit-speaking woman and the other is a man who sings in a low voice (the woman who speaks Sanskrit makes the sound *su su* like a heifer through whose nose a cord has been passed).

In general, a man should speak to a woman in Prākrit according to Pṛthvīdhāra (495,13) *strīṣu nā prākṛtaṃ vadet.*

Thus from all this we may gather that Prākrit is characterized as the proper language of women. On the other hand, women not only understand Sanskrit but speak it quite well as soon as they have to say something in verse (in other words, the correlation of linguistic variety with literary genre overrides the correlation of linguistic variety with sex). Thus the hetaera Vasantasenā in *Mṛcchakaṭikā* speaks mostly in Prākrit but in the Fifth Act [15-32] she speaks and says verses in Sanskrit (cf. 5.4).

Even the man of inferior social classes who speak usually Prākrit occasionally switch to Sanskrit, when they have to say something in verse (the correlation of linguistic variety with literary genre overrides the correlation of linguistic variety social class or occupation). Pischel (1900:32) gives examples from the dramas: Vidūṣaka, the gatekeeper, the barber. In *Mudrārākṣasa* Virādhagupta in the guise of a snake-charmer speaks Prākrit, but to himself and to the minister Rākṣasa in Sanskrit. The types of Prākrit to be used are described with much confusion and the amount of variation is large. The *Nāṭyaśāstra* gives seven different Prākrits correlated with various geographical and social/occupational specifications presented in Chart 5-1.

We also learn from the *Nāṭyaśāstra* (and from Mārkaṇḍeya in particular) that there were a number *vibhāṣās,* which would seem to be occupational dialects in some cases:

(i) Śākārī—attributed to Śakas and Śabaras
(ii) Śābārī—charcoal burners, hunters, wood-workers, and forest dwellers in general
(iii) Ābhīrī—herdsmen
(iv) Cāṇḍālī—Caṇḍālas
(v) Drāviḍī—Drāviḍas
(vi) Oḍrī—undescribed (presumably the men of Orissa)

Śākārī and Cāṇḍālī are definitely variants of Māgadhī.

The fact that the *Nāṭyaśāstra* uses the term *bhāṣā* 'language,

Chart 5-1. Correlation of Dialect with Geographical and Social/Occupational Specifications according to Nāṭyaśāstra.

Dialect	Geography	Social dimension (as used in drama)
(i) Śauraseni	the speech of Doab (the land between the Yamuna and Ganges)	i. female characters (+ their friends and servants) ii. men of the middle class
(ii) Prācyā	eastern dialect of Śauraseni (= eastern Doab)	Vidūṣaka
(iii) Āvantī	urban dialect of Śaurasen (spoken in the city of Ujjayinī)	gamblers or rogues (dhūrtas)
(iv) Ardha-Māgadhī		slaves (ceṭa), Rājaputras, guildsmen (śreṣṭhin)
(v) Māgadhī		i. men who live in women's apartments ii. diggers of underground passages iii. keepers of drink shops iv. watchers
(vi) Dākṣiṇātyā		soldiers, police officers, gamblers
(vii) Bāhlīkā		

speech' for the major varieties of Prākrits is very significant. As mentioned above, Pāṇini called his vernacular Sanskrit *bhāṣā*. However, in the 2nd century A.D. the Prākrit languages were viewed in a much favourable light, despite the cultural domination of scriptural and spoken Sanskrit. It should be mentioned that Pāṇini's commentators have already elevated Sanskrit to the same status as the Vedas and imposed their sacredness on Sanskrit at large. This extension of sacredness to non-Vedic Sanskrit was caused among other things by the fight against the Prākrit-using Buddhists and Jainas. The Brahmins elevated the status of non-scriptural Sanskrit and began treating it with the same sacredness which was previously accorded mainly to the Vedic texts. It is tempting to hypothesize that this was not the case in Pāṇini's days when Sanskrit was only a 'normal' upper class vernacular.

As mentioned above, the *Nāṭyaśāstra* gives no explanation of a principle regarding the divergent use of Sanskrit and different *bhāṣās* in the same play. Several explanations have been proposed by Indian and European scholars in the past. The 'realistic' explanation (Beames, Grierson) would maintain that the use of the plays copied the actual practice of Indian life. Grierson (Encyclopaedia Brittanica, 11th ed., Vol. 22, p. 254) wrote:

> 'In India there is nothing extraordinary in such a polyglot medley. It is paralleled by the conditions of any large house in Bengal at the present day, in which there are people from every part of India, each of whom speaks his own language and is understood by the others, though none of them attempts to speak what is not his mother tongue.'

Even the staunchest realists, of course, have to admit that we are not dealing with faithful reproductions of spoken vernaculars but rather with conventionalized and stylized forms of them.[1] As Bloch (1965:19) put it 'it would ... be fundamentally wrong to expect from it (=drama) information about the languages, which the characters are supposed to make use of. Thus, according to Bloch, Śaurasenī is not the speech of distinguished women and undistinguished men, but the language of the touring companies based on Mathurā, which popularized the drama in India. On the other hand, Bloch's opinion (1965:19) that dramatic Māgadhī is a product of stylization might be too strong. Bloch claims that this is evident from the fact that *-e* for Sanskrit *-aḥ* is only used for the Nom Sg of nouns and not on the other occasions as in Aśokan inscriptions. Thus in dramatic Māgadhī *-e* is not used in the Nom/Acc Sg of neuters whereas it is used in this function in the Gangetic Aśokan inscriptions (e.g., at Kālsī *phale* 'fruit', *dāne* 'gift', cf. under 1.3). Here we might prefer to think of the recategorization of the system of gender in inscriptional Māgadhī, (Kālsī) which reduced the three-way gender distinction to a two-way contrast of *-e* (Masc and Neuter) vs. *-ā* (Fem). Dramatic Māgadhī, on the other hand, was more conservative (perhaps influenced by Sanskrit) in preserving the inherited three-way distinction of Masc (*-e*), Fem (*-ā*) and Neuter (*-aṃ*).

Another explanation must be sought for the use of Māhārāṣṭrī which is limited to poetic passages in Sanskrit drama. As suggested by Woolner (1928:89), this is clearly a case of literary convention, due to the prestige of the school of lyric poetry developed in the Great Kingdom of the Sātavāhanas. Māhārāṣṭrī became another Middle Indo-Aryan literary koine, deemed appropriate for epic and lyric poetry, which spread far beyond the original borders of the Deccan (cf. under 1.2).

There can be no doubt that even in Middle Indo-Aryan times well-educated people (brahmins, kings, ministers) could speak Sanskrit in addition to their native Prākrit or Apabhraṃśa; the households of kings, merchants and hetaerae were a meeting place of people of diverse regional background speaking different geographic and social varieties of Middle Indo-Aryan.[2] Communication among these people could have certainly resulted in Sanskrit-Prākrit-Apabhraṃśa code-mixing. Another characteristic of these conglomerates of bidialectals and bilinguals was code switching which is amply documented in Sanskrit drama. It goes without saying that in the case of Sanskrit drama we are not dealing with the records of living speech but rather with literary stereotypes which are based on it. This, of course, is a dilemma faced by any historical linguist preoccupied with records in a dead language. The present study is based on the assumption that the function of written language is autonomous and that its records have to be studied in their own rights.

Summing up, it may be said that Northern India in Middle Indo-Aryan times was socially stratified and that its society was not only class-conscious[3] but also language- and dialect-conscious. Contemporary Indian playwrights exploited the social inequality of status and education, and the biological distinction of sex for the purposes of linguistic stereotypization on the stage. How far they succeeded in matching the dialects on the stage with those found in everyday life will remain controversial (the opinions of the scholars are spread along the continuum ranging from the realistic to the sceptical position).

In this context it might be of some interest to mention Ancient Greek parallels to the Indian usage. In Greek tragedy there is the Doric chorus, which sings in a stereotypical poetic language based on the regional Doric dialects. It is of interest to observe that the lyrical dialogues which have more in common with spoken part of tragedy display less of a Doric tinge than the choruses.[4] Often, in the same lyric passage, the code may change with the mood of the speaker. As we saw above, Māhārāṣṭrī, originally a regional dialect, was conventionalized as an appropriate code for melic passages in Classical drama. The change of the mood of the speaker accompanied by the change of the linguistic code is fairly common in Classical Sanskrit drama. The most famous example are the Apabhraṃśa songs in *Vikramorvaśīya* uttered by the Sanskrit-speaking king under the influence of an intoxicating drink. Or, to use an even more exalted example: in the same drama the divine nymphs Āpsarasas speak the feminine dialect (Śaurasenī) when they are on earth, but in heaven they switch to Sanskrit.

On the whole, the Indian playwrights exploited the phenomena of sex, education, social status and origin for linguistic purposes to a much larger degree than their Greco-Roman counterparts. In their focusing on sociolinguistic dimensions in terms of stereotyped social and regional dialects they are *sans pareil* in the world of dramatic literature.

5.3 Correlation of Dialect with Social Class, Occupational Group and Literary Genre in Mṛcchakaṭikā

No extant play exhibits anything like the variety of Prākrits found in *Mṛcchakaṭikā*, which seem almost as if they were intended to illustrate the precepts of the *Nāṭyaśāstra* in this respect:

Śaurasenī— M the director (after his Sanskrit exordium)
F Vasantasenā (the hetaera)
F Madanikā (Vasantasenā's servant)
M Karṇapūraka (Vasantasenā's slave)
F Vṛddhā (Vasantasenā's mother)
F Dhūtā (Cārudatta's wife)
F Radanikā (Cārudatta's maiden-servant)
M the Śresṭhin (guildsman)
M the officer of the court

Avantikā— Vīraka and Candanaka
(two policemen)

Prācyā— Vidūṣaka (Cārudatta's friend)

Māgadhī— Sthāvaraka (Śakāra's servant)

Saṃvāhaka (the shampooer who turns monk)
Kumbhīlaka (Vasantasenā's servant)
Rohasena (Cārudatta's son)

Śakārī- Śakāra (brother-in-law to King Pāḷaka, the villain in the play)

Cāṇḍālī— two Cāṇḍālas (executioners)

Ṭakkī

~ Ḍhakkī— the chief gambler

Sanskrit— Cārudatta (a brahmin merchant)
Viṭa (Śakāra's companion)
Āryaka (the royal claimant)
Śarvilaka (leader of the revolutionary party, a brahmin thief)

The distribution of Prākrits agrees with that of the *Nāṭyaśāstra* with some noticeable exceptions:

(i) The play ignores the Māhārāṣṭrī.

(ii) It does not assign the Ardha-Māgadhī to slaves (Vasantasenā's slave speaks Śaurasenī), Rājputs, or guildsmen (they speak Śaurasenī). In the case of Cārudatta's little son the anomalous Māgadhī ascribed to him has been largely converted into Śaurasenī in the manuscripts (note that Cārudatta's wife speaks Śaurasenī).

(iii) The *Nāṭyaśāstra* ascribes the Āvantī to gamblers (*dhūrtas*). This dialect has *s* and *r*. However, in *Mṛcchakaṭikā* this dialect is used by the two policemen. The second policeman identifies himself as a southerner, and we can hardly avoid the conclusion that the dialect is Dākṣiṇātyā which the *Nāṭyaśāstra* ascribes to warriors, police officers, and gamblers.

(iv) The Prācyā of the Vidūṣaka is more or less Śaurasenī (or rather its eastern sub-dialect).

(v) Ṭakkī ascribed to the gamblers (Māthura and Dyūtakara) is difficult to identify geographically, since it has features of all the dialects (Śaurasenī, Māgadhī and Māhārāṣṭrī).

(a) According to Pischel it was an eastern dialect (such as Māgadhī) in which *r* > *l* (*dūra* > *dūla, pari* > *pali, kuru* > *kalehi*) but to be sure many *r*'s are unchanged (*tarai* <

tarati, pidara < *pitaram*). Ṭakkī preserved two sibilants *ś* and *s* (*daśa* vs. *suvaṇṇa*) but some *ś*'s > *s* as in Śaurasenī (*yaśaḥ* > *jasaṃ*); also *ṣ* > *s* as in Śaurasenī *kṛṣṇa* > *kaṣaṇa*, *eṣaḥ* > *eso*).

(b) Hence, according to Grierson, Ṭakkī is a western dialect. But there is also *prasāda* > *paśāda* as in Māgadhī. In various directions shows also the development of *aḥ*: *-o* (as in Śaurasenī), *-e* (as in Māgadhī) and *-u* (as in Māhārāṣṭrī):

eso	eṣaḥ
laddhē	labdhaḥ
luddhu	ruddhaḥ

(vi) The Cāṇḍālī of the executioners is a variety of Māgadhī.

(vii) The Śākārī of villain Saṃsthānaka is another variety of Māgadhī (given as Śākārī as the language of the villains by the *Nāṭyaśāstra*). One of its salient features is the absence of the fricative weakening in the environment before *t* (*st* > *śt*, *ṣṭ* > *śt*); contrast *ciśṭadi* 'he stays' with *ciṭṭhadi*, *iśtiā* 'woman' vs. *itthiā* (in the speech of the Buddhist monk).

In terms of the rules proposed under 2.5, the derivational history of these forms may be outlined as follows:

	Śakāra	*bhikṣu*
	tiṣṭhati	tiṣṭhati
fricative weakening	-	tihṭhati
gemination	-	tiṭṭhati
palatalization	ciśṭhati	ciṭṭhati
dissimilation of fricativity	ciśṭati	-
voicing	ciśṭadi	ciṭṭhadi

In Śākārī *s* in the environment before *th* undergoes fricative weakening (followed by gemination and metathesis)—hence the contrast between *uvatthie* 'standing' (< *upasthitāḥ*) and *iśtiā* 'woman' (<*strī*). An exception appears to be *pottha* 'nourished' (< *puṣṭa*) which shows the effects of fricative weakening.

5.4 Code-Mixing and Code-Switching in Sanskrit Drama

As mentioned under 5.2, the phenomena of code-mixing and

code-switching are to be expected in the 'plural' society of Ancient India. The following comments are based on my analysis of Śūdraka's *Mṛcchakaṭikā* and Viśākhadatta's *Mudrārākṣasa.* In the Māgadhı passages in *Mṛcchakaṭikā* the expected form of the Gen Sg of *a*-stems is *-aśśa* (found in 83 instances); the form *-āha,* which is typical of Apabhraṃśa, is also found (23 instances). The villain, Śakāra, and the shampoer, Saṃvāhaka, also use the Śaurasenī form in *-assa* (4 instances). A complete statistical breakdown is given in the following chart:

Gen Sg of *a*-stems	*Māgadhī* -aśśa	*Śaurasenī* -assa	*Apabhraṃśa* -āha
Śakāra	40	1	14
Bhikṣu	8	3	
Cārudatta's Ceṭa	2		2
Śakāra's Ceṭa	8		2
Shampoer Saṃvāhaka	14	3	2
Vasantasenā's Ceṭa	5		
Caṇḍalās	6		

Examples of code-mixing involving Māgadhī and Śaurasenī are found in the speech of the villain and the shampoer:

Śakāra: ... imaśśa (=asya) ... śāhiaśśa (=sābhikasya) ... cāludattassa (=cārudattasya) [Mṛcch 2.6.53-7]
Saṃvāhaka: ... cāludattassa ... jīvaśi (=jīvasi) [Mṛcch 2.14.61-2]

The Apabhraṃśa form of the Gen Sg *-āha* co-occurs with the Māgadhī form *-aśśa* in the speech of slaves and the Buddhist monk in addition to the above two characters. Thus Cārudatta's Ceṭa uses both forms of his master's name:

... cāludattaśśa .. caludattāha [Mṛcch 6.12.8-9]
Śakāra: .. tāha ... tāha ... taśśa [Mṛcch 1.32.4]
Saṃvāhaka: ... śe (=asya) ... tāha [Mrcch 2.14]

The play which abounds in Sanskrit-Prākrit code-switching is Viśākhadatta's *Mudrārākṣasa* (ca. 800 A.D.). This is given by the plot of the play, full of spies, who while mixing with people use various dialects; when they report back to the minister they switch to Sanskrit. For instance, in the 2nd Act the snake-charmer uses Prākrit when he soliloquizes on the streets and in his discussion with the chamberlain; after being introduced to Rākṣasa as Virādhagupta he switches to Sanskrit and says a couple of verses in Māhārāṣṭrī.

The best known example of Sanskrit-Śaurasenī code-switching is found in the opening of Śūdraka's *Mṛcchakaṭikā*. The *sūtradhāra* 'stage-director', who speaks Sanskrit, reverts to Prākrit when he wants to speak to his wife. Here is the whole passage:

The director opens *Mṛcchakaṭikā* by invoking the god Śiva in Sanskrit verse:

> 'May the profound meditation of Śiva, fixed on Brahma due to the complete absorption caused by the absence of perception, protect you.'

But after a couple of double-verses he abandons the use of both Sanskrit and verse and switches to Prākrit Śaurasenī and prose:

> 'I again have finished my music programme ... my eyes with their pupils rolling about, are crackling through hunger, like the lotus-seed dried up by the rays of the fierce sun . . . So having called up the housewife, I shall ask her—'Is there anything for breakfast or not?' Here have I, oh gentlemen, become a Prākrit-speaker, owing to the exigencies of my business [with my wife] and dramatic representation.'

His wife appears and they start conversing on the subject of every day life:

Wife:	Here I am, Sir.
Director:	Lady, welcome to you.
Wife:	May the noble one command what duty is to be performed by me.
Director:	Is there something to eat in the house or not?
Wife:	Everything is there, Sir!
Director:	What things are there?
Wife:	It is as follows—Rice boiled with guḍa, ghee, curds, rice—everything regaling fit to be eaten by the noble one is there. May the gods bless you thus!

In the same play we find opposite case of Śaurasenī-Sanskrit code-switching when a female character approaches a male. In the Fourth Act courtesan Vasantasenā switches to Sanskrit (from her Śaurasenī) when Vidūṣaka approaches her. What is remarkable is that she does not expect to hear Sanskrit from Vidūṣaka (as mentioned above, this character speaks the eastern subdialect of Śaurasenī, so-called Prācyā); nevertheless, she continues using Sanskrit for some time in their conversation on an everyday topic:

Ceṭī (in Śaurasenī):	Sir, cast your eyes down. See Madam.
Vidūṣaka (in Prācyā):	Greetings to your ladyship!
Vasantasenā (in Sanskrit):	Oh! It is Maitreya! Welcome! Here is a seat. Please be seated here.
Vidūṣaka (in Prācyā):	Do you sit down!
Vasantasenā (in Sanskrit):	How is the son of the big merchant?
Vidūṣaka (in Prācyā):	Very well, Madam.

In the following conversation Vasantasenā is informed that Cārudatta went gambling. Vasantasenā switches back to Śaurasenī when she soliloquizes. An impulse to it came from her Śaurasenī-speaking maid:

Ceṭī (in Śaurasenī): Madam, congratulations to you! The noble one has become a gambler!

Vasantasenā (to herself in Śaurasenī): What? He says that the bunch of gold ornaments was gambled away at play although stolen by a thief? It is for this reason that I love him.

Both instances of code-switching (involving the use of a lower class dialect when a male character approaches a female; and vice versa, the case of a high class dialect when a female character approaches a male) look quite credible in the world of *Mṛcchakaṭikā.* Of course, we would like to ask a question whether they reflect more than a stereotype produced by Śūdraka (i.e., that one should not speak to a woman in Sanskrit and that the hetaerae should be conversant with a number of languages/dialects). The answer might be positive in view of the comment by Patañjali (cf. under 5.1) which makes the existence of bidialectal families in the post-Vedic period plausible. Vasantasenā's Śaurasenī-Sanskrit code-switching style seems to fulfill a certain social function. Vidūṣaka comes with a message from her Sanskrit-speaking lover Cārudatta and she, being eager to enquire about his well-being, adopts Cārudatta's linguistic code.[5]

NOTES

(1) In Woolner's words (1928:88) 'The systematisation of the Dramatic Prākrits is not surprising. Everything else about the Drama has been classified and codified, from the virtues of the various sorts of Hero to the 'faults' in the endless kinds of poetic ornament. The making of minute rules seems to have been characteristic of the Brahman in all ages.'

(2) A propos the royal courts, we know that their employees were recruited from all social strata in the period of Brāhmaṇas (cf. Rau, 1957:113-6). Among the officers of low social origin we may mention *pālāgala* 'runner' ('gewiβ ein Mann des Volkes, wie die undurchsichtige Form seines Namens zeigt'), *dūta* 'messenger', *goptṛ* 'watchman', etc.

(3) Venturing into the realm of sociological research, Bloch's caveat (1965:19) remains valid: 'the Sanskrit drama does not, like our comedy of manners, devote itself to portraying society. It is essentially, as S. Levi says, the transference of the epic and the story to the stage.'

(4) A.E. Haigh, *The Tragic Drama of the Greeks*, Oxford: Clarendon Press (1986) goes farther in observing that 'the choruses themselves, when written in sober metres, such as the iambic and trochaic, have a less Doric tinge than when written in dochmiacs and choriambics, and other measures of a passionate and exalted character'.

(5) The question whether any social prestige attached to the code-switching style in Ancient India needs a further examination. To mention a negative present day parallel, no prestige attaches to the Hindi-Punjabi code-switching style in contemporary Delhi (cf. Gumperz, 1962).

CONCLUDING REMARKS

In view of the enormous task of outlining the linguistic history of the northern part of the Indian subcontinent during the fifteen centuries, there is no need to excuse oneself for the unevenness in the treatment of all the above issues. The most serious handicap for linguistically oriented research in the field of MIA is the inherent incomparability of our primary data. These range from Aśokan inscriptions, deemed to be the best representatives of colloquial MIA varieties, to stylized literary 'koines' used by the Buddhist and Jaina writers. Needless to say, these data are not the product of systematic questionnaires designed by dialectologists and sociolinguistics but of historical coincidences which left us with considerable gaps in space and time. By comparison, the inscriptional corpus of MIA in terms of its regional coverage and time-depth is far behind the corpus available for Ancient and early Medieval Greek. The literary Prākrits are based on regional dialects but in the extant works they have been nivelized to literary koines. These works are available in late manuscripts of varying quality with a broad spectrum of variant readings. Not to mention the problems connected with manuscript tradition, there is no consensus among the philologists in how far to go in 'correcting' the Prākrit literature to conform with the rules of the grammarians (in addition, with one or two exceptions, there were no grammarians who would record the contemporary state of affairs). Compared with Ancient Greek dialectology, the diachronic-diatopical study of MIA documents is beset with serious and special problems of its own: the MIA dialects cannot be localized with any precision, and the absolute and even relative chronology of individual changes is very difficult or almost impossible. Another problem of MIA studies is the almost complete lack of specifically stated theoretical frameworks and methodological procedures. Most of the available studies are essentially philological data-oriented works whose conclusions are often incompatible. Methodologically, the whole field of MIA studies has yet to be elevated to the linguistic status comparable with that available for the middle stages of other IE languages (Hellenic, Romance, Germanic).

The growth and differentiation of various MIA dialects is only one aspect of MIA studies. The other is the influence of the prestigious Classical Sanskrit on Prākrits and that of Prākrits on Apabhraṃśa, observable especially on the level of syntax in most literary genres. Studies on a smaller scale than the present one (e.g., the studies of individual authors) may hope to capture various facets of these processes of Sanskritization and Prākritization.

I would like to conclude this monograph by identifying some of the problems which in my opinion should be subjected to further research. In Phonology instead of reducing the variation found in individual dialects to the presence or absence of a few 'low-level'-rules the sociolinguistic study of the respective phenomena should be attempted. Various mechanisms of the diffusion of phonological rules (regional, social, lexical, linguistic) can, of course, be studied only where the data are sufficiently homogeneous and without major gaps. In Morphology the role of animacy in the realignment of OIA gender should be further explored. The study of the phonetic erosion of morphological cases should be complemented on the syntactic side by the analysis of the functions of emerging postpositional cases.

In Syntax the fruitfulness of functional approach should be obvious. In the same time the postulate of an adequate consideration of the level of pragmatics makes up for a demanding study in the absence of native speakers. Here a further study of other syntactic problems (most notably subordination and the use of particles) in larger samples of Prākrit and Apabhraṃśa texts should be carried out. In 4.3 we saw that Sanskrit and Prākrit data enabled us to correct certain inaccuracies of modern sematics in what regards the addresshood and agentivity in jussive sentences. Further research should be done on the exploitation of passive imperatives in polite requests and demands, and into the relationship of deontic modality to subjective and epistemic modality, on the one hand, and to the category of mood, on the other hand. A more penetrating analysis of the emergence of ergativity (4.5) and that of the valency of lexicalized causatives (4.6) is another desideratum. All these problems whose solution is of fundamental importance for our comprehension of subsequent developments will be addressed in my (forthcoming) monograph *Historical Syntax of Apabhraṃśa and Early New Indo-Aryan Languages.*

A number of specific problems to be clarified arose in the context of a sociolinguistic approach to MIA data. It appeared that Ancient India is an example of a linguistic situation in which dialect was correlated not only with literary genre but also with social class and/or occupational group. How much of stereotypization had been involved between literary genre and social class or occupational group? For instance, what is the degree of the stereotypization of Kālidāsa's Prākrits on the face of evidence that the Apabhraṃśa passages in *Vikramorvaśīya* had been definitely written by him? Given the existence of strong social norms in Ancient India, was there any social prestige attached to the code-switching style? What can we infer from the dialectal passages in Sanskrit drama about the nature of dialect continuum in Northern India? What can we learn from the dialectal passages in Sanskrit drama about linguistic changes in MIA times?

Many aspects of MIA phonological, morphological and syntactic developments are of considerable importance from the point of view of general historical linguistics. It has been unfortunate that many of them tended to get lost in older philological presentations and are thus accessible only to a few specialists in Indology. I hope that the present monograph succeeded in identifying them and made some progress in their linguistic analysis. The whole fascinating field of MIA philology and linguistics remains open to those who want to use more up-to-date methods of presentation, systematization and evaluation of the great variety of data of MIA dialects.

SELECT BIBLIOGRAPHY

Alsdorf, L. (1937) *Apabhraṃśa-Studien*. Leipzig: Deutsche Morgenländische Gesellschaft.

—— (1974) *Kleine-Schriften*. Wiesbaden: Steiner.

—— (1980) 'Ardha-Māgadhī' in H.Bechert (ed.), *Die Sprache der ältesten buddhistischen Überlieferung*. Göttingen: Vandenhoeck & Ruprecht, pp. 17-23.

Ananthanarayana, H.S. (1973) *A Prakrit Reader*. Mysore: Central Institute of Indian Languages.

Andersen, P.L. (1980) 'Typological and functional aspects of word order in Aśoka', *General Linguistics* 19, pp. 1-24.

—— (1982/83) 'Amplified sentences in Aśoka', *Zeitschrift für vergleichende Sprachforschung*, Band 96, Heft 1, pp. 17-28.

—— (1986) 'Die *ta*-Partizipialkonstruktion bei Aśoka: Passiv oder Ergativ?' *ZfVS* 99, pp. 75-94.

Banerjee, S.R. (1977) *A Bibliography of Prakrit Language*. Delhi.

Barua, A. (1965) *Introduction to Pali*. Varanasi: Prācya Bhāratī Prakāśan.

Baumann, G. (1975) *Drei Jaina-Gedichte in Alt-Gujarati*. Wiesbadener Steiner.

Beames, J. (1872-9/1966) *A Comparative Grammar of the Modern Aryan Languages of India*. Delhi: Munshiram Manoharlal.

Berger, H. (1955) *Zwei Probleme der mittelindischen Lautlehre*. Munchener Indologische Studien, Heft 1. München: Kitzinger.

Bhandarkar, R.G. (1929) *Collected Works* (ed.) N.B. Utgikar. Poona: Bhandarkar Oriental Research Institute (Vol. IV contains Wilson Philological Lectures on Sanskrit and the Derived Languages, delivered in 1877).

Bloch, J. (1933) *L'indo-aryen du véda aux temps modernes*. Paris. (English translation by A. Master, Indo-Aryan from the Veda to Modern Times, Paris 1965.)

—— (1930) 'Some problems of Indo-Aryan philology' *BSOS* V, pp. 719-56.

Bronkhorst, J. (1982) 'The variationist Pāṇini and Vedic: a review article', *IIJ* 24, pp. 273-82.

Bubenik, V. (1983) 'Dialect consciousness and Middle Indo-Aryan Literary Languages' in *South Asian Horizons,* Vol. 1, (Proceedings of Fourth Asia Council, Vancouver), pp. 61-72.

—— (1986) 'Jussive Sentences in Sanskrit Syntax' in the Proceedings of the 7th South Asian Languages Analysis Roundtable, University of Michigan, 1985.

—— (1987) 'Passivized causatives in Sanskrit and Prākrits', *Linguistics,* 25, pp. 687-704.

—— (1989) 'On the origins and elimination of ergativity in Indo-Aryan Languages', *Canadian Journal of Linguistics,* 34(4), pp. 377-98.

Burrow, T. (1937) *The Language of the Kharosthī Documents from Chinese Turkestan.* Cambridge.

—— (1955) *The Sanskrit Language.* London: Faber and Faber.

Canedo, J. (1937) *Zur Wort- und Satzstellung in der alt- und mittelindischen Prosa.* Göttingen: Vandenhoeck & Ruprecht.

Cardona, G. (1974) 'The Indo-Aryan Languages'. *Encyclopaedia Brittanica.* 15th edition. Vol. 9, pp. 439-50.

—— (1976) *Pāṇini: A Survey of Research.* The Hague: Mouton.

Chatterji, S.K. (1926/70) *The Origin and Development of the Bengali Language.* London: Allen and Unwin.

Chatterji, S.K., and S. Sen. (1957) *A Middle Indo-Aryan Reader.* Calcutta: Calcutta University.

Chatterji, S.K. (1960) *Indo-Aryan and Hindi.* Calcutta.

Comrie, B. (1976) 'The Syntax of causative constructions: cross-language similarities and divergence' in M. Shibatani (ed.), *Syntax and Semantics,* Vol. 6. New York: Academic Press.

—— (1981) *Language Universals and Linguistic Typology.* Chicago: University Press.

—— (1985) 'Causative verb formation and other verb-deriving morphology' in T. Shopen (ed.), *Language typology and syntactic description,* Vol. III. Cambridge: University Press.

Dandekar, R.N. and A.M. Ghatage (eds.) (1970) *Proceedings of the Seminar in Prakrit Studies* (June 23-27, 1969). Poona: University of Poona Press.

Dani, J.B. (1944) *Easy Readings in Ardha-Māgadhī.* Part 1 (Prose). Poona.

Delbrück, B. (1888/1976) *Altindische Syntax.* Halle/Tübingen: Niemeyer.

Deshpande, M. (1975) 'Phonetics of short *a* in Sanskrit', *IIJ* 17, pp. 195-209.

—— (1979) *Sociolinguistic Attitudes in India.* Ann Arbor: Karoma.

—— (1981) 'Sanskrit gerund constructions: syntactic disputations', *IIJ* 23, pp. 167-85.

Dik, S.C. (1980) *Studies in Functional Grammar.* London: Academic Press.

—— (1989) *The Theory of Functional Grammar.* Dordrecht: Foris.

Elizarenkova, T.Ja. and V.N. Toporov. (1965) *Jazyk pali.* Moscow: Nauka (English translation in 1976).

Emeneau, M.B. (1956) 'India as a linguistic area', *Language,* 32, pp. 3-16.

Erhard, A. (1980) *Struktura indoíránskych jazyků.* Brno: Univerzita J.E. Purkyně.

Fairbanks, G.H. (1969) 'Comparative Indo-Aryan' in *Current Trends in Linguistics* (ed. by T.A. Sebeok, The Hague: Mouton), Vol. 5, pp. 36-42.

Franke, R.O. (1902) *Pāli und Sanskrit in ihrem historischen und geographischen Verhältnis auf Grund der Inschriften und Münzen.* Strassburg: Trübner.

Friedrich, P. (1975) *Proto-Indo-European Syntax: The Order of Meaningful Elements.* Journal of Indo-European Studies. Monograph No. 1.

Gaeffke, P. (1967) *Untersuchungen zur Syntax des Hindi.* The Hague: Mouton.

Geiger, W. (1916) *Pāli: Literatur und Sprache.* (English translation by B. Ghosh, Pāli Literature and Language, Delhi 1968).

Ghatage, A.M. (1941) *Introduction to Ardha-Māgadhī.* Kolhapur: School and College Bookstall.

—— (1962) *Historical Linguistics and Indo-Aryan Languages.* Bombay.

Ghosal, S.N. (1972) *The Apabhraṃśa Verses of the Vikramorvaśīya from the Linguistic Standpoint.* Calcutta: The World Press Private Ltd.

Givón, T. (1984) *Syntax: A Functional Typological Introduction.* Vol. 1. Amsterdam: Benjamins.

Gonda, J. (1951) *Remarks on the Sanskrit Passive.* Leiden: Brill.

—— (1959) *Four Studies in the Language of the Veda.* The Hague: Mouton.

Greenberg, J. (1966) *Language Universals.* The Hague: Mouton.

Grierson, G.A. (1903-28) *Linguistic Survey of India.* Calcutta.

Gumperz, J.J. (1962) 'Hindi-Punjabi code-switching in Delhi' in H.G. Lunt (ed.), *Proceedings of the Ninth International Congress of Linguists.* The Hague: Mouton.

Hamp, E. (1986) 'On the morphology of Indic gerunds', *IIJ* 29, pp. 103-8.

Hawkins, J.A. (1983) *Word Order Universals.* New York: Academic Press.

Hendricksen, H. (1944) *Syntax of the Infinite Verb-Forms of Pāli.* Copenhagen: Munksgaard.

Hinüber, von O. (1968) *Studien zur Kasussyntax des Pāli, besonders des Vinaya-Piṭaka.* München: Kitzinger.

—— (1986) *Das ältere Mittelindisch im Überblick.* Wien: Veroffentlichungen der Kommission für Sprachen und Kulturen Südasiens.

Hock, H.H. (1981) 'Sanskrit causative syntax: a diachronic study', *Studies in the Linguistic Sciences,* Vol. 11, No. 2, pp. 9-33.

—— (1982) 'The Sanskrit passive: synchronic behavior and diachronic development', *South Asian Review* 6, pp. 127-37.

Ickler, I. (1973) *Untersuchungen zur Wortstellung und Syntax der Chandogyopaniṣad.* Göppingen: Kummerle.

Jacobi, H. (1886/1967) *Ausgewählte Erzählungen in Māhārāṣṭrī.* Leipzig/Darmstadt: Wissenschaftliche Buchgesellschaft.

—— (1918) *Bhavisatta Kaha von Dhanavāla.* München: Bayerische Akademie der Wissenschaften.

Jamison, S.W. (1981) 'The case of the agent in Indo-European' in C. Watkins (ed.) *Indo-European Studies IV.* Cambridge: Harvard University.

Jaiswal, M.P. (1962) *A Linguistic Study of Bundeli.* Leiden: Brill.

Jeffers, R.J. (1976) 'The position of the Bihārī dialects in Indo-Aryan', *IIJ* 18, pp. 215-25.

Jha, M. (1967) *Magadhi and its Formation.* Calcutta: Sanskrit College.

Johansson, R.E.A. (1973) *Pali Buddhist Texts.* Oxford: Curzon Press.

Johnson, D.E. (1977) 'On relational constraints on grammar', *Syntax and Semantics*, 8, ed. by P. Cole and J.M. Sadock. New York: Academic Press.

Junghare, I.Y. (1979) *Topics in Pāli Historical Phonology*. Delhi: Motilal Banarsidass.

Katre, S.M. (1944) *Some Problems of Historical Linguistics in Indo-Aryan*. Bombay: University of Bombay.

—— (1945) *Prakrit Languages and their Contribution to Indian Culture*. Bombay: University of Bombay.

Keith, A.B. (1924) *The Sanskrit Drama*. Oxford: University Press.

Kelkar, A.P. (1968) *Studies in Hindi-Urdu*, I. *Introduction and Word Phonology*. Poona: Deccan College.

Lehmann, W.P. (1974) *Proto-Indo-European Syntax*. Austin: University of Texas Press.

Lesný, V. (1918). 'Die Entwickelungsstufe des Prākrits in Bhāsa's Dramen und das Zeitalter Bhāsa's', *ZDMG* 72, pp. 203-8.

Lüders, H. (1954) *Beobachtungen über die Sprache des buddhistischen Urkanons*. Berlin: Akademie-Verlag.

Lyons, J. (1977) *Semantics*. Vol. 2. Cambridge: University Press.

Macdonell, A.A. (1900/1968) *A History of Sanskrit Literature*. New York: Haskell.

—— (1916) *Vedic Grammar for Students*. Oxford: University Press.

—— (1917) *A Vedic Reader for Students*. Oxford: University Press.

Mayrhofer, M. (1951) *Handbuch des Pali*. Vols. I-II. Heidelberg: Winter.

Mehendale, M.A. (1948) *Historical Grammar of Inscriptional Prakrits*. Poona: Deccan College.

—— (1968) *Some Aspects of Indo-Aryan Linguistics*. Bombay: University Press.

Morgenroth, W. (1981) 'Zur Position der mittelindoarischen Literatursprachen in der indischen Sprachgeschichte' *ZfPSK*, Heft 1, Band 34, pp. 59-64.

Murray, R.W. (1982) 'Consonant cluster developments in Pāli', *Folia Linguistica Historica* 3.2, pp. 163-84.

Norman, K.R. (1958) 'Some absolutive forms in Ardha-Māgadhī', *IIJ* 2, pp. 311-5.

—— (1980) 'The dialects in which the Buddha preached' in H. Bechert (ed.), *Die Sprache der ältesten buddhistischen*

Uberlieferung. Göttingen: Vandenhoeck & Ruprecht, pp. 61-77.

Nitti-Dolci, L. (1938) *Les grammairiens prakrits.* Paris.

Ostler, N.D.M. (1979) *Case-linking: a theory of case and verb diathesis applied to Classical Sanskrit.* Cambridge. MIT PhD dissertation in Linguistics.

Pandit, P.B. (1961) *Prākṛta bhāṣā.* Banaras.

Panhuis, D. (1984) 'Is Latin an SOV Language? A Diachronic Perspective', *IF* 89, pp. 140-59.

Pischel, R. (1900) *Grammatik der Prakrit-Sprachen.* Strassburg: Trübner. (English translation by S. Jha, Comparative Grammar of the Prākrit Languages, Delhi: Motilal Banarsidass, 1965.)

Prakash, R. (1974). *Verb Morphology in Middle Indo-Aryan.* New Delhi: Munshiram Manoharlal.

Printz, W. (1921) *Bhāsa's Prākrit.* Frankfurt. Dissertation.

Rau, W. (1957) *Staat und Gesellschaft im alten Indien nach den Brāhmaṇa-Texten dargestellt.* Wiesbaden: Harrassowitz.

Renou, L. (1952) *Grammaire de la langue védique.* Lyon-Paris.

Saksena, A. (1983) 'A semantic model of causative paradigms', *Lingua* 59, pp. 77-94.

Saksena, B. (1937) *Evolution of Awadhi* (A Branch of Hindi). Allahabad.

Scharfe, H. (1977) *Grammatical Literature.* Wiesbaden: Harrassowitz.

Scheller, M. (1967) 'Das mittelindische Enklitikum *se*', *ZfVS* 81, pp. 1-53.

Smith, H. (1932) 'Désinences du type apabhramça en pali', *BSL* XXXIII, pp. 169-72.

Schneider, U. (1978) *Die Groβen Felsen-Edikte Aśokas.* Wiesbaden: Harrassowitz.

Schokker, G.H. (1969-70) 'The *jānā*-passive in the NIA languages', *IIJ* 12, pp. 1-23.

Schwyzer, E. (1939) *Griechische Grammatik.* I Allgemeiner Teil. Lautlehre. Wortbildung. Flexion. München: Beck.

Sen, S. (1953) 'Historical Syntax of Middle Indo-Aryan', *Indian Linguistics* Vol. 13, pp. 355-473.

—— (1960) *A Comparative Grammar of Middle Indo-Aryan.* Poona: Deccan College.

Sen, S.K. (1973) *Proto-New Indo-Aryan*. Calcutta: Eastern Publications.

Shapiro, M.C. and H.F. Schiffman (1983) *Language and Society of South Asia*. Dordrecht: Foris.

Singh, R.A. (1980) *Syntax of Apabhraṃśa*. Calcutta: Simant Publications India.

Sircar, D.Ch. (1943) *A Grammar of the Prakrit Language*. Calcutta: University of Calcutta.

Speijer, J.S. (1896) *Vedische und Sanskrit Syntax*. Grundriss der Indoarischen Philologie. I, 6. Strassburg: Trubner.

—— (1896/1973) *Sanskrit Syntax*. Delhi: Motilal Banarsidass.

Staal, J.F. (1967) *Word Order in Sanskrit and Universal Grammar*. Dordrecht: Reidel.

Tagare, G.V. (1948) *Historical Grammar of Apabhraṁśa*. Poona: Deccan College.

Turner, R.L. (1960) *Some Problems of Sound Change in Indo-Aryan*. Poona: University of Poona.

—— (1966) *A Comparative Dictionary of the Indo-Aryan Languages*. London: Oxford University Press.

Upadhye, A.N. (1975) *Prākrit Languages and Literature*. Poona: University of Poona.

Vaidya, P.L. (1941) *A Manual of Ardhamāgadhī Grammar*. Poona: Wadia College.

Vertogradova, V.V. (1978) *Prakrity*. Moskva: Nauka.

Wackernagel, J. (1926) *Vorlesungen über Syntax*. Basel: Birkhäuser.

Wallace, W.D. (1984) 'The interaction of word order and pragmatics in a Sanskrit text', *Studies in the Linguistic Sciences*, Vol. 14, No. 1, pp. 167-88.

Warder, A.K. (1963) *Introduction to Pali*. London: Pali Text Society.

Woolner, A.C. (1928/1975) *Introduction to Prakrit*. Delhi: Motilal Banarsidass.

INDEX OF NAMES

INDEX OF QUOTED PASSAGES